BUILDING THEORIES OF ORGAI

This volume explores the concept of communication as it applies to organizational theory. Bringing together multiple voices, it focuses on communication's role in the constitution of organization. Editors Linda L. Putnam and Anne Maydan Nicotera have assembled an all-star cast of contributors, each providing a distinctive voice and perspective.

The contents of this volume compare and contrast approaches to the notion that communication constitutes organization. Chapters also examine ways that those processes produce patterns that endure over time and those that constitute the organization as a whole. This collection bridges different disciplines and serves a vital role in developing dimensions, characteristics, and relationships among concepts that address how communication constitutes organization. It will appeal to scholars and researchers working in organizational communication, organizational studies, management, sociology, social collectives, and organizational psychology and behavior.

Linda L. Putnam (Ph.D., University of Minnesota, 1977) is a Professor in the Department of Communication at University of California-Santa Barbara. Her current research interests include discourse analysis in organizations, negotiation, and organizational conflict. She is the co-editor of eight books, including *Organizational Communication, The SAGE Handbook of Organizational Discourse,* and *The New Handbook of Organizational Communication.*

Anne Maydan Nicotera (Ph.D., Ohio University, 1990) is an Associate Professor in the Department of Communication at George Mason University. Her research is grounded in a constitutive perspective and focuses on culture and conflict, diversity, race and gender, and aggressive communication, with a particular interest in healthcare organizations. She has also published four books and numerous articles on these topics.

COMMUNICATION SERIES
Jennings Bryant/Dolf Zillmann, General Editors

BUILDING THEORIES OF ORGANIZATION

The Constitutive Role of Communication

Edited by Linda L. Putnam and
Anne Maydan Nicotera

Routledge
Taylor & Francis Group

NEW YORK AND LONDON

First published 2009
by Routledge
270 Madison Ave, New York, NY 10016

Simultaneously published in the UK
by Routledge
2 Park Square, Milton Park, Abingdon, Oxon OX14 4RN

Routledge is an imprint of the Taylor & Francis Group, an informa business

© 2009 Taylor & Francis

Typeset in Caslon by HWA Text and Data Management, London.
Printed and bound in the United States of America on acid-free paper by
Edwards Brothers, Inc.

Library of Congress Cataloging in Publication Data
Building theories of organization : the constitutive role of communication /
   [edited] by Linda L. Putnam and Anne M. Nicotera.
      p. cm.
   Includes bibliographical references.
   1. Communication in organizations. I. Putnam, Linda. II. Nicotera, Anne
   Maydan.
   HD30.3.B785 2008
   302.2–dc22   2008011140

ISBN10: 0-805-84709-X (hbk)
ISBN10: 0-805-84710-3 (pbk)
ISBN10: 0-203-89102-3 (ebk)

ISBN13: 978-0-805-84709-3 (hbk)
ISBN13: 978-0-805-84710-9 (pbk)
ISBN13: 978-0-203-89102-5 (ebk)

To Karl E. Weick for his inspiration on theories of organizing

Contents

Preface

For the past 25 years, scholars have treated organizations as social phenomena constituted by interactions, language patterns, sensemaking, and symbolic processes. Communication and social action, then, form the building blocks of organizational structure and change. Although communication is often treated as a cornerstone of organizing, research on the relationship between communication and organization is a more recent endeavor.

In the past decade, a plethora of publications have addressed the communication–organization relationship, either implicitly or explicitly. These studies have examined this relationship through treating organizations as conversations and texts (Cooren, Taylor, & Van Every, 2006), as sensemaking (Weick, 1995), as discursive constructions (Fairhurst & Putnam, 2004), and as emergent processes (Taylor & Van Every, 2000). Yet, no volume focuses specifically on ways to understand different orientations to this relationship. The burgeoning body of work in this area, both inside and outside the communication field, supports the need for critical consideration of this topic. This volume aims to fill this gap through comparing and contrasting different approaches to the notion that communication constitutes organizations (CCO). This book then moves beyond treating communication as simply a process of organizing. Rather chapters in this volume also examine ways that those processes produce patterns that endure over time and ones that constitute the organization as a whole.

Each chapter in this volume examines a number of issues that are central to theories about the communication–organization relationship. First, each responds to the four communication processes that McPhee and Zaug set forth in Chapter 2 as essential to constitute an organization. Some chapters take issue with these four processes while others extend them by focusing on ways that they intersect. Secondly, each chapter also provides a communicative description of the organization as a whole, the origin and development of structure, and the role and locus of communication in the CCO process. Thus, this volume focuses on questions that are central to developing theories about CCO. The chapters also serve as a comparison of inductive and deductive approaches to theory development in this area.

Moreover, by adopting a communication perspective, each chapter avoids reifying the organization as a static entity, a fixed structure, or an omnipresent agent. Thus, the chapters acknowledge that organizations have staying powers that extend beyond local, situated interactions, but that their endurance is not in the form of a fixture. Each one also presents different views as to how local interactions transcend time and space, what time and space mean, and the role of context in different processes. Thus, temporality and physicality surface as critical features of CCO theories.

In addition to temporality, each chapter highlights the role of speaking on behalf of the organization or referencing the "we" as a sign or a unit. This process is critical for boundary formation and for developing institutional relationships. Finally, the chapters in this book begin to explore the role of materiality or embodied practice in organizing. They do this through demonstrating how material objects and communication are intertwined in practice and through examining how interactions with nonhumans span time and space and thus stabilize communication.

This book emanated from a preconference held at the National Communication Association in November 2002. Over 50 young and established scholars gathered in New Orleans to examine what it means to say that organizations are constituted communicatively. Through position papers and case studies, participants focused on the implications of this work for research, teaching, and practice. This conference served as a springboard for continued discussions of this topic and for ways to develop theories.

It is our hope that this book will lead to future scholarship that expands on these theories, develops new approaches, and crafts communication-based organizational theories. These theories have the potential to advance research and maybe even move it to a new plane—one that roots concepts and constructs in the communication–organization relationship rather than in simply privileging one term over the other.

As Weick (2002, p. 4) noted in the paper that he prepared for this preconference, the topic of CCO is serious "because the idea that communication is constitutive is feedstock for most other assertions we make about organizing." He also urged us to drop our tools and the academic trappings that make it difficult to talk about how communication constitutes organizations. Given the abstract nature of this project, we have not fully dropped our tools, clarified our understandings, or reached a point of profound simplicity. Our hope, however, is that this project moves us one step closer to reaching this goal.

References

Cooren, F., Taylor, J. R., & Van Every, E. J. (Eds.). (2006). *Communication as organizing: Empirical and theoretical explorations in the dynamic of text and conversation*. Mahwah, NJ: Lawrence Erlbaum.

Fairhurst, G. T., & Putnam, L. L. (2004). Organizations as discursive constructions. *Communication Theory, 14*, 5–26.

Taylor, J. R., & Van Every, E. J. (2000). *The emergent organization: Communication as its site and surface*. Mahwah, NJ: Lawrence Erlbaum.

Weick, K. E. (2002, November). "Agile Theorizing about Constitutive Communication." Paper presented at the Organizational Communication Division Preconference of the National Communication Association, New Orleans, LA.

Weick, K. E. (1995). *Sensemaking in organizations*. Thousand Oaks, CA: Sage. Publications.

Acknowledgments

This book grew out of the willingness of contributors to continually orient their diverse perspectives toward a common thread. Through several iterations and repeated deliberations, we were able to find a common focus that would shape a conversation about the similarities and differences among CCO perspectives. Hence, we thank the contributors to this volume for their patience and for their continual revisions of chapters over the past several years. A nod of gratitude must also be extended to Megan H. Tucker, who under conditions of short time and meager reward, prepared our author index once the manuscript was in production.

We are also grateful to the *Electronic Journal of Communication* and to Timothy Stephen, the Editor, for granting us permission to reprint the McPhee and Zaug article, "The Communicative Constitution of Organizations," published in Volume 10, Issues 1 and 2. This article formed the common thread for this book and served as a springboard for the different chapters to react to it.

We also extend our appreciation to Karen L. Ashcraft at the University of Utah and Patricia S. Parker at the University of North Carolina for their work in organizing the NCA preconference, "Communication in

Action: The Communicative Constitution of Organizations and Its Implications for Theory, Research, and Practice" held in New Orleans in November, 2002. They planned this event with Anne Nicotera. Also, a special thanks to Marcia Clinkscales for providing facilitation at the event and to Maurice Hall for preparing materials. Each of the contributors to this volume made presentations at this preconference and reaped the benefits of questions, analyses, and critiques of CCO approaches. We appreciate Cynthia and Michael Stohl's contribution on the communicative constitution of terrorists' networks that was one of the invited presentations at the conference. Karl E. Weick was unable to attend the preconference, but wrote a provocative paper entitled, "Agile Theorizing about Constitutive Communication," that served as a stimulus for this project. So we are grateful to Karl for this paper and to the preconference participants who made this event an exciting intellectual endeavor.

Finally, a special note of appreciation goes to Linda Bathgate of Routledge/Taylor & Francis Group for her unconditional support, encouragement, and work on this project amid the transition from Lawrence Erlbaum Associates to Routledge. We were very pleased that the projects under contract with LEA were carried over to Routledge and we are grateful to Linda for her leadership in making this happen.

List of Contributors

Larry D. Browning (Ph.D., Ohio State University) is a professor of organizational communication and the John T. Jones Centennial Fellow in Communication in the Department of Communication Studies, University of Texas at Austin. His research areas include the role of lists and stories in organizations, information–communication technology and narratives, cooperation and competition in organizations, and grounded theory as a research strategy. In addition to over 60 articles, book chapters, and technical papers, he, along with his co-authors, have written two books: *Sematech: Saving the U.S. Semiconductor Industry*, Texas A&M Press (2000), and *Information and Communication Technologies in Action: Linking Theory and Narratives of Practice*, Routledge (2008).

François Cooren (Ph.D., Université de Montréal) is professor at the Université de Montréal, Canada. His research centers on the organizing properties of communication and questions related to organizations' mode of being and action. Recent publications include two edited volumes published by Lawrence Erlbaum: *Communication as Organizing: Empirical and Theoretical Explorations in the Dynamic of Text and Conversation* (co-edited with James R. Taylor and Elizabeth Van Every, 2006) and *Interacting and Organizing: Analyses of a*

Management Meeting (2007). He served as the Editor-in-Chief of *Communication Theory* (2005–2008) and the Chair of the Language and Social Interaction Division of the ICA (2004–2006). He is the recipient of the 2002 International Communication Association Young Scholar Award.

Gail T. Fairhurst (Ph.D., University of Oregon) is a professor of communication at the University of Cincinnati, USA. Her research interests include organizational communication, leadership, and organizational discourse. She has published over 50 articles in communication and management journals as well as book chapters, including contributions to *The Sage Handbook of Organizational Discourse* (2004) and *The New Handbook of Organizational Communication* (Sage, 2001). She is the author of *Discursive Leadership: In Conversation with Leadership Psychology* (Sage, 2001) and co-author of *The Art of Framing: Managing the Language of Leadership* (Jossey-Bass, 1996, with Robert Sarr). Her work has been the recipient of numerous awards, including the 2005 International Communication Association Award for "Outstanding Article" for the Communication discipline (with Linda Putnam), the 2007 and 1997 "Best Book Award" from the National Communication Association, Organizational Communication Division. She also serves on several editorial boards and is currently serving as an associate editor for *Human Relations*.

Ronald Walter Greene (Ph.D., University of Illinois) is an associate professor in the Department of Communication Studies, and on the graduate faculty in American Studies and Writing Studies at the University of Minnesota. His research areas include contemporary rhetorical theory, the communicative dimensions of capitalism, and film exhibition. He is the author of *Malthusian Worlds: US Leadership and the Governing of the Population Crisis* (Westview Press, 1999) and has published over 30 articles, book chapters, and reviews. In 2007, the Center for Teaching and Learning, University of Minnesota, awarded him a "Thank a Teacher" certificate in recognition of his excellence in teaching.

Joel O. Iverson (Ph.D., Arizona State University) is an assistant professor in the Department of Communication Studies at the University of Montana. His research focuses on communicative enactment of knowledge, mission, and community, in the context of nonprofit organizations. His publications include articles in *Management Communication Quarterly*, *Journal of Applied Communication Research*, *Nonprofit Management and Leadership*, and *Nonprofit and Voluntary Sector Quarterly*.

Robert D. McPhee (Ph.D., Michigan State University) is a professor in the Hugh Downs School of Human Communication at Arizona State University. Specializing in communication theory and methods and in organizational communication, he has served as Chair of the Organizational Communication Division of the National Communication Association, as Associate Editor of *Human Communication Research*, and as Book Review Editor of *Communication Theory*. Among his specific research interests are organizational hierarchies, organizational knowledge, the communicative constitution of organizations, and structuration theory. A book he co-edited, *Organizational Communication: Traditional Themes and New Directions*, won the NCA Organizational Communication Division Research Award.

Anne M. Nicotera (Ph.D., Ohio University) is an associate professor in the Department of Communication at George Mason University, where she teaches courses in organizational and interpersonal communication. Her research is grounded in a constitutive perspective and focuses on culture and conflict, diversity, race and gender, and aggressive communication, with a particular interest in healthcare organizations. She is an expert in African–American organizational communication, with emphasis on social service and healthcare settings. She has published her research in numerous national journals. She has also published four books including *Understanding Organization through Culture and Structure: Relational and Other Lessons from the African–American Organization* (Erlbaum, 2003, with Marcia Clinkscales) and several chapters. Her current research includes the examination of structurational divergence as experienced by hospital nurses and the unique organizational structure and form of hospitals.

David Obstfeld (Ph.D., University of Michigan) is a professor of strategy at The Paul Merage School of Business, University of California, Irvine. His research examines how the knowledge-intensive social processes that result in organizational change and innovation unfold at the local and firm levels. Currently, his interests focus on how social networks, combinatorial action, knowledge articulation, creative projects, and collective action yield new insights for strategy, organization theory, and leadership.

Linda L. Putnam (Ph.D., University of Minnesota) is professor of Communication at the University of California, Santa Barbara. Her work on social construction has infused her interests in negotiation and organizational conflict, discourse analysis in organizations, and gender in organizations. She has used transformative approaches to investigate labor negotiations and multiparty environmental conflict. Her recent co-edited books include *Organizational Communication: Major Works* (Sage, 2006, with K. J. Krone); *The Sage Handbook of Organizational Discourse* (Sage, 2004, with D. Grant, C. Hardy, and C. Oswick), and *The New Handbook of Organizational Communication* (Sage, 2001, with F. M. Jablin).

Sim B. Sitkin (Ph.D., Stanford University) is professor of Management and Faculty Director of the Center on Leadership and Ethics at Duke University's Fuqua School of Business. His research concerns the effects of organizational control and leadership on risk-taking and accountability, sensemaking, trust, learning, change and innovation. His publications have appeared in numerous scholarly and managerial journals and books. He recently completed serving on the Board of Governors of the Academy of Management, as Senior Editor of *Organization Science* and as Associate Editor of the *Journal of Organizational Behavior*.

Kathleen M. Sutcliffe (Ph.D., University of Texas at Austin) is the Gilbert and Ruth Whitaker Professor of Management & Organizations at the Ross School of Business at the University of Michigan. Her research focuses on processes associated with team and organizational learning and resilience, high–reliability organizing, and investigation of the social and organizational underpinnings of medical mishaps.

Her work has appeared in many academic journals including the *Academy of Management Review, Academy of Management Journal, Organization Studies,* and *Medical Care.* A recent book (co–authored with Karl Weick), *Managing the Unexpected: Resilient Performance in an Age of Uncertainty,* was released in 2007 by Jossey-Bass.

James R. Taylor (Ph.D., University of Pennsylvania, Annenberg School) organized a new graduate program of studies in Communication at the Université de Montréal beginning in 1970 and has since acted as chair of that department on three different occasions, as well as serving as advisor to 45 masters and 15 doctoral students. His work has been primarily directed to developing a research thrust centered on the development of a linguistic and discursive approach to the study of organization, on the principle that organization emerges in communication. A secondary focus of his work is the role of technology in organization. He is author or co–author of seven books, and some 70 published articles. He was recently named a fellow of the International Communication Association.

1

INTRODUCTION

Communication Constitutes Organization

*Linda L. Putnam, Anne Maydan Nicotera,
and Robert D. McPhee*

Organizational communication scholars have long been fond of claiming that communication is the essence of organization. Influenced by the work of Karl Weick (1969, 1979) to treat the concept of "organization" as a verb and not a noun, scholars have focused on how communication is the means by which human beings coordinate actions, create relationships, and maintain organizations. Thus, for decades, organizational communication scholars have claimed in our scholarship, pedagogy, and practice that *organizations are communicatively constituted*. This claim appears in a broad multidisciplinary body of work that examines the ways in which communication (often conceptualized and discussed as discourse) constitutes organization (e.g., Bargiela-Chiappini & Harris, 1991; Boden, 1994; Boje, 2001; Bougon, 1992; Bruner, 1991; Czarniawska, 1997; Grant, Keenoy, & Oswick, 1998; Heracleous, 2006; Pentland, 1995; Pentland & Reuter, 1994; Weick, 1995; Weick & Roberts, 1993). Communication scholars have also contributed significantly to the development of these ideas (see, for example, Browning, 1992; Browning, Sitkin, Sutcliffe, Obstfeld, & Greene, 2000; Cooren, 2000; Cooren & Taylor, 1997, 1999; Cooren, Taylor, & Van Every, 2006; Fairhurst, 1993; Fairhurst & Putnam, 2004; Kuhn & Ashcraft, 2003; McPhee & Zaug, 2000; Putnam & Fairhurst, 2001; Putnam, Philips, & Chapman, 1996; Stohl, 1997; Taylor, 1993, 1995,

Taylor & Cooren, 1997; Taylor, Cooren, Giroux, & Robichaud, 1996; Taylor & Van Every, 2000; Van Every & Taylor, 1998).

Despite the extensive and multidisciplinary nature of this literature, scholars have not satisfactorily explicated the claim that communication is constitutive of organizing (hereafter known as CCO). Some of the problem stems from rooting the claim in "unanchored abstractions, borrowed pretensions ... and the myth that organizing starts from zero" (Weick, 2002, p. 1). Specifically, both communication and organization are abstract constructs that are difficult to anchor individually as well as interdependently. Thus, unpacking one concept often leads to anchoring the other one as an abstraction. Borrowed presumption refers to the taken-for-granted response to the CCO claim—a response that says, "of course," without trying to explicate what this means. Scholars in other disciplines for whom communication processes are not as readily taken-for-granted have become more preoccupied with explicating CCO than have many communication scholars. But these efforts often treat organizations as if they were zero-history (Boden, 1994) and few organizations fit this specification.

Another reason that CCO has not been fully explicated is that the claim vacillates between superficial simplicity and confused complexity (Weick, 2002). CCO scholars recognize that communication is more than social exchange, information processing, or a variable that occurs within an organizational container. This treatment is too simple and lacks subtlety (Weick, 2002). Yet, when scholars theorize about CCO, they often become mired in complexity, immersed in abstract language, and unable to articulate similarities and differences among perspectives. Hence, scholars have not fully articulated the different processes of CCO, particularly as they become manifested in different perspectives.

The notion of the "communicative constitution of organization" has a variety of theoretical roots, among them (and in no particular order) speech act theory (Austin, 1962; Searle, 1969); rules theory (Cushman, 1977); systems theory (Luhmann, 1995); ethnomethodology (Garfinkel, 1967); phenomenology (Husserl, 1964, 1976; Schutz, 1967); conversation analysis (Sacks, Schegloff, & Jefferson, 1974); frame analysis (Goffman, 1959); critical discourse analysis (see Fairclough, 1995); structuration (Giddens, 1984); semiology (Barthes, 1954/1967);

narrative theory (Greimas, 1987); and critical theory (Derrida, 1988; Foucault, 1972; Heidegger, 1959).

In this chapter, we first examine what it means to say "communication constitutes." Second, we present a historical picture for understanding CCO. Then we offer a framework for examining CCO processes and their underlying assumptions (McPhee & Zaug, 2000). Each chapter in this book then responds to this framework and explores different theoretical orientations to CCO. The final chapter of the book compares each of the orientations and develops a matrix to demonstrate similarities and differences among the approaches. Overall, the book aims to unpack different ways to conceptualize the beguiling phrase of "communication constitutes organizations."

Definitions of Communication Constitutes

According to the *Oxford English Dictionary*, the term "constitute" refers to:

1. Setting up, establishing, founding (an institution, etc.)
2. Giving legal or official form or shape to an assembly, etc.
3. Framing, forming, or composing (by combination of elements) …
4. Making (a thing) what it is; giving it being, forming or determining.

(Compact Edition, 1971, p. 529)

In a similar way, the *Oxford English Dictionary* defines constitution as:

1. The way in which anything is constituted or made up; the arrangement or combination of its parts or elements, as determining its nature and character; make, frame, and composition.
2. The mode in which a state is constituted or organized; especially, as to the location of the sovereign power, as a *monarchical, oligarchical,* or *democratic constitution.*
3. The system or body of fundamental principles according to which a nation, state, or body politic is constituted and governed.

(Ibid.)

Thus, the typical definition of "constitute" and "constitution" highlights the forming, composing, or making of something in addition to describing the phenomenon that is constituted. These definitions also emphasize the mode or state in which something is formed. In effect, part of the attraction of the CCO term is the connotation derived from several of these definitions.

A related approach to the concept of "constitutive" is Hacking's (1999) discussion of "social construction." Constitutive and social construction are similar concepts in that both focus on forming, making, and composing. Both concepts also highlight the process or dynamic elements of a phenomenon. Yet, the two constructs differ in the role of the social as the primary factor that drives the forming of a phenomenon. In some ways, social construction is one form of constituting organizations. Moreover, an analysis of constitution tends to "unmask" a phenomenon, thus revealing the contingency of and work required to sustain an organization or to reveal the multiple forms of organizing. Specifically, constitution connotes one or all of the following notions of an organization, i.e., its historical emergence and contemporary reproduction, practices of organizing and participating, a body of knowledge about organizing, and the organization as a reified thing.

Thus, communicative constitution presumably embodies the material (composition or elements), the formal (framing or forming), and the efficient causes (principles or rules for governing) that bring organizations into existence. These definitions also call attention to the essence of a concept (those processes that make a thing what it is). When organizations routinely (and supposedly successfully) take on a variety of mutant forms, and when all or most forms of organization fail at an alarming rate (Starbuck & Nystrom, 1981), claiming that there is an essential character to this form is risky.

Herein lies the conundrum: "communication" is clearly more than an element of organization; just as an organization cannot exist apart from the communication process, but the broad claim of CCO essentializes both "organization" and "communication" in a dangerous way. To assume that an organization is constituted by (or "made of") communication is to treat "communication" and "organization" as equivalent. This philosophical position makes for engaging classroom discussions—but it becomes overly generalized and leads to the implicit assumption that an "organization" means "formalization"—another dangerous effect of essentializing this relationship (Taylor, Cooren, Giroux, & Robichaud, 1996).

This book employs communication theory as an explanatory mechanism for unpacking the ontology of organizations. We contend that organizational communication scholars are particularly situated to provide a deeper theoretical understanding of the CCO claim, conceptually, theoretically, and historically. Taylor, et al. (1996) summarize this task by challenging the assumption that organizations can exist independently of communication. "We err in thinking of communication as a transparent window on organizations; the properties that we recognize as organizational are *in the communicational lens*, not in the object they are focused on" (Taylor, et al., 1996, pp. 2–3, emphasis added).

The main reason for examining different orientations to CCO is theoretical. Namely, we say that communication is constitutive of organizations without fully understanding what this means, conceptually or empirically. We embrace it as an assumption that embodies disparate orientations, different theoretical roots, and different aims for organizing. We also talk about communicating and organizing as dynamic activities without unpacking the nature of these processes and how they are related to the elements that form an organization. Thus, to avoid essentializing, we treat constitutive as a faceless process or an inevitable outcome of organizing. Unpacking different ways that communication is constitutive adds to the theory construction process.

Moreover, having different orientations to CCO will aid in deciphering what goes wrong when organizing fails. By unpacking interrelationships among processes across perspectives, we can develop insights as to the arenas that need in-depth investigation. The goal of this volume, then, is to explicate different theoretical understandings of the claim that communication is constitutive of organizations.

Historical Background of CCO

Initial research in organizational communication treated organizations as objects, reified identities, or containers in which messages were sent up and down channels through superior–subordinate interactions and through internal communication networks (see Putnam & Cheney,

1983 and Redding, 1985 for a review of this work). Scholars presented definitions and characteristics of organizations based on administrative management, bureaucracy, or systems theory in which communication was cast as a separate, discrete phenomenon (see Tompkins, 1984, for a review of the role of communication in traditional organizational theories).

Other scholars began to question the very existence of organizations (Albrow, 1980) and cast them as interlocking behaviors or socially constructed processes (Barnard, 1938; Thompson, 1980). One particular theorist, Karl Weick (1969), viewed organizations as coordinated behaviors in which double interacts or act–response sequences formed the basic building block. These coordinated behaviors had the capacity to create, maintain, and dissolve organizations. In a similar way, Hawes (1974) urged communication scholars to examine "how organizations come into being in the first place, how such patterned behavior evolves, how the collectivities maintain themselves, and how they disengage" (p. 500).

The Conference on Interpretive Approaches to Organizational Communication in 1981 questioned the nature of organizations (Putnam & Pacanowsky, 1983). Through embracing a process view of communication, scholars challenged the notion that organizations were "social facts" that resided "out there." Adopting a social construction lens, they viewed organizations as emanating from communication. Communication, then, was not simply a variable or the transmission of information, "it created and recreated the social structures that formed the crux of organizing" through the use of language, symbols, and co-constructed meanings (Putnam, 1983, p. 53). Communication processes, then, enacted the ongoing, interlocking behaviors that constituted organizational life.

Other scholars also challenged the reification of organizations by treating them as systems of interacting individuals who were actively creating and recreating social orders (Conrad, 1985; Deetz, 1982; Johnson, 1977; Mumby, 1988; Tompkins, 1984). Yet, even though theorists embraced this new conception of organizations, very little research focused directly on unpacking the relationship between communication and organization. In 1993, Ruth Smith presented a conference paper that identified three major types of relationships between communication and organization. The first one, containment, treated organizations as objective, reified entities in which communication occurred. Thus, organizations were physical entities with height, depth, breadth, and fixed boundaries. Fixed boundaries provided an easy way to examine communication within the container or to focus on an organization's messages and audiences external to the corporation.

The second type, production, breaks into three sub-categories: communication produces organization, organization produces communication, and the two co-produce each other. The idea that communication produces organization is similar to treating social interaction as creating and recreating organizational structures. The view that organization produces communication also embraces a social construction lens, but conceives of the organization as being enacted before the communication. Finally, the notion that the two co-develop each other casts them as separate processes that are mutually constitutive. The production relationship treats communication and organization as distinct concepts in which one of them has a priori existence over the other or in which both of them develop concomitantly. The third approach, equivalence, takes a different tack and purports that the two constructs are the same phenomenon or a monastic unity. This perspective differs from the production relationship that views the two as distinct or separate processes. In the equivalence approach, communication is organization and organization is communication; the two processes are one and the same.

Other scholars have taken issue with Smith's categories and her notion of equivalence (Fairhurst & Putnam, 2004; Taylor, Cooren, Giroux, & Robichaud, 1996; Taylor & Van Every, 2000), but her thinking about these relationships paved the way for theorists in the field to develop different perspectives and ways to unpack this important relationship.

Since this time a steady stream of research in different arenas draws from and focuses directly on understanding the CCO relationship. It crosses research on lists and stories (Browning, 1992), knowledge management and the relationship among communities of practice (Iverson & McPhee, 2002); a communicative theory of the firm (Kuhn & Ashcraft, 2003); and discursive perspectives on organizations (Putnam & Fairhurst, 2001). The contributors to this volume have developed some of the most extensive and sophisticated theoretical projects that will be examined in light of different flows or types of social interactions deemed necessary for constituting organizations.

Discursive Constructions and CCO

Prior to discussing these flows, this chapter summarizes Fairhurst and Putnam's (2004) work on discourse and organizations—since it provides a framework for extending Smith's typology and for examining different perspectives on CCO. Fairhurst and Putnam present three approaches for understanding how discourse constitutes organizations. Discourse in this article is a sub-set of communication, one that excludes networks, information processing, or non-linguistic forms of organizing. However, the three orientations that they develop are directly applicable to understanding CCO. Specifically, Fairhurst and Putnam contend that organizations as discursive constructions can be interpreted in at least three ways: organizations as objects, organizations as perpetual states of becoming, and organizations as grounded in action. Although these categories resemble Smith's (1993) typology, the three are broader in scope and incorporate different assumptions than does the typology of container, production, and equivalence.

The object orientation is more than a container. It focuses on organizations as entities that exist independent of their participants' social interactions. So this orientation includes approaches that treat the organization as a bureaucracy, a structural form, or a material object. But it also includes researchers who focus on the organization as a product of social interactions or as the material consequences of previous social constructions. Thus, scholars who treat organizations as constituted by communication but focus on the outcome, product, or material consequences of this construction adhere to the object perspective.

The becoming approach focuses on communication as a dynamic process that creates, sustains, and transforms organizations. This perspective parallels the pleas of early interpretive scholars who called for a CCO focus. In this perspective, communication exists prior to the organization and shapes the context in which structural forms emerge. Thus, it privileges the micro activities of organizing and it aggregates or synthesizes social interactions into macro forms. In comparison with the object orientation, this approach brings agency back into the picture, but without accounting for how organizations develop identities, stable ways of acting, and the exercise of authority.

In the grounded in action perspective, the organization is anchored in the continuous flow of communication; thus, streams of interaction and organizing are reflexively and concomitantly constituted. Discursive forms and social practices flow continuously to create and recreate organizing but the organization as a whole mediates these communication processes. This approach aims for a balance between structure and agency rather than privileging one or the other. Organizations never emerge as entities per se, but as systems, objects anchored in social practices, texts, or memory traces derived from the properties of language and action. Communication and organization are not equivalent concepts per se, but they are mutually constitutive. The chapters in this volume fall into the grounded in action approach to CCO. They are similar in assumptions about CCO relationships, but they differ in how organizations emerge, ways to balance agency and structure, and ways that communication and organization are mutually constitutive.

Moreover, this typology of orientations fails to address what processes might be necessary for organizing to occur. The orientations and schools of thought within them address elements, forms, and CCO relationships, but only a few of them identify the types of dynamic processes that intertwine communication and organization in a CCO relationship. Thus, to expand CCO theory, scholars need to focus on the kinds of processes and interrelationships among them that occur in the ongoing streams of organizing. To address this concern, McPhee and Zaug (2000) set forth four flows as the conditions that are necessary to constitute organizations. These conditions focus on the multiple dynamic processes that anchor the continuous flow of experiences in social practices that endure in time and place. These four flows are developed in Chapter 2 of this volume, which is reprinted from *The Electronic Journal of Communication*, Vol. 10(1/2), 2000.

Theoretical Framework: McPhee and Zaug's (2000) Four Flows

The main idea of this framework is that there are four quite different processes (or groups of processes) that operate in constituting organizations. The term used for these processes is "flows." The flows allow for and integrate multiple forms of analysis; thus, they are analytically distinct. However, any one message or episode can contribute to multiple flows at once, and processes identified as part of one flow can overlap with interactions in other flows. Yet, the four processes are separate because any one of them constitutes the organization and makes it what it is. In like manner, the four flows are not unidirectional or topically coherent; hence, various interaction chains and conversational episodes can contribute in different ways to CCO.

The first flow, membership negotiation, focuses on the relationship of members to the organization. This relationship takes many forms—partial inclusion, commitment, identification, leadership—but it is continuous and often occurs in designated forums with particular scripts. The label "membership negotiation" is not limited to recruitment and assimilation; rather, it focuses on the ways that membership becomes a relationship formation. This flow highlights the role of human agency in constituting organizations through the actions of organizational agents and stakeholders.

The second flow, organizational self-structuring, refers to the enduring quality of reflexive design and control. This flow stems from "complex structure" as a feature that distinguishes organizations from mobs and neighborhoods. Whether such structures exhibit the purposeful design of master architects who strive to control complexity or the sediments of past organizing, they occur almost any time members retain activity patterns, develop trust relationships, coordinate work sites, legitimate authority, or gain control. Thus, self-structuring is a communication process among organizational members in that it refers to any interactions that steer the organization in a particular direction. Most importantly, this flow includes the forming of boundaries and loci that constitute the organizational identity that agents refer to. Self-structuring also encompasses formal organizational charts and policies as well as informal processes of influence that are retained, regularized, and normalized.

Organizational self-structuring is analytically distinct from, but often intertwined with, communication that coordinates member activities. The third flow, activity coordination, focuses directly on connecting and shaping work processes. As members work on novel, challenging, or exigent tasks, they must organize joint work through communication. In this flow, organizational members interactively adapt to preordained arrangements, overcome the hardships of joint work, and attempt to work out solutions to problems. In these processes members can also coordinate how to avoid work, seek external advantage for self, or enact new practices and policies for work. Thus, activity coordination is not necessarily cooperative and can lead to waste, conflict, or disaster. Theorists often cast the second and third flows as existing prior to organizing. When this occurs, these features become static elements or indicators of organizations instead of dynamic processes as conceived in examining organizational flows.

The fourth flow, institutional positioning, focuses on organizations and their societal interactions at the macro level with suppliers, customers, competitors, government regulators, and partners. Developing and maintaining a place in a larger social system is a type of identity negotiation. As an organization interacts with other agencies, it establishes itself as legitimate by developing an image of a viable relational partner. Positioning refers to this development and to carving a place in the larger social system. Organizations, then, are constituted in part through interactions that allow them to remain part of and occupy advantageous niches in inter-organizational systems.

The four flows model rests on a set of theoretic choices with important implications. First, communication is seen not merely as contributing to constitution, but as wholly constitutive of organizations, recognizing, of course, that events other than communication occur. The implication is that communication is seen as the one force that can bind such events into an organized system. Second, the four flows model suggests a choice of contextualist over structuralist thinking, the implication being that the constitution of organization must be seen as rooted in a process (or array of processes), not in characteristics of an abstract structure. These may include integrating processes that develop what Taylor calls collective agency, but also differentiating processes, drawing on varied structural resources. Third, the four flows model rests on a view of the structure/agency problem as one of duality, rather than dualism. Structure and agency are inseparably linked, following Giddens, rather than treated as separate processes. Finally, the four flows model resists the temptation to take a micro-level position. Although individuals communicate in situated, bounded episodes (and the constitution of organizations must take place in just such episodes), the model allows for relations among episodes to be treated as real and, indeed, the stuff of organizations. One of the strengths of a focus on constitution is that it forces on us a recognition of the importance of coping with the systems level to forge new and varied tools for discussing relations among communicative processes.

All four of these processes accomplish or contribute to organizational constitution in different ways (see Figure 2.1, p.33). Specifically, they relate to conditions generally recognized as necessary for organizational existence or the properties of organizations that need to be constituted communicatively. But despite the existence and interconnection among the flows, much of the organizational communication research focuses on only one flow, and on types of jobs in the work setting relevant to only one or another flow. Flows can also include events of organizational disorder or failure—a theater troupe can fail to retain its popular actors, to keep the writers from undermining the director, to "get its act together," or to get strong reviews that can keep its doors from closing.

Each flow (and cross-currents of the flows) involves generative mechanisms or contextual constraints that shape organizational research. These constraints include sensemaking and cultural regularities that favor interpretive analysis; dominance relationships, member/class identities, and resistance that align with critical analysis, and tensions and contradictions that the postmodernists examine. Similarly, the framework supports multiple ontologies of analysis: membership negotiation is amenable through measuring human actions, while reflexive self-structuring focuses analysis on the organization as a whole. Moreover, the notion of organizing as flows implies that the organization is becoming in discourse, as well as being grounded in action.

Overall, this framework counters the tendency to cast constitutive in a unitary or essentialistic way and to reduce the organization to any particular element. McPhee and Zaug in Chapter 2 contend that each dynamic flow is necessary for an organization to function. This framework also addresses the meso and macro-status of large-scale organizations and the processes of materiality that characterize politically powerful organizations evident in a global society. Despite the contributions of this framework, the flows are nevertheless arbitrary, in two ways. First, they "cut up the pie" of CCO in ways that may not be necessary and are open to redefinition. Other distinctions might be more basic or valued for particular concerns. The key ideas embodied in the four flows could be re-expressed, at least in part, through using other distinctions. But secondly, "an organization" as a social form is culturally and temporally defined. The four flows, even if ideal at one point in time, might be seen as historical in the future.

Organization of the Book

Each chapter in this volume highlights different reactions to the four flows, their interrelationships, or ways that the flows parallel concepts developed in other CCO theories. Hence, the four-flows framework serves as a stimulus to unpack different approaches to CCO that are represented in this volume. In particular, the emphasis on any one flow, the way each flow constitutes organizing, and the relationship among the flows differs across CCO approaches. These approaches also question the role of agency in the flows, the theory of communication that underlies them, and the betweenness that connects them. Hence, the chapters in this volume foster different ways to theorize about CCO through discussing the flows as well as focusing on different approaches to the conundrum of "communication constitutes organizations."

Chapter 2, a reprint of the McPhee and Zaug article, presents the definition and theoretical underpinnings of the term "constitutive," the derivation of the idea of "flows," and an in-depth description of each of the four flows. Drawing from a particular theoretical focus, this chapter presents the contributions of each flow and their interrelationships. In Chapter 3, McPhee and Iverson pick up on these flows to articulate a structurational conception of CCO. This chapter treats CCO as communication processes that are bounded and connected through the four flows. An organization emerges as a recognizable sign from enacting and reproducing these flows. Moreover, this chapter uses an actual case, *Comunidad de Cucurpe*, to illustrate how constitution proceeds differently for each flow and how the interrelationships of the flows leads to developing an organization as a sign.

In Chapter 4, Browning, Greene, Sitkin, Sutcliffe, and Obstfeld propose that constitution happens at the intersections between the flows, creating vast systems that transcend, yet carry, discrete instances of organizing. Using an example of Air Force technicians as military entrepreneurs and a civilian review board, they illustrate how pairs of the four flows come together to monitor and control legitimacy, to enact practices that reconstitute membership identity, and to develop integrative complexity through testing and altering the rules of self-organizing. In effect, they show how intersections of different pairs of flows are fundamental for organizational survival. They also contend that strengths in one flow can overcome weaknesses in another one.

In Chapter 5, Cooren and Fairhurst take issue with McPhee and Zaug's framework and find it too deductive and too limiting regarding the role of agency. Their inductive, bottom-up approach examines the ways in which associations between human and nonhuman agents produce the flows. They contend that any approach to CCO needs to emphasize both the process of organizing and the development of an organization as a complex social form. Through expanding the notion of social interaction, they show how organizations evolve through associations among human and nonhuman actors whose present interactions transcend space and time. Collective action, as a product of these associations, enables some actors to speak on behalf of others and to contribute to stabilizing and structuring organizations.

Similarly, Taylor in Chapter 6 takes issue with McPhee and Zaug's framework. He contends that the four flows need a more precise theory of communication to trace their grounding in communication processes. Using coorientation as a fundamental process, Taylor situates organizations in the ways that actors develop communities. Thus, in Taylor's view, agency transfers from individuals to collectives through a coorientation process that parallels how individuals engage in activity coordination and membership negotiation. Through retrospective sensemaking, organizational members develop meta-stories or narratives in which groups of people identify with the organization or unit as a whole.

In effect, this book explores how McPhee and Zaug's four flows framework developed in Chapter 2 can provide the ground to enrich current theories and develop features or characteristics of CCO. The four flows are intertwined processes with constitutive force, although each is not independently sufficient in its own right to constitute an organization. But further, the flows represent different sites of organizing and the role of communication in constituting organizations may be a function of the relationships among the sites, the features that cross different perspectives, and the ways that different approaches articulate what a CCO perspective contributes. The theoretic construction of the flows thus allows for a powerful connection between constitutive processes and sites for that constitution.

References

Albrow, M. (1980). The dialectic of science and values in the study of organizations. In G. Salaman and K. Thompson (Eds.), *Control and ideology in organizations*. Cambridge, MA: MIT Press.

Austin, J. L. (1962). *How to do things with words.* Oxford: Oxford University Press.

Bargiela-Chiappini, F., & Harris, S. J. (1991). *Managing language: The discourse of corporate meetings.* Amsterdam and Philadelphia, PA: John Benjamins.

Barnard, C. (1938). *The functions of the executive.* Cambridge, MA: Harvard University Press.

Barthes, R. (1954/1967). *Elements of semiology.* Trans. A. Lavers, & C. Smith. Boston: Beacon Press.

Boden, D. (1994). *The business of talk: Organizations in action.* Cambridge, U.K.: Polity.

Boje, D. M. (2001). *Narrative methods for organizational & communication research.* London: Sage.

Bougon, M. G. (1992). Congregate cognitive maps: A unified dynamic theory of organization and strategy. *Journal of Management Studies, 29,* 369–389.

Browning, L. D. (1992). Lists and stories as organizational communication. *Communication Theory, 2,* 281–302.

Browning, L. D., Sitkin, S., Sutcliffe, K. M., Obstfeld, D., & Greene, R. (2000). Keep 'em flying: The constitutive dynamics of an organizational change in the U.S. Air Force. *Electronic Journal of Communication,* Vol. 10(1/2). www.cios.org/www.ejc/v10n200.htm. Accessed October 15, 2001.

Bruner, J. (1991). The narrative construction of reality. *Critical Inquiry, 18,* 1–21.

Conrad, C. (1985). Chrysanthemums and swords: A reading of contemporary organizational theory and research. *Southern Speech Communication Journal, 50,* 189–200.

Cooren, F. (2000). *The organizing property of communication.* Amsterdam and Philadelphia, PA: John Benjamins.

Cooren, F., & Taylor, J. R. (1997). Organization as an effect of mediation: Redefining the link between organization and communication. *Communication Theory, 7,* 219–259.

Cooren, F., & Taylor, J. R. (1999). The procedural and rhetorical modes of the organizing dimension of communication: Discursive analysis of a Parliamentary Commission. *The Communication Review, 3*(1/2), 65–101.

Cooren, F., Taylor, J. R., & Van Every, E. J. (Eds.) (2006). *Communication as organizing: Empirical explorations into the dynamic of text and conversation.* Mahwah, NJ: Lawrence Erlbaum Associates.

Cushman, D. P. (1977). The rules perspective as a theoretical basis for the study of human communication. *Communication Quarterly, 25,* 30–45.

Czarniawska, B. (1997). *Narrating the organization: Dramas of institutional identity.* Chicago: University of Chicago Press.

Deetz, S. (1982). Critical interpretive research in organizational communication. *The Western Journal of Speech Communication, 46,* 131–149.

Derrida, J. (1988). *Limited inc.* Evanston, IL: Northwestern University Press.

Fairclough, N. (1995). *Critical discourse analysis: The critical study of language.* London: Longman.

Fairhurst, G. T. (1993). The leader-member exchange patterns of women leaders in industry: A discourse analysis. *Communication Monographs, 60,* 321–351.

Fairhurst, G. T., & Putnam, L. L. (2004). Organizations as discursive constructions. *Communication Theory, 14,* 5–26.

Foucault, M. (1972). *The archeology of knowledge.* Trans. A. M. Sheridan Smith. New York: Pantheon. (Original work published in 1969.)

Garfinkel, H. (1967). *Studies in ethnomethodology.* Englewood Cliffs, NJ: Prentice-Hall.

Giddens, A. (1984). *The constitution of society: Outline of the theory of structuration.* Cambridge, U.K.: Polity Press.

Goffman, E. (1959). *The presentation of self in everyday life.* New York: Doubleday Anchor.

Grant, D., Keenoy, T., & Oswick, C. (1998). Organizational discourse: Of diversity, dichotomy and multi-disciplinarity. In D. Grant, T. Keenoy, & C. Oswick (Eds.), *Discourse and organization* (pp. 1–13). London: Sage.

Greimas, A. (1987). *On meaning: Selected writings in semiotic theory.* Trans. P. J. Perron & F. J. Collins. Minneapolis, MN: University of Minnesota Press.

Hacking, I. (1999). *The social construction of what?* Cambridge, MA: Harvard University Press.

Hawes, L. C. (1974). Social collectives as communication: Perspectives on organizational behavior. *Quarterly Journal of Speech, 60*, 497–502.

Heidegger, M. (1959). *An introduction to metaphysics.* Trans. R. Manheim. New Haven, CT: Yale University Press.

Heracleous, L. (2006). *Discourse, interpretation, organization.* Cambridge, U.K.: Cambridge University Press.

Husserl, E. (1964). *The idea of phenomenology.* Trans. W. Alston, & M. Nakhnian. The Hague, Netherlands: Martinus Nijhoff.

Husserl, E. (1976). *Logical investigations:* Vols. 1 & 2. Trans. J. N. Findlay. London: Routledge & Kegan Paul.

Iverson, J. O., & McPhee, R. D. (2002). Knowledge management in communities of practice: Being true to the communicative character of knowledge. *Management Communication Quarterly, 16*, 259–266.

Johnson, B. M. (1977). *Communication: The process of organizing.* Boston: Allyn & Bacon.

Kuhn, T., & Ashcraft, K. L. (2003). Corporate scandal and the theory of the firm: Formulating contributions of organizational communication studies. *Management Communication Quarterly, 16*, 1–38.

Luhmann, N. (1995). *Social systems.* Trans. J. Bednarz, Jr. & D. Baecker. Stanford, CA: Stanford University Press.

McPhee, R. D., & Zaug, P. (2000). The communicative constitution of organizations: A framework for explanation. *Electronic Journal of Communication, 10* (1/2), www.cios.org/getfile/McPhee_V10n1200. Accessed October 15, 2001

Mumby, D. K. (1988). *Communication and power in organizations: Discourse, ideology and domination.* Norwood, NJ: Ablex.

Oxford English Dictionary. (1971). Compact ed. (p. 529). Oxford: Oxford University Press.

Pentland, B. T. (1995). Grammatical models of organizational processes. *Organization Science, 6*(5), 541–546.

Pentland, B. T., & Reuter, H. H. (1994). Organizational routines as grammars of action. *Administrative Science Quarterly, 39*, 484–510.

Putnam, L. L. (1983). The interpretive perspective: An alternative to functionalism. In L. L. Putnam & M. E. Pacanowsky (Eds.), *Communication and organizations: An interpretive approach* (pp. 31–54). Beverly Hills, CA: Sage.

Putnam, L. L., & Cheney, G. (1983). A critical review of research traditions in organizational communication. In M. S. Mander (Ed.), *Communication in transition: Issues and debates in current research* (pp. 206–224). New York: Praeger.

Putnam, L. L., & Fairhurst, G. T. (2001). Discourse analysis in organizations: Issues and concerns. In F. M. Jablin & L. L. Putnam (Eds.), *The new handbook of organizational communication: Advances in theory, research, and methods* (pp. 78–136). Newbury Park, CA: Sage.

Putnam, L. L. & Pacanowsky, M. E. (Eds.). (1983). *Communication and organization: An interpretive approach.* Beverly Hills, CA: Sage.

Putnam, L.L., Philips, N., & Chapman, P. (1996). Metaphors of communication and organization. In S. R. Clegg, C. Hardy, & W. R. Nord (Eds.), *Handbook of organization studies* (pp. 375–408). London: Sage.

Redding, W. C. (1985). Stumbling toward an identity: The emergence of organizational communication as a field of study. In R. D. McPhee & P. K. Tompkins (Eds.), *Organizational communication: Traditional themes and new directions* (pp. 15–54). Newbury Park, CA: Sage.

Sacks, H., Schegloff, E. A., & Jefferson, G. (1974). A simplest systematics for the organization of turn-taking for conversation. *Language, 50,* 696–735.

Schutz, A. (1967). *The phenomenology of the social world.* Evanston, IL: Northwestern University Press.

Searle, J. R. (1969). *Speech acts.* London: Cambridge University Press.

Smith, R. C. (May, 1993). Images of organizational communication: Root-metaphors of the organization–communication relation. Paper presented at the International Communication Association Conference, Washington, DC.

Starbuck, W. H., & Nystrom, P. C. (1981). Why the world needs organizational design. *Journal of General Management, 6*(3), 3–17.

Stohl, C. (1997). *Organizational communication: Connectedness in action.* Thousand Oaks, CA: Sage.

Taylor, J. R. (1993). *Rethinking the theory of organizational communication: How to read an organization.* Norwood, NJ: Ablex.

Taylor, J. R. (1995). Shifting from a heteronomous to an autonomous worldview of organizational communication: Communication theory on the cusp. *Communication Theory, 5*(1), 1–35.

Taylor, J. R. (2000). What is an organization? *Electronic Journal of Communication, 10*(1/2). www.cios.org/www.ejc/v10n200.htm. Accessed October 15, 2001.

Taylor, J. R., & Cooren, F. (1997). What makes communication "organizational"? How the many voices of the organization become the *one* voice of an organization. *Journal of Pragmatics, 27,* 409–438.

Taylor, J. R., Cooren, F., Giroux, N., & Robichaud, D. (1996). The communicational basis of organization: Between the conversation and the text. *Communication Theory, 6,* 1-39.

Taylor, J. R., & Van Every, E. J. (2000). *The emergent organization: Communication as its site and surface.* Mahwah, NJ: Lawrence Erlbaum Associates.

Thompson, J. (1980). Organizations as constructors of social reality. In G. Salaman and K. Thompson (Eds.), *Control and ideology in organizations.* Cambridge, MA: MIT Press.

Tompkins, P. K. (1984). The functions of communication in organizations. In C. Arnold and J. Bowers (Eds.), *Handbook of rhetorical and communication theory* (pp. 659–719). New York: Allyn & Bacon.

Van Every, E. J., & Taylor, J. R. (1998). Modeling the organization as a system of communication activity: A dialogue about the language/action perspective. *Management Communication Quarterly, 12*(1), 127–146.

Weick, K. E. (1969). *The social psychology of organizing.* Reading, MA: Addison-Wesley.

Weick, K. E. (1979). *The social psychology of organizing* (2nd ed.). Reading, MA: Addison-Wesley.

Weick, K. E. (1995). *Sensemaking in organizations.* Thousand Oaks, CA: Sage.

Weick, K. E. (November, 2002). Agile theorizing about constitutive communication. Paper presented at the National Communication Association Conference, New Orleans, LA.

Weick, K. E., & Roberts, K. H. (1993). Collective mind in organizations: Heedful interrelating on flight decks. *Administrative Science Quarterly, 38,* 357–381.

2

THE COMMUNICATIVE CONSTITUTION OF ORGANIZATIONS

A Framework for Explanation*

Robert D. McPhee and Pamela Zaug

Abstract

In this paper we argue that the communicative constitution of organizations requires not just one, but four types of messages, or more specifically types of message flow or interaction process. Such a variety of message flows is required because complex organizations require distinct types of relations to four "audiences". They must enunciate and maintain relations to their members through membership negotiation, to themselves as formally controlled entities through self-structuring, to their internal subgroups and processes through activity coordination, and to their colleagues in a society of institutions through institutional positioning. These four sorts of communication are analytically distinct, even though a single message can address more than one constitutive task; we need to recognize that complex organizations exist only in the relatedness of these four types of flow.

---

* Reprinted from: McPhee, R. D., and Zaug, P. (2000). The communicative constitution of organizations: A framework for explanation. *Electronic Journal of Communication*, 10 (1–2).

Introduction

Max Weber founded modern organization studies by offering an interpretive analysis of bureaucracy (1922/1968). His account can be summarized as follows: members use the ideal type conception of bureaucracy to understand the conduct of other members and to guide their own actions; because they all act in patterns organized by the ideal type, their actions coordinate in such a way that organizations consequentially and meaningfully exist. Thus, from its beginning, organization studies have pursued the central question of how large-scale, purposefully-controlled organizations are constituted. In this paper, we will attempt to help answer this question by presenting a theoretical framework for the communicative constitution of complex organizations. We will begin with a selective and partial review of important theories that basically argue for a communicative approach to understanding the nature of organizations. Then, we discuss the meaning of the phrase "communicative constitution of organizations" by specifically defining the terms constitution, organization, and communicative. The central focus of the paper will be the presentation of our theoretical framework consisting of four types of constituting communication processes or what we call "flows." The four flows involve the processes of *membership negotiation*, *organizational self-structuring*, *activity coordination*, and *institutional positioning*. Through the explication of these four flows we will be able to argue for a theoretical framework that takes both micro- and macro-level issues into consideration in analyzing the communicative constitution of organizations.

Theoretical Underpinnings of the Analysis

Weick (1979) brought to the forefront for modern communication theorists the idea that organizations were not mere objects or systems that existed physically. For Weick, organization was the process of organizing, of interpreting an enacted environment in a way that led to orderly action. His theoretical move from organization being a static entity to a dynamic process was a dramatic turn in how organizational communication could be studied and explained. The basic theme for his organizational model can be found in the recipe for sensemaking:

"How can I know what I think until I see what I say?" (Weick, 1979, p. 133). This recipe is understood as a combination of three processes: enactment, selection, and retention; patterns of sensemaking action and communication reflectively identified and retained by members add up in retrospect to a social entity called "an organization."

Sensemaking occurred as organizations, or at least organizational members, talked to each other and retrospectively made sense of the talk which could then be stored as knowledge for future use (Weick, 1979). While Weick was far from the first theorist to take what we might call "the process turn," his varied and equivocal formulation was tantalizing enough to exert far-reaching influence across many camps of organizational communication research. But Weick's image of organizing allows it to occur even among people, in the minimal social situation, who are unaware of each other's existence. We seek an account that focuses specifically on entities more like the complex formal organizations of today's world.

Another theorist, with motives quite different from those of Weick, was Smith (1993) who explicated the relation between communication and organization by identifying root-metaphors that undergirded the discourse of organizational communication. The notion of root-metaphor, while allowing critique of theories, also offers an entry-point into the ontology of organizations. Root-metaphors capture a fundamental, underlying worldview and are able to undergird broad areas of meaning (Smith & Eisenberg, 1987). Smith's work made the organization–communication relation a central problem recognized by the field; and furthermore, suggested that reconceptualiztion of the object/unit of analysis could avoid the problems of reification and marginalization. She argued that organizational communication theories were cast in terms of containment (that organizations involve spatial limits within which communication processes occur), production (that either communication or organization is the produced, even causal outcome of the other process), and equivalence. Because of limitations in the employment of the first two metaphors, she states that many writers have argued for an equivalency position—the idea that communication is organization and organization is communication. For Smith, the weakness in this position is that, "If organization and communication are equivalent, to explicate Organizational Communication in terms of organization–communication would be tautological" (Smith, 1993, p. 28). While she does not offer an elaborated answer to the question of the communication–organization relation, she sharpened our perception of the importance and neglect of that question and moved the field toward potentially greater rigor. But she also, through the very generality of her metaphors, allowed the impression to persist that the constitution problem can have a basically simple answer.

Boden (1994) approaches the constitution issue by examining how single communication events such as telephone calls, gossip, or planning meetings structure organizations. Her goal was to demonstrate that interactive mechanisms could implicate organizational properties. By applying the technique of conversation analysis to ordinary communication events that occur in organizations, one should be able to observe the interface between talk and social structure. For example, if a researcher studied a planning meeting, she could not only analyze the adjacency-pairs of turn-taking, but examine how people use "turn-making" to advance their own political position (p. 18). However, Boden's argument is weakened by lack of a justified list of necessary and sufficient organizational properties—she discusses one organizational phenomenon after another, but does not show or argue that they "add up" to organization. Furthermore, Boden gets her list of phenomena from established organizational theories, not from specifically communication theory. Thus, her argument shares the weakness of many reductionist arguments, that it does not capture the emergent relations among phenomena that are essential to organizational studies. Studying the fragments of conversation that occur between organizational members does offer insight at the micro-level of how talk creates structure; yet this position does not provide an explanation of how all the single communication events synthesize to constitute an entire organization at the macro-level.

Taylor (1993) also tackled the discussion of what organizational communication theory should entail as he states that, "The goal of organizational communication theory ought to be to bridge the micro/macro gap, by showing how to discover the structure in the process and delineating the processes that realize the structure" (p. 261). The processes of communication create a patterning that constitutes the structure of organization and the organization itself simultaneously.

To develop his conception of communication, Taylor turns to Greimas (among, we should hasten to note, many other theoretic strands), who contends that all communication has an underlying deep narrative structure that organizes conversation through various speech acts. The constitution of an organization would involve the deep narrative structuring of a great number of elementary transactions conducted by human agents. Another main tenet is his claim that communication involves two aspects, conversation and text, with the latter (the medium of organizational structure) stabilizing and grounding, but also being enacted and potentially transformed by, the former (the medium of organizationally communicative action). Since communication creates the structure of organization, Taylor argues that it makes sense to study organizations from the communication perspective. A key point to his position, which seems to be comparable to Weick's, is that organization is an effect of communication and not its predecessor. Taylor vastly extends the range of communication theory applied to the constitution problem, but his fascination (even as a pronounced interpretivist) with structuralism leads him to root his answer to the constitution problem in a grammatical rather than a systems conception.

Deetz & Mumby (1990) provide an additional view of how organizations are constituted. First they remind us that organizations are not simply given in their current form and persist through time, but they have to be produced and reproduced continually. Second, these organizations also exist within a superstructure over time and space that includes values, laws, rules, ideology, and other institutions— indeed, their development represents a quantum leap in social abilities to concentrate and exert power. Finally, although they agree that communication is constitutive of organizational reality, Deetz and Mumby integrate the issue of power into the constituting process. Their position is that

> power is an inevitable and constitutive element in all social and institutional interaction … . All communication necessarily involves the use of power, and the role of a radical theory of organizational communication is to explicate the processes through which power is manifested and thus shapes organizational reality. (p. 37)

Discursive practices that are employed every day by members of organizations aid in the constitution of meanings in their organizational lives. Furthermore, communication is understood to be ideological because it produces and reproduces particular power structures to the exclusion of alternate power configurations. As organizational members engage in communicative practices in certain ways, they are indeed shaping and constituting their organization into a unique formation that is very different than other organizations. Deetz and Mumby bring our attention usefully to the historical, practical, and power-relevant sides to the constitution question, and discuss vital processes that we shall redescribe below. However, their main concern is not to provide a general account of how organizations are constituted, but to argue how central the question of power is to organizations.

In short, we might single out four contributions, tagged simplistically by keyword labels, that past theory has made to the constitution question: the idea of process, the question of equivalence, the idea of structure, and the idea of power. In the theoretic framework presented below, we seek to draw on these ideas while introducing a fifth: the idea of multiplicity.

Terms, Assumptions, and Context of the Model

A definition or explication of terms is very important for a paper on this topic. There are three important ones for us, to be discussed in the following order: constitution, organization, and communicative.

In his magisterial *Constitution of Society*, Giddens (1984) mentions "the constitution of day-to-day life," context as drawn upon by actors in "constituting communication," and "the phenomenon of talk … as constitutively involved in encounters" (pp. xxii, 71, 73). However, he never explicitly defines "constitution," or places it in his index, or gives it sustained focal discussion. Therefore, it might be useful for the sake of guidance to spend a little time explicating the phrase "communicative constitution of organizations." "Constitution" is a technical term in philosophy, especially in Kantian philosophy, Marxism, and phenomenology. It is rooted in the Kantian notion that objects and causal relations have reality only due to the activity of the transcendental ego. "Constitution" has a variety of philosophical meanings ranging between the epistemological (we, as researchers, know reality by constituting concepts of it) and the ontological (we, as members of society, constitute our reality, or social reality), between the cognitive and the practical/active, between creation and making sense of what already exists (Outhwaite, 1983). It also has technical meaning in speech act theory, especially in the distinction between regulative and constitutive rules (Searle, 1969; Giddens, 1984, p. 20). Constitutive rules are those which define an institutionalized speech practice, making it what it is.

All of these schools seemingly influence Giddens, the last most strongly. We would claim that he uses "constitute" so as to point to his concept of the duality of structure. As agents behave, they constitute interaction and its meaningful units because meanings, communicative acts, and episodes are what they are only due to the knowledgable, empowered, contextually positioned action that implicates them. This reflexive dependence of action and meanings extends to institutions as well: "The fixity of institutional forms does not exist in spite of, or outside, the encounters of everyday life but is implicated in those very encounters" (1984, p. 69). His sense of constitution is primarily ontological and practical, but rather than creation involves reproduction and transformation.

We use roughly Giddens' sense of "constitution" below: a pattern or array of types of interaction constitute organizations insofar as they make organizations what they are, and insofar as basic features of the organization are implicated in the system of interaction. This relevance is not necessarily outside the knowledge of members and others who are communicating—while they may see themselves as powerless to destroy or fundamentally change the organization, they typically do know how to make their communication compliant to dominant organizational directives, or resistant, or irrelevant and non-organizational. After too many resistant choices by members, the climate of the organization may change and its legitimacy may sink, even in the face of top member resource control. So communication even by members low in power still does forceful work on the constitutive task.

Following McPhee, Corman, & Dooley (1999), we see much to admire in Jelinek and Litterer's (1994) definition of an organization as a "deliberately created and maintained social institution within which consciously coordinated behaviors by members aim to produce a limited set of intended outcomes" (p. 12). We do approve the emphasis in this definition on institution-hood, though the idea that all organizations are institutions may exaggerate their fixity and conscious coordination with purposeful intent (however, see Giddens' (1976, 1984) critique of these concepts). Nonetheless, we explicitly do not assume that the institutionalized organization is an unquestionable given, that interaction across or outside institutional boundaries is inessential, or that most behavior "inside" the organization, even contributing to its persistence, is either conscious or coordinated. More importantly, this definition implies a model of the organization as behaviors inside an institutionalized container, coordinated by prior plan or cognition. So we would prefer to transform the definition to "a social interaction system, influenced by prevailing economic and legal institutional practices, and including coordinated action and interaction within and across a socially constructed system boundary, manifestly directed toward a privileged set of outcomes."

We can go farther in framing our paper if we explicate the notion of "communicative constitution of organizations" more specifically. We emphasize, first, that all communication has constitutive force. At the very least, it constitutes socially recognized agency: when we communicate, an unstated presupposition accompanying our words is that the speaker is a conscious, capable agent; when hearers interpret our words, they use the presumption of agency to help make sense of our words (Grice, 1987). On the other hand, a listener who ignores our words or rejects their validity partly undermines the establishment of agency, so the whole communication process, rather than any one act or exchange, is the locus of constitution. A second point to note is that, although communication relatively straightforwardly constitutes the agency of the communicating parties and aspects of their relationship, the constitution of outside objects, especially complex organizations, is itself more complex. Two people conversing can no more constitute, say, General Motors or the Redheaded League than two Birchers can conversationally constitute a Communist conspiracy. (Here it is important to be precise: of course two conversants can constitute a conspiracy as a topic or assumption of conversation, but generally not as the type of thing it is claimed to be in fact. Insofar as we seek to explain organizations as complex distantiated systems, the preceding argument holds.) It seems logical to expect that, in order to constitute a complex organization, a complex relation among organizational communication processes is required. Third, it is important to emphasize that not all communication is organizational. For instance, a casual chat between friends certainly makes them into a communication system, coordinates their perspectives to some degree, and even involves some conversational organization. But the friends are usually not "an organization" as a result of having communicated, in the sense relevant to the tradition of organizational communication or the definition of organization stated above.

Fourth, we will suggest relatively broad and abstract ways in which communication, including both single messages and interactive episodes, constitutes organizations. In other words, we will pitch our analysis one or more levels of abstraction above that of Boden (1994). While she showed that conversational processes can help constitute organizations, we want to identify broad but clear types of processes being carried out in the conversation. We doubt that proceeding inductively by identifying scripts or longer recurrent conversational segments will work, given the variety of organizational cultures and ways constitution can be carried out. Instead, we will proceed more deductively, identifying types in terms of their necessity for a complex organization to exist and have the impact it does in society.

For us emphasizing communication means emphasizing circulating systems or fields of messages. We will follow Mintzberg (1979), and more recently Lash & Urry (1994), in calling these "flows," but we emphasize that these flows involve crosscurrents, and are considered as constitutive communication, not merely information transmission. Thus each episode of communication is interactive, involving multiple participants with only partly shared goals and understandings; the results of communication episodes are by no means physically "transmitted," but become conditions mediated in later interaction episodes involving the initial parties or others. As a result of "chains" of interaction episodes, certain topics and ideas become manifest in successively larger domains of the organization (Sperber & Wilson, 1986), but any resemblance of an organizational communication process to an electrical network is the result of a definite array of social practices strategically engaged in by agents, admittedly under institutional and other conditions that bolster the "networkness" of the result.

The need for a larger and more general unit of analysis might be easier to convey metaphorically. Think of an organization as a collection of member cells, with messages as the blood, the hormones, the nerve impulses that affect and relate them. Of course, specific chemicals and nerve-signals affect specific cells. However, once we recognize those effects, another problem remains—how do we account for the nature and growth of whole organs or bodies? We need to register the whole array of necessary influences and types of influence on the organ and the pattern of their effects.

Similarly, it is vital to begin by identifying the types of flows that make an organization what it is, and to plot their interrelations. To state the argument less metaphorically than above, organizations are complex and have varied defining facets, so that no one grammatical or communicative form is sufficient to constitute them. On the other hand, they are so varied in size, origin, and "member" status, and thrive so persistently through changes of membership and structure, that a theory of constitution must be highly general, allowing organizations to occur in a variety of ways. Although specific messages can be decisive in the outcome of a decision-making session, for instance, no specific message or even decision session is necessary or decisive for making the group of members an organization. But decision-making sessions, as a type of message flow or interaction process, might be essential.

Our analysis compares and contrasts with two threads of argument implicit in the theoretical writings of Taylor and his colleagues. In one thread, they argue that specific grammatical forms (for instance, ditransitive forms or, more narrowly, commands, or as another instance, narrative form (Taylor, 1993; Taylor, Cooren, Giroux, & Robichaud, 1996)) are constitutive of or fundamental to organizations. Usually they argue this by showing how important organizational processes can be represented/enacted, or can only be represented/enacted, by using the grammatical form in question. We see this kind of argument as valuable in pointing out how essential functions of organizing are rooted in communication, and possibly in identifying formal communicative features to focus on in analysis of discursive transcripts. On the other hand, the necessity Taylor and his colleagues face in focusing on broad grammatical features is that the grammatical forms have limited power to distinguish and explain complex social forms such as organizations. For example, commands and narratives occur importantly in marriages and casual chat just as in corporate communication. And in focusing on the "command" form, they may abstract it from a type of discourse flow in which it is an important but incomplete part, like a cell nucleus studied apart from its role within a cell.

A discussion of the ongoing constitution of an enduring systemic form such as an organization automatically raises the issue of functionalism. Are we presuming the existence, stability, orderliness, universal utility, and even self-sustaining powers of organizational systems in a way which derogates the agency of human individuals or their unequal power and treatment? No—we explicitly deny these assumptions. But we believe that a more limited version of functionalism is unavoidable or at least useful in discussing the topic of the persistence of organizations and societies of organizations. Organizations are a social form created and maintained by manifestly and reflexively reifying practices of members—the members think of, treat, and relate to organizations as real, higher-order systems, and make provision for their survival. In addition, some communication patterns may contribute to the existence and persistence of organizations as an unintended consequence, and may even be necessary for their survival. Any analysis that points this out will sound functionalistic; we do not presume that the commonsense existence of organizations is real in any sense beyond its reality within and conditioning of the practices of members, or that such "reality" is free from ambiguity, aporias, or contradictions. But interpretive, postmodern, and even some critical analyses are sometimes phrased so as to imply that organizations are unreal figments—that "General Motors" is not a thing that could be causally relevant to lives of hundreds of thousands of people or the existence of automobiles on roads. This implication, we think, is silly. More scarily, the form of our theory is eerily suggestive of Parsons' (Parsons & Smelser, 1965) four-function scheme that dominated 1950s sociology and stimulated the currently fashionable ire against functionalism. His model's acronym is AGIL, which represents the four basic functions necessary for the persistence of a social system such as an organization. The letters of the acronym stand for Adaptation—the problem of acquiring and using resources; Goal attainment—the problem of setting, legitimizing, and implementing goals relative to higher-order systems; Integration—the problem of maintaining solidarity or coordination among subsystems; and Latency—the problem of creating, preserving, and transmitting the system's distinctive culture and values (see Rollag, n. d.). This approach was criticized for conservatism, in underplaying the role of contradiction and change in systems, and for mechanism, in using an oversimplified model of agency. In contrast, our analysis will expose the critical and interpretive edges of organizational constitution.

For instance, we see this theory as having three values. First, it sketches an explanation of the power and efficacy of organizations in the West-dominated world today. They are the kind of thing that can have such power because they constitute themselves in the four ways noted below. As Perrow indicates (1979), such theories have critical import. Second, its four flows of messages are actually more or less hidden implications of conversations and reports within and outside organizations, operating on a level that may not be obvious or seem important to members. Explicating such implications and presuppositions is a hermeneutic task, potentially allowing members to understand their own communication better. Third, these flows are arenas in which organizations do vary and can be changed in their fundamental nature. Many authors have claimed, over the decades, that new forms of organizations have emerged, as a result of various social and technological developments. A theory such as this one gives us a template by which to detect, diagnose, and assess novel organizational phenomena.

Before beginning the specific description of the four constitutive communication processes, a brief overview might be useful. We want to argue that organizations are constituted in four different communicative flows, not just one, and that the flows are different in their main direction and in their contribution to organizational constitution, with each making a different and important contribution. Furthermore, we argue that organizations and communication are varied enough so that we cannot go much further in explaining constitution at this level of generality than by discussing types of flow. We see our theory as building on and elaborating the theoretical underpinnings reviewed above, summarized by the four keywords of process, equivalence, structure, and power. Our emphasis on communicative flow takes up Weick's idea of process; our four flows escape tautology in showing the equivalence of communication and organization. In each flow, a sort of social structure is generated through interaction; and by allowing for one flow to control or condition another, the model allows for specifically organizational power. The types of flow are analytically different—while they are often distinct, a single message can and often does make more than one type of contribution. Also, as mentioned above, each kind of "flow" is actually a kind of interactive communication episode, usually amounting to multi-way conversation or text passage, typically involving reproduction of as well as resistance to the rules and resources of the organization. The four flows link the organization to its members (membership negotiation), to itself reflexively (self-structuring), to the environment (institutional positioning); the fourth is used to adapt interdependent activity to specific work situations and problems (activity coordination). Figure 2.1 gives a schematic of an organizational system and the four directions of flow.

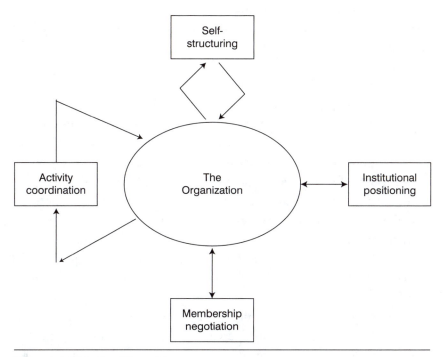

Figure 2.1 Explication of the model

Membership Negotiation

Organizations always must include members and are distinct in nature from the members. Thus, one process vital to an organization is the communication that establishes and maintains or transforms its relationship with each of its members. We should emphasize the obvious—"membership" in any one organization is not a natural property of people, and is instead constituted by/in this flow of communication. But in constituting members, the communication process importantly constitutes the organization, since one must be a member of something.

One of the best-known examples of member constitution is member recruitment and socialization (Jablin, 1987). Prospective members must be evaluated and categorized; both the new member and the organization must decide to create a relationship; and the new member must be incorporated into the routines and structures of the organization, and vice versa. However, in the course of this socialization process, the organization is simultaneously framed as having prior existence, a multitude of other members, and the power to induce a relation of co-membership (as well as other relations like supervision and mentorship) between members. This facet of the individual–organization relationship is well recognized; although some others are less so.

One other facet is the shaping of the member relation itself. What does it mean for Al to be a member of or related to organization O, and how is the answer to that question worked out? A fairly good example is embedded in Delany's new-wave science fiction novel *Dhalgren* (Delany, 1974). His amnesiac hero, the Kid, occupies an anomalous position on the outskirts of a gang in an anomic future world. The Kid is accepted by the gang, even has some leadership status and respect, yet both he and the gang are constantly aware that he is not a member. Similar membership issues are faced by engineers or managers "loaned" from one organization to work in another. This facet shades over quickly into a second relationship, involving identification and identity (Tompkins and Cheney, 1985).

Interaction processes that might be expected given the nature of this flow include, first, a dialectic of reputation and courtship, including all the varying strategies exhibited during job-seeking and recruitment. It is common knowledge that both the organization and the person typically take the most positive line possible, often tacitly offering to redefine themselves to fit the other's expectations more closely. A second web of processes involves identification or positioning by individuals, and inclusion by organizations: these terms are classically used to refer to the problem of membership construction. Finally, we must not forget that the problem of relation between individual and organization exists even for members very high in status; power-claiming and spokesmanship are processes of negotiation of relations of power over organizational resources or the whole organization. For instance, Pacanowsky (1987) notes how Bill and then Bob Gore are clearly in charge of Gore, Inc., yet avoid many labels and rituals common in other companies that would coalesce their power as formal position. Instead, they try to manage an ambiguous role as equal, yet inevitably "more equal," organization member.

Why is this process a vital facet of communicative constitution of organizations? One answer is that organizations, like all social forms, exist only as a result of human agency (Giddens, 1984). By many definitions of communication, only individual humans can communicate, so when communication constitutes organization, the relation of the communicators to the organization is important. We would want to go farther, though, to emphasize that organizations ineluctably involve members, almost, as the metaphor suggests, as parts or limbs of the organization. Organizations exist when they draw members in, and lead them to take part in and understand the interactional world unique to the organization.

Organizational Self-Structuring

Organizations do not draw members and coordinate work automatically or as a result of natural tendency; some individual or group typically works hard to bring the organization into being, make decisions about such matters as member time and resource investment. In short, organizations are the objects not merely of reflexive attention but of reflexive control and design—of self-structuring. We would claim that this reflexive self-structuring distinguishes organizations from groupings such as lynch mobs or mere neighborhoods; it is essential to the explanation of the power of formal organizations in history, especially but certainly not only Western economic history (McPhee, 1985). It is important to emphasize that self-structuring is a communication process among organizational role-holders and groups; it is analytically distinct from, though often part of the same messages as, communication that helps coordinate the activities of members. It is unique in that it does not directly concern work, but rather the internal relations, norms, and social entities that are the skeleton for connection, flexing, and shaping of work processes.

Examples of communication like this are easy to give—if anything, they are stereotypical of organizational communication. Official documents such as charters, organization charts, policy and procedure manuals; decision-making and planning forums; orders, directives, and the more casual announcements that often substitute for them; processes of employee evaluation and feedback; budgeting, accounting, and other formalized control processes—all these are mainly media for organizational self-structuring. Self-structuring communication includes any process that serves to steer the organization or part of it. It also involves processes that design the organization, the setting up of subsystems, hierarchical relationships, and structural information-processing arrangements (Galbraith, 1973). Johnson (1981, chap. 7) gives examples of how recursively evolving and dialogic communication is responsible for creating and documenting formal structure. Examination of several borderline cases reveals the impact and uses of self-structuring communication. Larson (1992) discusses the process of network organization construction among entrepreneurial firms. In the cases she examined, contracts and other legal self-structuring mechanisms were not present or at least emphasized. In their place she found an extended process of mutual exploration based on reputation and early cooperation followed by trust building and expectation clarification that laid the groundwork for operational and strategic integration of plans and knowledge stocks. The self-structuring process for the network had to go beyond mere considerations of economic advantage to achieve low uncertainty, high mutual knowledge, and high goal alignment before full cooperation could be risked. If we decide to call Larson's sort of network dyad an organization, we do so partly because of this meta-layer of self-structuring process that grounds and solidifies the collaboration. Another seemingly borderline example is Pacanowsky's (1987) discussion of Gore, Inc. Gore operates while avoiding reliance on hierarchy, formal structure, and rigid controls. However, even Pacanowsky's account recognizes how senior organization members engage in sustained reflection on organizational operations and stimulate extensive communication about work decisions, to allow for widespread responsibility over work operations rather than centralized responsibility. Self-structuring is made globally collective rather than centralized. In addition, Pacanowsky notes in passing that this diffused responsibility does not eliminate processes that control and monitor the division of labor. In short, there are many forms of self-structuring, but the process itself is vital.

Why is it vital? McPhee (1985) argues that the communication of formal structure—one form of self-structuring, though a narrower concept than ours—has two important impacts within organizations. First, it substitutes for what we have called collaborative communication above, by pre-fixing work arrangements and norms rather than let them emerge during collaboration. And next, it is authoritative metacommunication that guides but also controls the collaboration and membership-negotiation processes, that takes organizational processes as an object so that the organization as a whole can deal with its environment and be exploited by powerful interests. In the process of achieving these outcomes, the organization is inevitably internally differentiated or distantiated. In addition to these effects of formalized structuring, we would point to several others as not merely useful (for organizational survival or profit) but constitutive. It is in the process of self-structuring that the organization as a system takes control of and influences itself, not merely to handle immediate problems but to set a persistent routine procedure for response. Only through developing this analogue to a sense of self can an organization avoid problems of over-adaptation, incoherence, and confusion. And this kind of reflexive communication constitutes the organization for itself, a basic process in its overall constitution.

However, by taking self-structuring to be a communication process, we avoid the illusion that it itself is unidirectional, internally coherent, or successful by definition. Self-structuring communication is subject to discrepancy, dispersal, and ambiguity, with varying consequences for the system, subsystems, individuals, and outside interests. It is an interpretive and political process, stuck in socioeconomic traditions that, in the West, favor corporate bureaucracy.

Nonetheless, to contribute even at a minimum to the constitution of the organization, communicative interchanges of this sort must assume and implicate a sense of the organization as a differentiated yet purposeful whole. In relatively complex organizations, communication usually must tacitly recognize a governance structure with legitimate power, and whether in implementing, serving, subverting, or resisting it, must reproduce it.

Activity Coordination

Organizations, by definition, have at least one manifest purpose, and the activity of members and subgroups is partly directed toward it. To a substantial extent, these activities are coordinated as a result of the organization's self-structuring, which creates a division of labor, a standard task-flow sequence, and a series of policies and plans for work. However, such structural directions can never be complete or completely relevant, are never completely understood, and are frequently amended in an informal patchwork of adjustments. In addition, exceptions and problems arise frequently and require coordinated adjustments out of the ordinary (Perrow, 1967). The process of adjusting the work process and solving immediate practical problems requires the sort of communication we call activity coordination.

The clearest exponent of activity coordination as a vital organization-constituting process is probably Barnard (1938), who presents organizations as cooperative systems. All the activities of executives are dependent, in Barnard's view, on the cooperative work they support and the cooperative stance taken by workers toward executive arrangements. More recently, developers of systems of computer-assisted cooperative work have devoted tremendous effort to the analysis of cooperative work interaction. For instance, Filippi and Theureau (1993) studied work in a control room for the Paris metro, uncovering a complex weave of mutual assistance and attentiveness that resolved train system breakdowns. They found some general principles of coordination. For instance, the Controller "who starts handling a disruption is responsible for it during its entire course, because he knows all the surrounding circumstances and the consequences of his own decisions." As well, all Controllers "actively listen ... to the details of the solving of an incident ... to be able to anticipate delays and amendments ... on their own sector" (pp. 182, 181). Of course, the real challenge comes when circumstances force principles like these to be violated.

Exemplary accounts of coordination are well developed by structural contingency theory (Mintzberg, 1979). In Mintzberg's description there are five (later seven) kinds of coordination processes. The most obviously relevant example is mutual adjustment, with highly skilled or mostly unorganized members working out solutions to problems on the spot. Nevertheless his other processes also involve activity coordination, as workers, say, determine how to substitute for one another on an assembly line and how to relieve the pressures of line work.

In activity coordination, as in the other flows, one finds multiple processes and attitudes toward the organization. For example, members can coordinate on how not to do work, or coordination may be in abeyance as members seek power over one another or external advantage for themselves from the system. Nonetheless, what seems inescapable is that members presume that they are working not just on related tasks but within a common social unit with an existence that goes beyond the work interdependence itself. This presumption may be a result of self-structuring discourse.

Institutional Positioning in the Social Order of Institutions

One other type of communication flow remains to be discussed, communication outside the organization, to other entities, "at the macro level" in systems or functional terms. Such entities include suppliers, customers, and competitors and collaborators, including merger or acquisition candidates. Probably also more powerful organizations such as potential buyers and governmental regulators could be added. Sometimes this communication is presented as a direct product of the focal organization to which it is responsible as a formal entity. More often the communicators are individuals on boundary-spanning roles who negotiate terms of recognition of the organization's existence and place at the same time as they negotiate their own relationships. "Identity negotiation" is an appealing label for this type of communication; we have chosen the broader term "positioning" because the latter includes both identity establishment and development and maintenance of a "place" in the inter-organizational or larger social system. Since identity is inescapably comparative and relational, these two processes merge inextricably.

For example, much of the work of the "institutional school" of organizational theory contains examples of this sort of communication, since an "institution" is recognized as such by and within a community of its peer and related organizations—its "organization-set" in Evan's words (1966). Thus, Meyer and Rowan (1977) note how a formal organization chart and similar documents are valuable in establishing the image of legitimacy and rationality presented to fund-suppliers and other peer institutions in the community. The whole process of relationship building involved in capital acquisition is an example of this sort of communication flow. Another broad array of examples is surveyed by DiMaggio and Powell's (1983) article on the "iron cage" of institutional isomorphism. The forces bringing about isomorphism are all direct or indirect communication processes, and many of them have force because they create the conditions for future communicative relations. In communication, Cheney's analysis (1991) of the National Council of Catholic Bishops' pastoral letter on disarmament illustrates the concern to address other organizations, including other branches of the Church, the Papal See, and both Catholic and general popular audiences.

Of course, all sorts of "business" are transacted between an organization and other agents in its environment, but in the process a number of constitutive moves are required to establish any organization as a "presence" in the inter-systemic institutional order. Thus, whether an organization sells a line of merchandise, attracts capital or donations, or certifies that it has met governmental standards, several processes seem almost unavoidable. The focal organization must actually connect with and induce return communication with important elements of its environment, and vice versa. It must establish or negotiate an image as a viable relational partner—customer, supplier, neighbor, for example. This image minimally implies creating an impression that the organization meets the acceptability conditions set up by the government and other vital stakeholders. Classically, Apple Computers gained respect only when its managers negotiated an image that allowed them to secure capital and marketing access; start-up companies are often marginal because they lack such reassuring features as institutional status (that protects their property), routine practices, and relations to suppliers and customers. Illegal organizations like the Mafia are also marginal, though even they depend on relations to dummy corporations and use force partly because they lack access to some usual economic institutions. More secure organizations build relationships of trust with important others, and even try to gain control of the uncertainty in their environments in various ways (Pfeffer & Salancik, 1978).

This sort of communication is vital for constituting organizations because organizations exist in human societies that already are organized, that already have institutional ways of maintaining order, allocating material resources, regulating trade, and dividing labor— and, of course, that already have ways of communicating about all these practices. Without an institutional backdrop, any but the most primitive human organization is unthinkable; certainly today's complex organizations depend on political, cultural, economic, social, and communicative institutions for their constitution. If each new organization had to reinvent the concepts of property rights and contracts, membership and management, as well as the kind of organization they are (corporation, social service agency), there would be few organizations in existence today. Moreover, institutions like these exist partly because they allow inter-organizational relations— they allow each organization to draw on other organizations for the variety of resources that it needs to accomplish its goals and maintain itself. Whether or not a completely autonomous organization could exist, in practice, most depend on others, and so, in this dependence, organizations must constitute themselves as practical relational partners.

However, as the proliferation of new organizational forms suggests, there is no one configuration that an organization must use to present its identity to the institutional community. The minimum necessary process seems to be negotiating inclusion, and the measure of inclusion is a purely practical one.

Summary and Implications

We hope the accounts of the four flows above convey both their relatedness and their difference.

The four flows allow four divergent descriptions of organizational processes: the first recounts the struggle of individuals to master or influence their member roles, statuses, and relations to the organization. The second articulates how organizational leaders design, implement, and suffer problems with decision and control mechanisms. The third focuses on members engaging in interdependent work or deviating from pure collaborative engagement. The fourth describes the organization as a partner, often anthropomorphized, in exchange and other social relations with other organizations.

We definitely do not mean to say that if the four kinds of flows exist, an organization automatically has been constituted and exists. To illustrate the problem, we might consider a neighborhood bar. Suppose one evening two bar patrons discuss going out tomorrow to clean up the neighborhood; in another corner, out of earshot of the first, two other patrons discuss the rules that ought to be followed in clean-up efforts (not too early, etc.); and so on for other groups of patrons. Even if all four types of conversation took place, would the neighborhood be constituted as an organization? We would say not. The four flows would need to be more interrelated, more mutually influential.

For one thing, the four flows need to develop and share a realm of mutual topical relevance, within which the relevance of the other flows themselves is also recognized. This sphere of mutual relevance is what we might call organizational knowledge (McPhee, Corman, and Dooley, 1999). One other requirement would seem to be that the legitimate authority of self-structuring, relative to the other flows, is recognized in the other flows. We do not have reason to believe that this set of relations is sufficient, but we cannot think of others. At any rate, we hope it is clear that all of these flows are required, and that a constituted organization is not just a set of flows, but a complex relationship of them.

To go back to the four keywords we used earlier to reference past theories—process, equivalence, structure, and power—we agree with the arguments that organization is rooted in or "painted on" the communication process (Taylor, 1993), though for us the relation is emergence of a higher order system. In a sense this is equivalence, and in a sense not. Organization is not simply communication, but a relationship among distinct types of analytically separable processes, so saying that it "is communication" is misleading, especially from the point of view of level of analysis. Among our communication processes are some that are purposefully designed to generate, and more likely than others do generate organizational structure. This requirement is partly due to the inescapable need for structure in organizations, and partly due to a corporatist and systemic ideology rampant in the world today. But perhaps a deeper sense of structure, on a level with Taylor's text-conversation dyad, as it specifically applies to organizations, is the structured relation among the four flows/crosscurrents of organizational communication that inform, enable, and constrain one another. Finally, in various ways, these four currents, especially self-structuring, depend on and generate power imbalance and communicative distortions. Yet they ground a unique approach to critical theory, and are not simply reducible to general theories of ideology, distorted communication, power-knowledge relations, or self-practice relations.

We would claim that the practical and theoretical implications of our model are broad but difficult to trace because they could be developed in many ways. For instance, Child (1980) argues that a number of problems of decision-making and coordination, which for us would be "activity coordination," as well as motivation, which might be included in "membership negotiation" in our model," actually stem from inappropriate organizational structure (or "self-structuring"). If problems apparent in one flow can really develop due to patterns in another flow, we clearly must be aware of all four flows and their potential effects when we diagnose organizational problems. On the other hand, problem-solving efforts must also recognize that problems arising in one flow might nevertheless be capable of solution mainly within another flow, as when problems of member resistance to perceived exploitation are alleviated by creation of a structure wherein members can be promoted frequently (Edwards, 1979). Of course, the same points made about practical diagnosis and remedy must apply to theory: theories focused on one of the flows may be blind to implications of other flows for them. For instance, consider attempts to theorize formal organizational structure (McPhee, 1985; Smith, 1990). Students of information technology and new organizational forms have frequently noted that in some important ways, intra- and inter-organizational cooperation (i.e., activity coordination and institutional positioning) based on informal relations and trust have come to supplant formal structure as modalities of organizational control (Morton, 1991). Whether or not these developments alter the theories of formal structure, clearly the latter must take the former into serious account.

We have argued that organizations are constituted in four different communication flows, not just one; that the flows are different in their main direction and in their contribution to organizational constitution, with each making a different and important contribution. Membership negotiation, organizational self-structuring, activity coordination, and institutional positioning underpin the theoretical framework that was presented in this paper. We have argued that such a variety of message flows is required because complex organizations require distinct types of relations to four "audiences." They must enunciate and maintain relations to their members through membership negotiation, to themselves as formally controlled entities through self-structuring, to their internal subgroups and processes through activity coordination, and to their colleagues in a society of institutions through institutional positioning. These four sorts of communication are analytically distinct, even though a single message can address more than one constitutive task. Finally, we hope that this theoretical framework provides a unique explanation of the complex ways in which organizations are constituted communicatively.

Authors' Note

This paper was presented at the Western States Communication Association Convention, where it won a Top Three award from the Organizational Communication Division. The first author thanks the Herberger Professorship in Communication at Arizona State University for support during the development of this paper.

Afterword: Robert D. McPhee

This article about CCO drew a degree of attention that was, at least to me, surprising. A central concern motivating our article was reactive: We wanted to oppose the search for a single process of CCO, and the assumption that there should or had to be a single process. We didn't argue for a multiple model very rigorously, but we did seemingly connect with a broad consensus that many different sorts of organizational communication have constitutive force. However, the implied theoretical question, whether the strongest account provides just one model, or a small number of different but related models, or an unruly plethora of accidentally constitutive processes, still hasn't generated much debate.

References

Barnard, C. (1938). *The functions of the executive.* Cambridge, MA: Harvard University Press.

Boden, D. (1994). *The business of talk: Organizations in action.* Cambridge, U.K.: Polity Press.

Cheney, G. (1991). *Rhetoric in an organizational society: Managing multiple identities.* Columbia, SC: University of South Carolina Press.

Child, J. (1980). *Organization.* London: Harper & Row.

Deetz, S., & Mumby, D. (1990). Power, discourse, and the workplace: Reclaiming the critical tradition. In J. A. Anderson (Ed.), *Communication yearbook, 13* (pp. 18–47). London: Sage.

Delany, S. (1974). *Dhalgren.* New York: Bantam.

DiMaggio, P. J., & Powell, W. W. (1983). The iron cage revisited: Institutional isomorphism and collective rationality in organizational fields. *American Sociological Review, 48,* 147–160.

Edwards, R. (1979). *Contested terrain: The transformation of the workplace in the twentieth century.* London: Heinemann.

Evan, W. M. (1966). The organization set: Toward a theory of interorganizational relations. In J. D. Thompson (Ed.), *Approaches to organizational design* (pp. 173–188). Pittsburgh, PA: University of Pittsburgh Press.

Filippi, G., & Theureau, J. (1993). Analyzing cooperative work in an urban traffic control room for the design of a coordination support system. In G. de Michelis, C. Simone, & K. Schmidt (Eds.), *Proceedings of the third European conference on computer-supported cooperative work* (pp. 171–186). Boston: Kluwer Academic Publishers.

Galbraith, J. (1973). *Designing complex organizations.* Reading, MA: Addison-Wesley.

Giddens, A. (1976). *New rules of sociological method.* New York: Basic Books.

Giddens, A. (1984). *The constitution of society: Outline of the theory of structuration.* Berkeley: University of California Press.

Grice, P. (1987). *Studies in the way of words.* Cambridge, MA: Harvard University Press.

Jablin, F. M. (1987). Organizational entry, assimilation, and exit. In F. M. Jablin, L. L. Putnam, K. H. Roberts, & L. W. Porter (Eds.), *Handbook of organizational communication: An interdisciplinary perspective* (pp. 679–740). Newbury Park, CA: Sage.

Jelinek, M., & Litterer, J. A. (1994). Toward a cognitive theory of organizations. *Advances in managerial cognition and organizational information processing, Vol. 5* (pp. 3–41). Greenwich, CT: JAI Press.

Johnson, B. M. (1981). *Communication: The process of organizing.* Boston, MA: American Press.

Larson, A. (1992). Network dyads in entrepreneurial settings: A study of the governance of exchange relationships. *Administrative Science Quarterly, 37,* 76–104.

Lash, S., & Urry, J. (1994). *Economies of signs and space.* London: Sage.

McPhee, R. D. (1985). Formal structure and organizational communication. In R. D. McPhee & P. K. Tompkins (Eds.), *Organizational communication: Traditional themes and new directions* (pp. 149–178). Beverly Hills, CA: Sage.

McPhee, R. D., Corman, S. R., & Dooley, K. J. (1999, May). Theoretical and methodological axioms for the study of organizational knowledge and communication. Paper presented at the annual convention of the International Communication Association Convention, Chicago.

Meyer, J. W., & Rowan, B. (1977). Institutionalized organizations: Formal structure as myth and ceremony. *American Journal of Sociology, 83,* 340–363.

Mintzberg, H. (1979). *The structuring of organizations: A synthesis of the research.* Englewood Cliffs, NJ: Prentice-Hall, Inc.

Morton, M. S. S. (1991). *The corporation of the 1990s: Information technology and organizational transformation.* New York: Oxford University Press.

Outhwaite, W. (1983). *Concept formation in social science.* London: Routledge and Kegan Paul.

Pacanowsky, M. (1987). Communication in the empowering organization. In J. Anderson (Ed.), *Communication yearbook, 11.* Beverly Hills, CA: Sage.

Parsons, T., & N. J. Smelser (1965). *Economy and society.* New York: Free Press.

Perrow, C. (1967). A framework for the comparative analysis of organizations. *American Sociological Review, 32,* 194–208.

Perrow, C. (1979). *Complex organizations: A critical essay.* Dallas, TX: Scott, Foresman.

Pfeffer, J., & Salancik, G. (1978). *The external control of organizations: A resource dependence perspective.* New York: Harper & Row.

Rollag, K. (n. d.). Parsons' social system (Structural functionalists), *Encyclopedia of organizational theory* [Online]. Available: http://faculty.babson.edu/krollag/org_site/encyclop/parsons.html. Accessed 4/28/08.

Searle, J. R. (1969). *Speech acts: An essay in the philosophy of language.* Cambridge, U.K.: Cambridge University Press.

Smith, D. (1990). *Texts, facts, and femininity: Exploring the relations of ruling.* New York: Routledge.

Smith, R. C. (1993). Images of organizational communication: Root-metaphors of the organization-communication relation. Paper presented to the Organizational Communication Division at the International Communication Association Convention, Washington, D.C.

Smith, R. C., & Eisenberg, E. (1987). Conflict at Disneyland: A root-metaphor analysis. *Communication Monographs 54,* 367–380.

Sperber, D., & Wilson, D. (1986). *Relevance.* Cambridge, MA: Harvard University Press.

Taylor, J. R. (1993). *Rethinking the theory of organizational communication: How to read an organization.* Norwood, NJ: Ablex.

Taylor, J. R., Cooren, F., Giroux, H., & Robichaud, D. (1996). Are organization and communication equivalent? Paper presented at a conference on Organizational Communication and Change: Challenges in the Next Century, Austin, TX.

Tompkins, P. K., & Cheney, G. (1985). Communication and unobtrusive control in contemporary organizations. In R. D. McPhee, & P. K. Tompkins (Eds.), *Organizational communication: Traditional themes and new directions* (pp. 179–210). Beverly Hills, CA: Sage.

Weber, M. (1968). *Economy and society.* Berkeley: University of California Press. (Original work published 1922.)

Weick, K. (1979). *The social psychology of organizing* (2nd ed.). Reading, MA: Addison-Wesley.

3

AGENTS OF CONSTITUTION IN COMMUNIDAD

Constitutive Processes of Communication in Organizations

Robert D. McPhee and Joel Iverson

In the Mexican state of Sonora, around the county (*municipio*) of Cucurpe, certain land and water rights are legally under community control. Land rights are exercised through a (actually, several) peasant corporations, or corporate communities, especially the *Comunidad de Cucurpe* (which means roughly "where the dove calls") (Sheridan, 1988; we will mainly use Sheridan's extensive analysis of *Cucurpeno* corporate community throughout this chapter). Although the communal model evolved under the guidance if not control of Jesuit missions in the 17th century, the legitimate existence of the collective corporations wavered with Mexican political change, was opposed by rich private ranchers, and was advocated in the 19th and 20th centuries based on skimpily documented traditions of joint usage.

The specific *Comunidad de Cucurpe*, for existence, dated from early times, but had to be fought for by a series of leaders and committed members for over a century of governmental neglect and rancher subversion of the advocacy process (Sheridan, 1988, Ch. 8 *passim*). The fight culminated in 1975, when the government officially recognized, under the Federal Law of Agrarian Reform, the *Comunidad's* status "as a full-fledged 'Indian community'" (p. 160) and right to over 21,000 hectares of land, and simultaneously recognized 240 peasants as official members with rights to that land. The *Comunidad* governs its common resources through a president and other elected officers, and a monthly general assembly.

By law, the *comunidad* owns and controls all the land within its boundaries. However, by tradition, arable land, the most valuable, has been controlled and worked by households for decades if not centuries, and only in 1975 was their right to inherit or sell their land abrogated by the government. There are roughly four groups in contention: ordinary *comunidad* members, members who claim rights to sections of land, Cucurpe residents who claim communal lands by tradition even though they are not *comunidad* members, and rich ranchers who legally own (due to government grant) sections of land that was once communal, and try to take advantage of common grazing land as well, even fencing it in for the use of their herds. The first three groups are united in striving to recover expropriated lands from the ranchers, and they agree on the value of common grazing land (since it cannot be practically developed by household efforts, nor is it practical to raise cattle on plots of the size individual householders could claim), but they are divided in their attitudes toward household ownership of arable land developed and farmed by the household. Poorer members, tending to be in the first group, tend to want land to be distributed by the *comunidad*, and taken away from nonmembers for redistribution, while members with traditional title to land want that title to be respected. On the other hand, all the groups share a vision of individual household ownership and working of the land; communal ownership, a political vision of the Mexican state and bureaucracy of the late twentieth century, is a residual solution for the peasants themselves. Across Mexico, conflicts among groups like these have been so disruptive to the development of corporate communities that a new land tenure regularization program (COMPREDE) was instituted in 1992 (Appendini, 2001).

The *Comunidad de Cucurpe* is an organization that is legally recognized, has clear powers, and exercises them in impactful ways. It has continually, since before its legal recognition, been a focus and medium of community, legal, and economic conflict. It is intertwined with a system of other organizations and institutions, including the purportedly more basic economic unit of the household (Sheridan, 1988; Appendini, 2001). Undoubtably, the organization is alive in the discourse of its members, opponents, and regulating bureaucrats. How is that possible? How does discourse create, sustain, or otherwise support this sort of social reality?

The phrase "communicative constitution of organization" (abbreviated CCO in the rest of this chapter) has come to refer to a number of interconnected questions: "How do a set of people, or practices, or messages, become an organization? How do people come to represent themselves as identified with or agents of organizations? How do 'external' audiences come to represent organizations as social actors? How do organizations possess the powers that have let them become so powerful and impactful in modern society and global processes?" The article that serves as a springboard for this one (McPhee & Zaug, 2000) emphasized that last question, but recent scholarship has emphasized how important and puzzling all of them are. Questions like these have become more important as the traditional "systems view" of society (Parsons, 1951) has broken down, and as social creativity in the institutional sphere has accelerated. The rapid cycle of organizational creation and dissolution, the decline of norms of lifelong employment and mutual loyalty, and the strategic creation of organizations to exploit innovations that serve and exploit other going organizations (Microsoft in the 1980s), or tax laws (Enron), or international boundaries, has eliminated the image of organizations as given, enduring realities. Instead, we have today multiple images, of organizations as Chinese boxes, or churning coalescences, or ... webs of words.

One approach to CCO has emphasized the constitutive power of communication generally, the equivalence of communicating and organizing, and the nature of "organizations" as resultants emerging from autopoetic communication processes. Both the concept of organizing in Karl Weick's work, and the conception of coorientation as the basic unit of organization in James Taylor and Elizabeth Van Every's work (2000; Taylor, 2000) fall under this basic description. Especially for the latter, a key idea is that we can see the basic building block, if not the essence, of organizations in a single statement or a single, relatively short conversation (cf. Cooren, 2004).

The conception in McPhee and Zaug (2000) differed from this image in several important ways. First, constitutive communication was conceptualized as *multiprocessual*: the "four flows" it described (discussed more below) are importantly different communication processes, related to each other in complicated ways. No one process or flow is sufficient to constitute an organization, although all have constitutive force. Second, the four flows implied different "sites" of organizational communication. The sites are typically physically and temporally different—contract negotiations for a baseball player don't occur too often in the dugout during a game, though both are vital in different ways to constitute a ballteam. Different people, different professions are present, often under conditions that are spelled out in other organizational communication. Thus, constitution was conceived as essentially multisite, and worked only as a function of the relations among the sites.

McPhee and Zaug based their conceptual argument on the assumptions of Anthony Giddens' theory of structuration (Giddens, 1976, 1979, 1984; cf. McPhee and Poole, 1980; Poole, Seibold, & McPhee, 1985a, b). One problem with the foundation of McPhee and Zaug is that Giddens was notoriously brief in his discussion of communication. He presented his social theory as a revision of interpretive social theory that fully registered the social and structural bases and consequences of interpretation processes. Communication is analyzed mainly as an element or dimension of all human praxis, a dimension that is not really focal in Giddens' theorizing. In particular, due to his opposition to structuralism and post-structuralism (1987a), his position gives little room to the constitutive dimension of communication.

In this chapter, we want to do two main things. First, we will review and synthesize recent work done to articulate more fully a structurational conception of communicative constitution. Second, we will use that conception, in addition to analysis of examples, to explain and elaborate, perhaps even amend the four flows of McPhee and Zaug.

Constitution, Communication, and Organization

The Context of Communication

Communication is a dimension of social interaction and practice, specifically the dimension in which meaning is marshaled in the course of practice; communication draws on and reproduces the signification resources of a social system, but always in practical contexts. This is a different image than that conveyed by theories of social construction—structural resources, including an array of signification resources and communicative practices, are not generated or negotiated from scratch, so much as maintained or transformed. That idea changes but only begins to address the constitution problem, which becomes, how, from the resources of the past, do humans organize a meaningful present?

For communication theory in general, "constitution" has (at least) three common meanings—constitution of a sign as meaningful within a system of meanings; constitution of a party as an agent in interaction or communication; and constitution of a social relationship or system as an institution. The first is a matter of practice or language game—a sign or element has been constituted as meaningful if we know how to go on with it in a language-game (Wittgenstein, 1953). Note that this definition conceals a number of complexities: if one man yells, "Brick," and another brings him a brick, the word "brick" has evidently worked as a sign. But what about the physical brick carried by the second man? What if the second man brings too large a brick, from another pile? What if the second man demurs, explaining that he dislikes this game? Perhaps more importantly, the definition gives a criterion of completion, not an account of how constitution is accomplished in process or, for that matter, initially comes about—how is the game set up? How are ambiguities and puzzles worked out, so that "knowing how to go on" comes to be treatable as routine? How is it tested for adequacy as a game, and modified if inadequate? How does it come to be an accepted part of a culture or economy? All of these questions are relevant to the *comunidad de Cucurpe*—both early and late in its history, we can imagine members confronting the practical issue, "Where do we go from here? How will the laws about being a *comunidad*, or its officers, or its powers, work here, and how does our committee relate to this new reality of '*comunidad*?" There is a difference between the meaning of a sign and its constitution: neither is simply reducible to the other. And this difference brings the constitution of signs into question.

The second meaning of "constitution," constitution of an agent, involves recognition of the powers of the agent to, e.g., make claims or otherwise participate in interaction. It is widely understood that not every human being, in every situation, is an agent—if someone in a coma falls off the bed and crushes an ant, or if someone does it unaware that the ant is there, the results are not attributed to the person's agency or agentive powers, nor should they be.

One theoretical challenge is that contextual factors are vital in constituting agency: a person of age 15 cannot legally purchase liquor or vote in the United States, and linguistic knowledge, vocal chords, low noise level, and recognition from other conversants are necessary for someone to participate in a conversation. This sense of socially enabled/constrained agency is important in everyday conduct and in a long tradition of social theory: the agency of classes, women, and the subaltern have all been topics of devoted inquiry. So has the agency of the organization, especially the corporation: Bakan (2004; cf. Lippmann, 1937) notes the questionable origins but also the immense impact of U.S. recognition of corporate powers to own property, Taylor and Van Every (2000) emphasize attribution of agency to organizations in popular discourse, and Allison (1971) distinguishes three models for understanding organizational decisions, some of which emphasize member agency while others gloss it in emphasizing organizational agency. This issue has puzzling implications for the communicative constitution of organizations: How can we theoretically account for the commonsense power of organizations to act, issue communications, and own property, while avoiding these dangers: derogation of the powers and contributions of it members and constitutive communication processes; metaphysical (in the worst sense) imputation of human agentive powers of cognition and action to organizations, with romantic but logically indefensible implications of group mind and functional explanation; and ideological misrepresentation of "organizational" communications and actions as articulating a group viewpoint or serving a group interest, without power imbalance or conflict among members? How can we see the *comunidad de Cucurpe* as the outcome of the organizing work of its members, as the medium of their (partly) historically-effective agency, and as the site of their agentive attempts to control it and achieve the ends it expresses?

The third, constitution of a relationship or system (especially the convoluted relationship that is commonly called a "complex organization"), differs importantly from the first two. An organization, or any other relationship, is not merely a sign (which can stand for a real, or dead, or imaginary organization), but is enacted through a broad system of related communication processes. It is not an agent, but includes agents who help enact and constitute it, and has powers, consequences of the powers, sedimented structure, and coordinated activity of its members that tempt us to regard it as an agent. Its spatiotemporal range depends on the nature of the relationship, but must extend beyond any one language game if the relationship demands it (as "complex organization" does). Complex organizations are fundamentally different from the fleeting social acquaintanceship created in a single conversation. They are bound together by the constitution of a system of common signs that is part of "lamination" as described by Boden (1994) and by Taylor and Van Every (2000). But that answer, partly illuminating about discourse structure in any social order (e.g., a friendship), is in vital need of supplement at the level of the specific discourse of organizations. These binding processes are initial but inadequate answers to the question: how do systems of relations and practices become constituted as organizations, despite (or perhaps through?) the distance in space and time, the conflict and anomie, and the diversity and fragmentation that are characteristic of organizational systems such as the *comunidad de Cucurpe*?

We can only pretend to have complete answers, by sketching a framework that will outline more specific insights we will try to offer about the four flows. We will elaborate the answer to the question about the constitution of signs by discussing the "structurational hermeneutic" implicit in structuration theory (McPhee & Iverson, 2002); then we will very briefly describe the structurational approach to agency, repeatedly elaborated elsewhere, and its implications for constitution. Finally, we will note Giddens' portrayal of the relation of interaction contexts to more complex social systems and, again, its implications for constitution.

The Structurational Hermeneutic

Structuration theory stems from hermeneutic philosophy, among other sources; Giddens is famous for his argument that interpretive social science is "strong on agency, weak on structure" (1993, p. 4). In particular, he consistently works from the interpretive assumption that human beings live and interact in a life-world, an actual social context that they find understandable and practically relevant. We must recognize some basic parallels between the duality of structuration and Gadamer's account of hermeneutic process. In early work, Giddens analyzes Gadamer's and related accounts of human being and understanding; he selectively appropriates them, but also develops his basic concepts in a way that corresponds closely to Gadamer's conceptual structure. We can summarize Giddens' appropriation of Gadamer's hermeneutics (sketchily and unsatisfactorily) in a few terse propositions:

- Languages and cultural traditions are not to be taken as objects or instruments or methods; rather, we "live within them," and they mediate our experiences and plans (and vice versa).
- In interpreting discourse or engaging in conversation (always from within a tradition), we must begin from a prejudiced preunderstanding of the discourse, and we progressively understand the discourse by accomplishing the mutual mediation of old and new reference frames.
- This mutual mediation involves a "hermeneutic circle," wherein we understand a part of the discourse in the light of our overall understanding and standpoint, then recast our understanding of the whole text, and our earlier standpoint, in the light of the part confronting us, in a process of bimodal reflection and linguistic/cultural articulation. This process is not a method, but a dimension of human life; it is always potentially contextually adaptive, creative, and judgment-based, even though it typically takes advantage of routine patterns available.

In his concept of the duality of structure, Giddens broadens the domain of the hermeneutic process to other aspects of structure and even spatiotemporal context:

Interaction ... is temporally and spatially situated. But this is no more than an uninteresting truism if we do not see that it is typically used or *drawn upon* by actors in the production of interaction: anticipations of the responses of others mediate the activity of each actor at any one moment in time, and what has gone before is subject to revision in the light of subsequent experience. In this way, as Gadamer emphasizes, practical social life displays ontologically the characteristics of the "hermeneutic circle". "Context-dependence", in the various ways in which this term can be interpreted, is aptly regarded as integral to the production of meaning in interaction, not as just an embarrassment to formal analysis (1976, p. 105).

As Giddens indicates, the hermeneutic circle applies to everyday life in general, not just understanding of texts or communications, and in particular it applies to "the production of interaction." This is a circle, not between local and global understanding of a text, but between local experience and action, and global consideration of *and transformation of* structural and contextual resources that can have implications for social reality beyond the current encounter. We can carry this a little farther, along lines elaborated by McPhee (1990).

First, as is well known, in interaction people dually produce and, more obviously, reproduce the structural rules and resources they draw on in interacting. By using English, say, they maintain it as a living language, a live option for communicating and the medium of their expressed meaning. But less well recognized is that communicative "production" is no less production of "structure," if by that we mean rules and resources able to be drawn on in later interaction. The whole point of communicating is to get across a meaning, or at least a resource, that will be used by others in mediating their later acts and responses. If we say, "My office is too small," we want the topic of office size to occupy this and later conversations and decisions. Both interpretation and action involve circling between the meaning of specific statements or acts, and the overall state of structural resources—especially the manifest meaning-state of the conversation—that the specific statements are transforming.

One fact about agent knowledgability and communication in a complex organization is that members *know* they are in one setting among quite a few others, that they influence some discussions but hardly others, and that their production of structure has local but rarely organization-wide impact. Members often seek information from other settings, but they also often protect their own setting from outside influence, resisting ideas that threaten the autonomy of settings with which they identify. One of us (Bob) can somewhat seriously write: "Where I regard my research resources as a needed right vital to the intellectual advance of humankind, that should be able to be taken for granted, my boss regards those same resources as a precious accomplishment she has had to fight for and deserves commendation (i.e., constant flattery) for, and *her* boss regards them as part of a larger pot of resources that she claims as a right and power resource, and has to manage carefully (i.e., penuriously) in the face of varied self-serving demands by people like my boss." As self-centered as the typical scholar, but at least aware of the relation between local and other contexts.

What are the implications of the structurational hermeneutic for the constitution of signs? As noted above, one way to understand the constitution of signs is praxically—they are constituted if we know "how to go on" in contexts of their significatory use. The structurational hermeneutic says that "going on" is an interpretive process, rooted not in deduction from rules but in judgment, and that it "produces," not just local meaning but meaning and use-pattern as structural resources with relevance beyond the immediate context. For instance, McPhee and Iverson (2002) argue that the organizational context can transform traditional illocutionary acts into what they call *conlocutions* because in context they have a force that involves a perlocutionary effect on the hearer's response:

> Another example, adapted from Taylor and van Every (2000), … illustrates this point.
>
>> Suppose a boss is giving a Powerpoint presentation and says to a subordinate, "Bill, would you get the lights?" Now, it's well understood that "get the lights" is quickly understood as "turn the lights off/down enough for people to see the presentation," with a need for skilled performance or problem-solving. And it's equally well known that this is an indirect speech act, question converted to request. As Taylor and van Every indicate, the request in this situation must equally be interpreted as an order, and it brings about a (re)formation of an instrumental bond between boss and subordinate, with the result that the boss, via collective or mediated or corporate agency, accomplishes turning off the light. Unlike an audience member, the subordinate "has to" turn off the light. We might say that an order is a boundary-spanning kind of speech act—it does not allow the typical range of response choices for the hearer. An order changes, narrows, the amount of room available for legitimate response choice (or it reaffirms the fact of limited choice), by definition. (p. 7)

Of course, the creativity and consequentiality of sign use are simultaneously constrained (and enabled) by the fact that we are always also reproducing, in a transformed way, the social systemic resources available to us in context. In short, our approach urges looking for transformed language games or practices, and what they imply about the new organization of communicative resources available to people communicating about the organization.

Agency and its Constitution

Giddens is famous for arguing that functionalism and, to a lesser extent, Marxism are weak on agency, and for positing a widely-criticized "stratification model of the agent" to ground theory-development that avoids the agency weakness. According to Giddens (1984), "Agency concerns events of which an individual is the perpetrator, in the sense that the individual could, at any phase in a given sequence of conduct, have acted differently" (p. 9). Giddens constructs a model (or perhaps a pair of models) that identifies discursive and practical consciousness, and the unconscious, as constituents of any agent; and also emphasizes processes of reflexive monitoring, rationalization, and motivation as essential to ongoing agency. Agents possess the capacity to explicitly talk about actions that they and others do (discursive) while other actions are simply known and done (practical). Whether or not words can be used to describe a particular practice, the agent can still rationalize those actions which they consciously choose to do through practical or discursive consciousness "within the ongoing Praxis of day-to-day life" (Giddens, 1993, p. 92). Agents do not have to consciously think about every action. Routinization accounts for the unconscious portions of agency, but the unconscious should not be misunderstood as determinism or inevitability. Cohen (1989) explains:

> Social practices do not reproduce themselves, social agents do, and it must be borne in mind that from the standpoint of structuration theory social agents always are seen to retain the capability to act otherwise than they do. (p. 45)

Agents reflexively monitor their actions as well as the actions of others. As a result, agents "maintain a continuing 'theoretical understanding' of the grounds of their activity" (Giddens, 1984, p. 5). Giddens provides a model of agency where the capacity to think about actions and to consider consequences as well as the capacity to act otherwise. It seems fair to note how all of these concepts are, in a sense, powers—they are states an agent *can* be in and processes one *can* engage in, not processes that must all or constantly be exhibited. These powers that ground such public demonstrations of agency as purposeful conduct, accounts, judgment, anxiety management, and competent interaction. And they are, to an overwhelming extent, specifically individual human powers—we can be skeptical about whether it will ever be defensible to say that a computer or a mob, or an organization, can explain its situation and conduct, or be (un)conscious or motivated in any sense.

Further, such processes and powers are partly social in origin—development and education, acquisition of contextual knowledge and practice of social skills, all transpire through social involvement. But all require and develop inchoate human powers and natal resources for power development: oysters, computers, and committees could not even develop agentive powers in the way that people typically do. They would all fail if placed in the usual situation of nurturing.

While his model is certainly not exhaustive (Emirbayer & Mische, 1998), it serves its intended grounding role: it organizes attacks on empiricist, psychoanalytic, and structuralistic models of agency, and directs our attention to the importance of reflexivity, accounting, and physical positioning for social analysis. But Giddens, equally importantly, leaves room for social process in the constitution of agency, and not merely as a fabric of experience for the developing agent. Mastery of the rules and resources labeled "structure" by Giddens is a necessary condition of agency; so is social recognition of that mastery; so is the socially and situationally constrained power to use that mastery. In a recent article, McPhee (2004) noted that Anthony Giddens supplies primarily an "internalist" conception of agency as using human powers in social interaction. This contrasts with the "externalist" conception available in, e.g., Benveniste (1971) or Cooren (2000), where the agent is the floating and divided referent/referee of the shifting symbol "I", or the a place in a discursive relational system, or a node in a network of effects. Giddens synthesizes the internalist and externalist ideas in a way that neglects, or is weak on, neither, but emphasizes their dialogue.

How, on this model, is human agency constituted in organizational communication? We assume that childhood socialization has developed the basic powers of agency. Three contextual developments seem vital, though. First, the person must be contextually *knowledgable*— knowledgable of structural resources, contextual and traditional background facts, acquainted with relevant others in the social network, etc. These are factors that would result from membership negotiation. Second, an agent must be a legitimate member or position-holder, recognized by others as empowered and appropriate in using his/her powers. Legitimacy might be formally based, but it might also depend on informal factors such as reputation and trust. Finally, for full agency, a person must have access to organizational action contexts—of work, of decision-making, of information dissemination. These are requirements of agency that might be affected by or involved in any of the flows.

Constitution of the Organization as a System

An organization is not sufficiently explained by the practices that allow people to name it and its parts, or to act in roles and communicatively constituted interactions attributable to it; it is typically a spatiotemporally-distributed, materially effective reality. The structurational answer to its constitution is analogous to the answer—actually, answers—Giddens gives to the question of the constitution of society, and of the relation of interactional episodes to societal systems and institutions. Giddens' answer is quite complex, and occupies at least one book (1984), but a few themes can especially be singled out. First, interaction episodes are typically not closed, as micro-theories often tacitly assume. Yes, they are bounded, but their boundaries are themselves practically constructed, and thus connect as well as limit the encounters. Encounters "shade off" into other contexts as new people appear, conversants move or take up conversations anew, and more globally as people follow out time–space trajectories while maintaining stable locales of coordinated interaction. Second, and as another facet of the first, people can interact, and their contexts can be integrated, at a spatiotemporal distance, via various media of "system integration." From primitive postal services to recorded teleconferencing, contexts very separate in space and time can interact as parts of the same society or even organization. Third, modifying the second, relations among contexts can be designed to create relatively determinate and purposeful coordination and control. Giddens (1987) emphasizes the importance of centralized records of personnel surveillance, and the concentration of administrative staff to allow face-to-face adaptivity in planning and decision, as key contributors to the development of complex organizations. By contributing to, or resisting or transforming, relations like these, flows of organizational communication can lead to a level of effective integration that allows a set of people engaged in social practices to be realistically identifiable as an organization.

The Four Flows

The preceding analysis of the constitutive power of communication has direct consequences in the four flows of organizational communication distinguished by McPhee and Zaug (2000). As reviewed above, their central argument was that communication constitutes organizations in four analytically distinct but interdependent ways, called "flows" as a shorthand for "circulating systems or fields" of evolving discourse. In this section of the paper, we discuss each of the flows in more depth, simultaneously paying attention to the question of their interrelatedness and distinctive constitutive effects. We will use more specific examples from Sheridan (1988), but will note the unusual character of that example as well.

For each of the flows, we will argue that a rather distinct set of communication processes characteristic of it can be identified. Specific processes, including conlocutions and broader interaction units, are often especially useful in the processes carried to some constitutive effect in the flow, and the specific, unique effects of conlocutions implicate and are implicated by the existence of the organization that they thereby help constitute; sometimes more complex communication patterns prototypical of the flow can be identified; the distinctive way the flow is grounded in the underlying structurational hermeneutic of the organization can often be posited; and characteristic power strategies in the flow may be noteworthy.

We will also explore more deeply the question of how the flow helps constitute an organization. It is not sufficient to say that communication is constitutive because it points out, or formulates, or reveals, or reifies the organization; that may work to explain the organization as a communicative focus or referent of a sign, but not as a complex within which the communicator claims, e.g., membership. Moreover, the distinction of four flows makes sense only insofar as constitution proceeds differently for each flow. We will note how the organization's constitution involves constitution of a field of signs; how it involves the constitution of agency; and how it is constituted as an institutional system.

First Flow: Membership Negotiation

In the Cucurpe community certain individuals, and/or the households they represent, were recognized and named members of the *comunidades* and *ejidos* that attempt to control communal land and water resources, in the census that was part of the legal process confirming the *comunidad*'s status as a corporate entity. But that recognition only started a very changeable process, because in the next census of members, almost 140 were absent from the rolls, replaced by 78 proposed new members. People who met all the official membership requirements in 1981 still had to fight to win membership recognition, failing in at least one case due to political machinations of members who preferred their own relatives (Sheridan, 1988).

These examples illustrate several basic ideas. First, organizations must have members: the formal licensing of the *comunidad* was simultaneous with the identification of the 240 "original" *comuneros*. Second, despite this first fact, membership is often not a simple yes-or-no or once-and-for-all issue: an unchallengable list even of founding members never existed, no definite and general membership criteria exist, and membership has constantly been varied in nature and contested over time. The concept of "membership negotiation" can take account of these facts, and more.

A. Communication Processes.

As McPhee and Zaug note, the clearest site for the membership negotiation flow is the entry process for new members. The words "You're hired" are one step in an extended and complex process wherein an individual comes to be thought of as a "true member" rather than an outsider. But membership negotiation continues as the relationship between individual and organization is reproduced, transformed, or even severed for a departing member. Membership is collectively enacted and socially interpreted. But at any rate, it seems justifiable to separate the process of negotiating new membership from that of reproduction of established membership.

What communication processes are especially prototypical of new membership negotiation? We can start by conceiving of becoming a new member as a process of crossing organizational boundaries: the boundary of ignorance, the boundary of illegitimacy, the boundary of disconnection … . Communication that recognizes these boundaries is automatically communication that helps constitute the organization, because these boundaries imply and give practical impact to the organization's existence. Thus, for instance, a central communicative act relied on by new members is the question, or request for information (Miller & Jablin, 1991), which begins the conlocutory process of instruction. An old member reacts to a new one's question by recognizing the implication that the latter stands outside the boundary of ignorance, and instruction is question-answering that recognizes and brings the hearer across that boundary. But it also recognizes the hearer's right to such an answer—i.e., the hearer's legitimate status as new member. The *comunidad* example, however, reminds us of the circumstantiality of such processes: no potential *comunidad* member has questions because they have all grown up in the neighborhood of Cucurpe and had their questions answered as children—legitimate learners of another sort.

Two other conlocutions that recognize the boundary of ignorance are storytelling and dismissive reaction. The multiple functions of the story process have been analyzed well by Orr (1996), but one clear function is conveying contextualized information to new members, and stories for this purpose can be more elaborated and adapted to the newcomer's perceived level of knowledge (Boje, 1991). Such storytelling may legitimately usher a newcomer past the boundary of ignorance (so that s/he can be chided for making a mistake after a cautionary story), but it also confirms the newcomer's legitimate status as organizational initiate. Similarly, if the newcomer makes a suggestion, publicly in a meeting or privately, they are uniquely open to chiding in words such as "That's not how we do things here." Their proposal is not subject to more typical sorts of argument or rejection because they have not yet crossed a membership boundary of ignorance.

Two other types of conlocution have special relevance for new members: the introduction and the initiation. Introductions recognize that the member is not typically connected up in the organization's social network (where everyone knows all relevant others already); newcomer introductions are nuanced to reveal both the newcomer's status and enough of the old member's status to make their organizational position clear. The process of initiation, similarly, moves the newcomer past the key boundary of legitimate membership.

Of course, the negotiation of more established membership is much more varied, involving members of variable power and status and often affecting their status. While their knowledgability is well beyond that of typical newcomers, negotiation of new duties, or rights, or placement in the organization, often brings changes in knowledge, legitimacy of actions, and access.

The broadest level of constitutive force comes from the immersion of specific interaction in the structurational hermeneutic process. It is part of everyday organizational reality that the organization exists, people are members, new members are assimilated, and the status of members can involve local problems. These recognitions are typically reproduced and elaborated as shared background for live membership negotiation.

The hermeneutic takes on an importantly different form for new member negotiation because of the continuing issue that it is unclear (sometimes even to the newcomer) how fully the newcomer understands and accepts the established context. So communication can be redundant or puzzling to the newcomer, but, interestingly, both of those phenomena help confirm the unquestionable existence of the established organization.

For more established members, ordinary organizational processes confirm the established member relation, and thus simultaneously the organization's existence. The hermeneutic becomes noteworthy only when the implications or continuation of membership becomes a live issue. In either case, the accustomed member relation can't be taken for granted. If the negotiating member can change his/her relation to the organization, how far do the implications of that stretch for other members? In the extreme, does it threaten the existence or nature of the organization? Extreme examples might be the impeachment or expulsion of a leader, more revolutionary in some cases than others, or negotiation with a central sports-team member.

B. How the Flow Constitutes the Organization

To a certain extent, the preceding discussion has begun to address this issue: Whether by implicating the existence of organizational boundaries, or of standard assumptions about a membership relation, membership negotiation communication reifies the organization in the grammatical process of direct or indirect reference and the psychological processes of presumption and projection. But while communication can thereby constitute the organization as a static sign, we need to go further and analyze how such communication has constitutive force for the new member's agency and in the system integration of practices the new member engages in.

This analysis must have two foci: the local communication process and its continuity with the broader range of organizational contexts. Any episode that involves membership negotiation necessarily makes reference, however indirectly, to the organization—"Oh, you're a member of the council of vigilance"—of what organization? There seem to be three broad modes of reference. First, one speaker speaks on behalf of or as representative of the organization ("Welcome to our department," or "We think your salary demands are unreasonable"). This usage, especially the term "we," is sometimes clear and clearly legitimate, but can also be extremely tricky; as McPhee (1989) notes, the apparent reference for "we" can float from the whole organization to top leadership, from a specific group to a vague unidentifiable one to the single speaker, in a process that has never been fully analyzed. But in the clearer cases, a local interaction is treated as standing in for member–organization negotiation.

Second, the organization is referred to as an absent third party. Joseph K can talk to castle residents and officials about the castle and its rulers, but the latter group is not seen, always deferred, and a source of puzzlement. No matter how high the speakers are in status, they can refer to the rest of the organization and its character to account for anything—"I didn't know what was going on," says Ken Lay (or

Ronald Reagan). Admittedly, this latter example involves a somewhat different process—negotiating a distinction or difference between the organization and the self, to shield the latter from blame.

Third, for fairly small organizations, enough of the membership may be present in a decision forum for "we" to stand for the immediately present group. For the *Comunidad de Cucurpe*, such general assemblies allow the communicatively constituted organization to have a temporarily tangible reality. Of course, such a meeting is not equivalent, even temporarily, to the organization, which is a relationship poorly and illusorily reflected in the distorted communication processes of any instantiated meeting. In the usual *comunidad* general assembly, most members fearfully keep silent while a few powerful members run things.

All three of these modes of reference, especially the first two, have constitutive force for the organization especially because the interaction episodes or documents where they occur "shade off," as Giddens puts it, into other episodic interaction contexts that have continuity with the first, a continuity that "is" the organization. When a new member is recognized as crossing a boundary, that fact has impact in other settings, either directly or after argument that often runs along very routinized lines ("Show us your ID card."). The complex relations of micro to macro, which carry out the process of constituting the organization begun in any interaction context, occur along five dimensions noted in McPhee (1998).

But a deeper sense of how membership negotiation constitutes organizations goes beyond reference and labeling of the member and the organization. A member has, sometimes as a result of anticipatory socialization and sometimes through experience as a member, a sense of what the organization and membership in it is like. Similarly, organizational representatives and communicators have a sense of the member, whether from an initial interview or introduction or as a result of past tenure. But the future of the membership relation is unclear; negotiation helps to fill in, however tentatively, the murky terrain of future membership. As it does so, it is generating relations among members and of the focal member to such organizational entities as tasks, issues, subunits, records, and organizational locales. In expanding the newcomer's contextually supported agency and his/her integration in the more extensive system, it is thus constituting the organization as a known system.

Second Flow: Reflexive Self-Structuring

Communication to self-structure by the *Comunidad de Cucurpe* is fairly well illustrated in a couple of accounts by Thomas Sheridan. First is the relatively recent history of the chartering of the *comunidad* (Sheridan, 1988, pp. 153–160). In response to encroachment by ranchers, the community first elected a representative, then formed the "Agrarian Committee of the Ancient *Ejidos* of Cucurpe" (1960), then the "Committee for the Defense of the Ancient Lands of the *Comunidad* of the Pueblo of Cucurpe" (1965). These committees petitioned the government to intervene in disputes, to confirm their rights to ancestral lands, and to institute a survey to solidify those rights. They developed arguments and evidence to oppose the wiles of the rich ranchers. (For instance, after one survey was completed in 1967, "wealthy ranchers" met the surveyor at his hotel, "got him drunk, and then drove him to Nogales, where they bought him clothes and gave him money. Once he sobered up, he had lost all of the documentation concerning the *comunidad* ... ." (p. 155).

The ranchers also hired an attorney, who argued that the peasants of Cucurpe did not constitute a *comunidad* (based on long-standing traditions of peasant ownership), but rather were a more recent *ejido*, to which the law gave much more restrictive land rights without recognition of traditional boundaries. The Department of Agrarian Reform did end by siding with the *comunidad* about its status, but accepted some of the attorney's arguments about private land grants that abrogated the *comunidad's* claimed acreage (Sheridan, 1988, pp. 158–9).

A second instance of self-structuring occurred after the Mexican supreme court ruled that the *comunidad* had the right to seize the land of four nonmembers who had long occupied and farmed it, and after 42 *comuneros* or members seized the land and planted spring crops (pp. 181–3). Matters came to a head at an acrimonious general assembly meeting, where the nonmembers bemoaned their right to the land ("We were born here!" "I'm not a foreigner! I'm a Mexican! Don't rob me of my land!" (pp. 180, 182), and government bureaucrats proposed a commission (agreed to by the *comunidad*, and filled with radicals), then argued that the 42 members should leave the land till the commission made its decision. The *comuneros* refused: they noted that they had waited for a supreme court decision and further had "agreed to abide by the opinion of a lawyer appointed to review the case," who said they had legal right to the land. After long debate, a bureaucrat called for a vote and, despite the fact that outside the meeting a majority opposed expropriation, almost every member stood up in refusal of the government's (obviously illegitimate and craven) demand that the land be vacated.

> Although a number of the *comuneros* undoubtedly were swayed by the determination of their neighbors, the comunidad clearly and unequivocally stood its ground. The defiant members even signed a statement expressing their resolve to remain on the land. ... By occupying the fields, the comuneros had taken a major step toward making those fields their own. Given its fear of conflict and agrarian unrest, it seemed unlikely that the Mexican government would risk possible bloodshed for the sake of a few relatively insignificant private landowners. Such turned out to be the case. (p. 183)

Our normal images of reflexive self-structuring are of classic organizational design and organizational knowledge codification. The first image involves a planner drawing up an organization chart, or a new set of policies, or a set of orders, then getting them approved by necessary decision-making bodies, and finally disseminating them to part or all of the organizational membership. Henry Mintzberg (1979) gives a prototypical analysis and depiction of this process in his "Regulated Control" and "Regulated Staff Information" flows—vertical, functional, transmitting information upward and imperatives downward. We should not too hastily discard this image, because it conveys a useful partial picture, overlapping in interesting ways Foucault's image of the Panopticon and discipline-based organization. This image is in part the focus of strenuous developments by information system developers and planners.

An alternate but important image is of the organization, through action of its officers or others, laying claim to what we can broadly call "resources." McPhee and Zaug give the example of organizational knowledge stocks, a highly discursive resource that accords well with Weick's (1979) concept of retention, a step that is absolutely crucial to Weick's specific consideration of the constitution of an organization (pp. 3, 141–3, 225–9). That same example is central to Giddens' (1987b; cf. McPhee, 2004) argument that information gathered through surveillance and recorded in texts is central to the special economic efficacy of organizations. But we would argue that self-structuring is involved in any process that leads to practical organizational possession and processing of a resource. The allocation of money through budgetary processes is carried out communicatively and has communicative significance, since money is itself basically symbolic and linguistically mediated (Searle, 1995; Simmel, 1990). Logos and inventories are additional evidence, if it were needed, that self-structuring communication is involved in the physical manipulation of even the most material organizational resources.

But the examples from Cucurpe help supplement our set of images. The *comuneros* who collectively organize and press their claims are avowedly agonistic rather than neutral; the constitution of the *comunidad*, to originate it and to take control of "its" resources, are focally political, strategic acts. In both cases, the process of self-structuring involves various nonmembers. In the history of the *comunidad*, its founding members initiate a process of survey and legal certification that is carried out by the government. The structuring is only in a sense self-structuring, since members initiate but do not control the substance of the corporate entity. Its governing officer roles are determined by law, its membership and jurisdiction by external inquiry and decree. But the *comuneros* collectively decide to keep the *comunidad* alive as an organization, they elect specific officers, and the officers make decisions that further structure the *comunidad*. In particular, they decide not to oppose the tacit appropriation of arable land by member households, despite the fact that the ideology behind the Agrarian Reform law justifies their doing so. In the second instance, the supreme court decision gave the *comuneros* rights to the land they seized, but they had to "enact" those rights by first physically occupying the land, then making it an organizational policy to do so in the general assembly meeting. The term "they" is dangerously ambiguous here, because the activists (called *bolsheviki* by their opponents) who actually seized the land did not do so after immediate approval by regular *comunidad* processes—the vote in the general assembly could have gone against them. Yet their action was a crucial step in affirming the *comunidad's* actual appropriation of both their land and their powers.

We should also note how self-structuring is involved in the example of membership negotiation in Cucurpe. The focal issue was membership, but the issue was intertwined with the rules of the *comunidad*, its status as a "traditional community," and its reflexively controlled land resources. As McPhee and Zaug note, the flows can overlap, and the *comunidad* is perhaps distinctive as a type of organization in which this overlap is frequent.

A. Communication Processes

As McPhee and Zaug note, reflexive self-structuring includes the most unnatural or at least unusual communication processes, in the extent to which they involve explicit discursive work. Two ideas are especially central in most accounts of constitution. One is a conlocution, pretty well analyzed by Searle (1995) as the illocutionary act *declaration*. Searle argues that constitutive rules can be analyzed as taking the form "X counts as Y in situation C;" such rules allow socially-based status functions to be assigned to objects with "collective agreement, or at least acceptance, both in the imposition of that status on the stuff referred to by the X term and about the function that goes with that status" (p. 44). Social realities have a special dependence on language for their construction, since *"[i]n general, when the X term is a speech act, the constitutive rule will enable the speech act as a performative declaration creating the state of affairs described by the Y term"* (p. 54). Searle uses the example of a game as involving numerous performative acts of constitution—"That's a strike." Searle does note that not all institutional facts can be created by declaration in this way: Institutional facts are constructed on a nest of prior constructions, and some institutional facts can be established only by physical acts or other changes.

Searle's analysis is more rationalistic than structuration theory would allow. An emphasis on declarations can lead social theory toward a position akin to contract theories of the state. A structurational analysis of self-structuring must equally stress the reproduction of the structure, in unacknowledged and even unknown conditions and with unintended consequences.

The example of Cucurpe illustrates both the centrality and the conditionality of declarations in organizational constitution. A declaration by properly empowered government officials gave the community official status, an initial membership, and an initial allotment of land. But the declaration itself is part of a list of similar findings in the history of the community, until it is acted on, especially by *comuneros* themselves. However, their subsequent actions may not be simple conformity. Some *comuneros* themselves opposed the idea that the *comunidad* had power over arable land worked by their household for decades, and resident nonmembers, from the outset having an anomalous status relative to the *comunidad*, saw the declarations by Mexican and community officials as threats. But they recognized their implications and the new assumptions and processes they set up, the new forums for argument for action that they created. In that sense, the self-structuring declarations functioned as authoritative metacommunication if not metapractice, informing if not accepted by other levels of discourse (McPhee, 1985).

A second central idea of communicative process is the notion of the decision forum, or more generally Bryson and Crosby's forums, arenas, and courts (1992). The general assembly required of the *comunidad* by Mexican law is an important locale for communication, as the second example described above illustrates. It is a distanciated site, far from the land tracts at issue in many deliberations. The deliberations have a routine, a set of guiding norms (set up in the legal declarations that serve as foundational documents for the *comunidad*), and a regular constituency, all of which promise a coherence and predictability that members count on when they plant their crops and decide where to graze their cattle.

However, we should note that self-structuring is not limited to "official" declarations and meetings. Daily interactions can offer self-structuring by establishing coherence, predictability, and form over time. The *self-structuring* is enacted in the daily interactions in Barley's (1986) description of two radiology departments that differed greatly after the introduction of new CT scanner technology. In one, the radiologists maintained power and authority, whereas the self-structuring gave the technicians more power in the other. In each case, it was not new orders or policies that resulted in a structuring shift, but enactment of rules and resources.

This image of communication processes is consonant with the structurational hermeneutic: as interaction accomplishes reflexive self-structuring, it also assumes and reproduces the organization as an ongoing enterprise. Even a governmental proclamation confirming the legal status of the *comunidad* is taken by the *comuneros* as a meaningful, practical part of their organized reality, transforming their status but continuing their efforts to gain collective control of traditionally communal land, and serving as a new locus of rules and resources for future action. Equally, the processes that develop organizational knowledge are simultaneously production and reproduction, whether accomplishing productive outcomes that exercise and confirm the self-structured organizational knowledge stocks they draw on, or meta-level knowledge codification and reification activities that produce an (intendedly) valuable organizational resource while at the same time reproducing the organization as a stratified action domain where some people are especially qualified to do such structuring work.

B. How the Flow Constitutes the Organization

Communicative constitution of an organization may typically begin with reflexive self-structuring, as a group of people begin to represent themselves as (part of) an organization, or a series of actions begins to be considered as regular enough to regard as a system. Self-structuring is an important step in the process whereby the organization is constituted as a legitimate sign, as a group begins to refer to itself, and to be referred to, as an organization. When the Cucurpe community represented itself as first one committee, then another, it could refer to itself as a unity, as a potential political and economic force. And when Mexican President Echevarria issues a resolution of recognition and entitlement to the *comunidad*, he supplies a foundation for other references to the *comunidad* as an organization with legitimate rights and powers.

However, many self-structuring processes do not focus on signs for the whole organization. They involve plans and information about production and other programs and processes, diagnoses of organizational problems and opportunities, and data about organization members, resources, and commitments. These processes of course produce and reproduce an organizational signification system including jargon and reified forms (Iverson, 2003); organizational boundaries and access are named and articulated with membership negotiation processes. This system is a resource for practices of organizational control, but also resistance and personal strategies, as the second Cucurpe example illustrates. In short, self-structuring has constitutive force partly because it generates an internal system of signs that are used as resources shaping and allowing coherence across discourse episodes.

But in this same process, member (and nonmember) agency is altered, enabled, and constrained. Members come to have more or less consensually and legitimately recognized powers. The 42 *comuneros* who seized land now can develop it as a site to which they have individual rights. And the *comunidad* membership generally now has a new level of practical rights over their communal land. Having exercised this power, they are energized and perceive an expanded horizon of possibilities, with the organization as a medium of action and a site of decision about such possibilities. We need not call the organization an agent, in the structurational sense; it is sufficient to analyze it as a complex resource with important implications for individual agency.

We should emphasize two other facts about agency and self-structuring, though. First, insofar as self-structuring is distanciated from other flows and sites, some people will be atypically powerful by having legitimate access to self-structuring interactions. More than for anyone else, even stockholders or owners, the organization is a medium of agency for the designing managers. Second and correlatively, self-structuring includes the collection and use of information, especially about work operations and performance through surveillance. "Alienation," "deskilling," "the separation of conception from labor" (Braverman, 1974), and "discipline" (Foucault, 1977) are terms frequently used to describe this kind of reflexivity (Giddens, 1987b), which leads to classically reduced labor agency in many ways. Even in Cucurpe organization brings with it new threats and conflicts to the membership.

Finally, self-structuring constitutes the organization as a system. First of all, it exemplifies the complexity of the system: self-structuring includes the generation of structure and resources in one locus that has potential general relevance and influence in other sites at later times (McPhee, 1985; McPhee & Poole, 2001). Indeed, the collection of information resources through surveillance, and their organization for use by management, guarantees the system integration of organizational sites in ways that are likely to work in the interests of powerful organizational members, with further direct and indirect implications for member agency (Giddens, 1987b; McPhee, 2004). However, structures of whatever sort do not obviate the fact that organizational members are agents and that organizational power rests on that fact—clearly argued by Giddens in his concept of "dialectic of control." Agents do not lose their local knowledgability or their powers to rationalize and reflexively monitor—indeed, the next flow shows the continued existence and importance of just those powers.

But we should recognize that self-structuring does not just generate an imposed layer of control: it typically penetrates the very fabric of organizational life. Gerardo Patriotta (2003) presents an analysis of organizational knowledge that is quite enlightening about the self-structuring of social systems. He argues that organizational knowledge becomes background (a term that he prefers to "tacit") as a result of three processes: "history: ... the sedimentation of learning experiences over a time span; ... habit: when knowledge is deeply internalized and institutionalized we tend to use it in an almost automatic and irreflexive way [; ... and] experience [as formulated in organizational discourse, especially narratives]" (p. 61). He argues that these suggest three lenses for the study of knowledge (time, breakdowns, and narratives), but we can equally argue that they are three connected processes through which self-structuring "takes root" in interconnected member practices.

Third Flow: Activity Coordination

Since the *comunidad* is, in a sense, a regulatory organization, much of its "productive work" is best described as self-structuring—making decisions about rules for membership and the allocation of land rights, rather than actually allocating land or doing anything else. This inactivity itself is prejudicial and is the result of self-structuring: the *comunidad* has tacitly decided not to try to reclaim lands traditionally worked by member households or to proceed further against the wealthy ranchers who hold land that, by right of tradition, would seem to belong to the community. They also have refrained from communal work to protect the common pasturelands from overgrazing or to develop them, in part because of the typical commons dilemma facing members: work done by particular members brings them little benefit and is likely to be exploited by other members. In the vicinity of Cucurpe, there are water cooperatives that do engage in more active allocation and conservation work (Sheridan, 1988).

However, members do work together to protect their pastures against ongoing encroachment efforts by ranchers, who try to run their cattle on it, or even to fence it for their own use. Sheridan describes work by another communal land organization (in this case, an *ejido*) to protect their land after finding a group of two ranchers, four employee cowboys, a lawyer, and a purported state policeman who fires several shots at the *ejidatarios*.

> The *ejidatarios* disarmed him anyway, capturing one of the ranchers and two of the cowboys in the process. Time and again we hear the the story of the capture, especially the part about how quickly the bravado of the policeman dissolved into abject fear. ... "I'm nothing," he kept repeating as he cried and begged for mercy. "I have a family. I have children." The *ejidatarios* replied that they had children, too, which is why they were defending their land.
>
> Earlier that day, the rancher and the policeman had been turned over to the authorities unharmed. The two cowboys, on the other hand, remain prisoners of the *ejidatarios*, who gather now to decide what to do with them. As the discussion progresses, most of the *ejidatarios* agree with one of their spokesmen, who concludes that the cowboys "are not guilty. They're workers, nothing more. They had to follow the orders of their bosses or lose their jobs."
>
> Finally, after a consensus is reached, the cowboys are brought before the informal tribunal. The *ejidatarios* ask them to sign an *acuerdo* (resolution) in which they admit their guilt and implicate the ranchers. The *ejidatarios* then formally pardon them of their crimes.
>
> ... I then ask [a leader] how the conflict over the land will be resolved. He replies that it never will be. "*Este problema sigue toda la vida.*" (This problem lasts your whole life.) (Sheridan, 1988, pp. 1–3 passim)

This example borders on reflexive self-structuring, but seems to be a local adaptation to a problem. The "informal tribunal" is not making decisions that have evident status as precedents—it is trying to come up with a fair solution to a tricky problem. And the coordination involved in the earlier attack disarming the policeman and capturing the cowboys was no doubt equally accomplished by local coordination more than any standard plan.

Of course, this rather extreme example can be supplemented by more mundane cooperation, for instance in the annual fall cattle round-up (Sheridan, 1988, pp. 83–84). The cowboys scatter to envelope a section of rocky range, then converge herding the cattle, cooperating to chase down unruly steers, and helping one another when they fall and are injured, meanwhile maintaining joking interchanges.

A. Communication Processes

Because it is a "residual" category—the interaction needed or open for member initiative once the structure generated in self-structuring has taken effect—activity coordination involves many types of acts and processes. A taxonomy by Robertson (1997), based on a study of a distributed software design company, seems unwieldy in its dispersion and variety: it includes communication categories like "conversing," "looking at the same thing at the same time," all the way to "doing something else" apart from the group's interaction. However, three processes seem worthy of note. One is work on, or structuration of, a group task representation. This representation may be based on self-structuring results, context, and/or results of past coordination and work; in any event, it must be maintained, and it is the map upon which members locate themselves and their needed moves. Robertson's taxonomy recognizes the importance of this kind of process in its category of "calling attention."

Another important activity coordination category is renegotiation of the division of labor. General task roles developed in self-structuring activities never fit exactly the demands of the current context, and people have the power to adapt to this contingency. Robertson's taxonomy does not include categories that specifically reflect this process—perhaps "breaking into smaller groups and reforming"—but its categories seem based on a very stable task arrangement. A good example of this process is Hutchins' (1991/1996) statement that the most important thing the lead navigator said during their crisis coping was:

He pushed the calculator at the [other navigator] and said, "Here, add these things." There is no need to attribute a global awareness of the process to [the leader] to account for this. He doesn't have enough time to do his own work, much less reflect on the overall division of labor. He is just acutely aware that he is falling behind and that he needs help to catch up. This is a case of local design. (1991, pp. 52–53)

A third process, perhaps overlapping the second, can be simply labeled "support". If a cowboy of the *comunidad* falls and seriously injures himself, someone rides over and helps him. Aronsson and Sätterlund-Larsson (1987) have shown "how doctors' 'thinking-aloud sequences' require active patient collaboration. Patients' opposition, as revealed in avoidance strategies and minimal feedback, resulted in vague … medical decisions" (p. 1).

Also on account of it being a "residual" category, activity coordination naturally exemplifies the structurational hermeneutic: it is often terse and unelaborated because self-structuring has generated structure that substitutes for explicit communication (McPhee, 1985). The *comuneros* who disarmed the policemen may have earned prestige by doing so; they may be more likely to step forward in other risky situations; and they may be more inclined toward skepticism or disparagement of State force. Activity coordination is the realm of emergence, of unintended consequences, of the slow sedimentation of organizational culture/ knowledge.

On the other hand, we should point out here the unease of the distinction of the third flow from the second. Yes, Aronsson and Sätterlund-Larsson's doctors and patients are engaged in adaptive work, but also may be reflexively planning treatment—a self-structuring sort of activity. The distinction of the second and third flows pretends that reflexivity and self-structuring can be absent from adaptive interaction in ongoing work. It supports but also confounds this problematic structuring/adaptation distinction with several others—distanciated vs. local communication, managerial vs. worker interaction, and retained vs. occasional organization. Yet each of these distinctions fails at times, as people simultaneously work adaptively and structure their work.

On the other hand, this simultaneous adaptation and structuring may simply be a case where the flows are carried out conjointly, as McPhee and Zaug allow. This phenomenon should not lead us to overlook the fact that, often and even characteristically, distanciated, managerial, retained structuring is separated from adaptive, local, occasional worker coordination.

B. How the Flow Constitutes the Organization

In the activity coordination flow, communication mainly uses and reproduces the sign system that represents the organization, already available as a result of self-structuring, so constitution of basic organizational signs is mainly routine reproduction in application. But activity coordination is probably the main process where ordinary members express themselves as productive agents. For instance, Hutchins (1991) shows the development of coordinated agency in what he calls a division of cognitive labor. We would argue that the case presented by Hutchins is actually a case illustrating extreme individual agentive adaptability. The crew members cannot fully rationalize their activity—they don't know the overall social problem-solving pattern to which their actions contribute. But they can make enough sense of the other's manifest activity to know what is called for from them, and to make their contributions fit.

The main constitutive contribution of activity coordination is in the integration of work processes, though. This flow allows practices to endure and adapt to contingencies. For instance, in the water cooperatives of Cucurpe, soil fertility is maintained by taking advantage of nutrient rich sediments deposited by flooding. But the flooding, when too severe, demolishes the irrigation canals, and members have to work together to rebuild the canals, coordinating their activity by ingrained knowledge of the canal system, but also by communicating to cooperate. Their efforts maintain a fairly extensive canal system that serves the fields of multiple farmers. It is possible that the *comunidad* suffers from a lack of solidarity due to the infrequency of coordinated, mutually supported activity.

In another example, Hutchins (1991/96) describes interaction that gets cooperative work done and simultaneously develops the adaptive interaction pattern that he calls distributed cognition. This contribution to organizational constitution is not a distinctive one, since we can imagine the same adaptive capacity in an informal group (though

Hutchins does describe the organized conditions of role and material tools that facilitate his example of distributed cognition). But the kind of cooperation he describes, albeit at a more minimal level, may be a necessary constituent of complex organization, since the institutional features whose constitution is described above is typically set up to facilitate at least a basic form of cooperation.

Finally, because the analysis of this flow has sounded, and tends to sound, most functionalistic, we must emphasize the power-ladenness of processes of activity coordination. Coordinated activity, by definition, pursues a single task goal or at least a consistent, even parallel set of goals; almost always, the goals are not chosen in this flow but are results of outside or distantiated self-structuring. Coordination does not imply equality of power—as Aronsson and Sätterlund-Larsson's (1987) example of doctors and patients makes clear, active and voluntary coordination can occur in, and reinforce, situations of definite power imbalance. Moreover, Sherry (1995) notes that even the arrangements and technologies of coordination can be externally imposed, inimical to local cultures, serve larger systemic power blocks, and involve strategic resistance as well as cooperation. On the other hand, as the site where self-structuring reveals itself as requiring worker adaptation and supplementation, this flow is also the prime foundation for the dialectic of control.

Fourth Flow: Institutional Positioning

Partly because the *comunidad* is a community-based organization, institutional positioning is constant. The general assembly, or *junta*, where membership is debated and voted is held in response to government requirements, and bureaucrats from the Department of Agrarian Reform attend and try to influence the meeting. The seizure of nonmember land by activist *comuneros* was in response to a supreme court decision, and was followed by another general assembly meeting involving bureaucrats and the nonmembers of the *comunidad*. Even the cattle round-up is an economic endeavor in which U.S. buyers wait until February to purchase cattle, driving down prices and empowering a group of Mexican middle-man cattle purchasers, who buy cheap in the fall, then sell at higher prices in February. *Comuneros* think there is collusion among the buyers, but have found no strategy to resist (Sheridan, 1988, p. 120).

Because of the ubiquity of other organizations, skill in institutional positioning is a prime leadership qualification. Sheridan describes the current *comunidad* president, Juan:

> Meanwhile, Juan, in his gray felt cowboy hat and his boots with the silver toe tips, slips easily through the crowd [at a post-*junta* party], joking with the dignitaries and swigging *lecheguilla* with his friends and neighbors. He's the bridge, the broker, the man who brings the bureaucrats and the *comuneros* together. He understands the expectations and the limitations of both groups, and he constantly explains one group to the other, lining up support among the *Cucurpeños* in order to manipulate the powers-that-be in Magdalena and Hermosillo. Even his followers laugh and say he's *sin vergenza*—without shame—but no one else in the comunidad knows how to move through the Mexican bureaucratic jungle as deftly. (1988, p. 148)

A. Communication Processes

The array of disciplines and specialties that involve institutional positioning is impressive: public relations, investor relations, labor relations, lobbying, purchasing, marketing and customer relations ... . These jobs each involve a wide range of communication processes, so that no list of narrow processes is of much use. Some broad processes, or aspects of many processes, will be noted below.

First is an aspect that might be called face-presentation, though it is what Davies and Harré (1990) (one of the sources for McPhee and Zaug's notion) meant by the term "positioning." Face-presentation is external rationalization, giving the external parties a sense of the nature of the organization, what it is trying to accomplish, and its character as a partner in cooperation or negotiation. Of course, representation is carried out by varied organization members, to varied audiences or their representatives, but organizational leaders typically try to coordinate and control the self-representations of the organization by its members. Foster (1969) gives an example of how varied professional members of a construction company can cooperate to present a consistent narrative to a customer (or, equally, can undercut one another).

A second aspect of institutional positioning is environmental exploration, the process of gathering information about potential connections and competitors, opportunities and constraints. Both active and passive information gathering strategies are available to reduce or otherwise manage uncertainty about the environment (Kramer, 2004).

A third broad aspect of communication process is negotiation. Of course, this aspect is seamlessly interwoven with the others, as the process of finding and sizing up partners, and of presenting a strategic image to them, is a constant part of negotiation.

The "local ecology" of organizations, and a place in its web of connections, can be considered as part of the resource base of any organization. Thus, institutional positioning too can be interestingly described in terms of the structurational hermeneutic. As organizational representatives act, they reproduce the rules and resources that have been produced (generally or with specific reference to particular partners) in earlier interaction, and past resources and present resource-proposals give meaning to, and enable or constrain, each other. Thus, the *comunidad* has an image, a perceived character, in the eyes of Agrarian Reform bureaucrats, and every self-presentational or negotiating move is constrained by and reinterprets that character.

B. How the Flow Constitutes the Organization

Institutional positioning is especially relevant to the "external face" of the organization (despite Cheney and Christensen's, 2001, point about their overlap). Initially, it is usually vital to constitute the organization as a sign, with a recognizable and significant place in the local ecology of organizations. Branding, logo development, image advertisement are relatively new names for a very old process of changing the signification system. In the history of the Cucurpe *comunidad*, the peasants organized two distinct initiating committees, both reflecting in their names the tradition of communal peasant property that they wanted the government to recognize. In particular, the issue of whether Cucurpe's peasants could claim to be a tradition-based *comunidad* or a more modernity-rooted *ejido*, a social form created to express the ideals of the Mexican Revolution, was debated and consequential for the land range granted to the *comunidad*.

Institutional positioning in large measure rests on individuals representing the organization, especially spanning boundaries as representatives communicating with outside constituencies. The freedom and pressure this status provides to consider one's own interests as distinct from the organization's is immense and well documented. So boundary-spanning legitimacy and access are dangerous, but necessary, for organizations. Juan, the president of the Cucurpe *comunidad*, is regularly tempted to favor his own values and interests in representing the *comunidad*, and other members are suspicious of him for this.

However, institutional positioning is also vital to secure resources, support, income, and legitimacy for the organization—closed systems such as communes very rarely endure. The resources secured have to be distributed throughout the organization (in a self-structuring operation), and this resource flow is one of the chief and primordial processes of system integration upon which the distinctive power, and even the existence, of the organization depends. Indeed, it is typical that institutional positioning consumes a large proportion of the organization's resources, since the system is differentiated to deal with different constituencies. For instance, banks have tellers but also personal bankers at several levels, to serve customers with different requirements and levels of wealth.

Conclusion

In our eyes, the key contribution of this chapter is its analysis of how each of the flows contributes to the constitution of a complex organization. We feel we have clarified the relation between constitution and agency, by noting how organizing changes the powers and range of agency without creating an organization as mega-agent or group mind. We have tried to sketch the ways in which the agency of members is differently, complexly, and interpretively involved in different flows, so that any structural description of their connection to the organization is likely to misrepresent the nature of the communication. We have also analyzed the constitution of signs of the organization as a necessary but incomplete part of the general process of constitution, to emphasize the ways in which local discourse analyses of constitution (of which Boden,

(1994) is an example which goes unusually far toward a fuller analysis) need to be supplemented to get an adequate account.

We also think the *Comunidad de Cucurpe* is an excellent addition to the stock of standard examples to refer to in accounts of organizational constitution. It is not a profit-oriented organization, is marginally and debatably effective in achieving its goals, is far from a total organization, is perhaps an NGO and perhaps not, is quite politicized but interestingly politically ambivalent, and is a contemporary organization constituted along both traditional and romantic lines. Sheridan's (1988) account leaves us convinced that it is an organization, not mainly a community or mass movement or party. It has faced recurrent challenges to constitute itself as real and efficacious, and it has met those challenges reasonably well. It sheds valuable light on the nature of constitution, even while stretching traditional definitions of organization.

References

Allison, G. T. (1971). *Essence of decision: Explaining the Cuban missile crisis.* Boston: Little, Brown.

Appendini, K. (2001). *Land regularization and conflict resolution: The case of Mexico.* Rome: Food and Agriculture Organization, Rural Development Division, Land Tenure Service. www.fao.org/Regional/LAmerica/prior/desrural/tenencia/pdf/mexico.pdf. Accessed on December 8, 2006.

Aronsson, K., & Sätterlund-Larsson, U. (1987). Politeness strategies and doctor–patient communication: On the social choreography of collaborative thinking. *Journal of Language and Social Psychology, 6,* 1–27.

Bakan, J. (2004). *The corporation: The pathological pursuit of profit and power.* New York: Free Press.

Barley, S. (1986). Technology as an occasion for structuring: Evidence from observation of CT scanners and the social order of radiology departments. *Administrative Science Quarterly, 31,* 78–108.

Benveniste, E. (1971). *Problems in general linguistics.* (Trans. M. E. Meek). Coral Gables, FL: University of Miami Press.

Boden, D. (1994). *The business of talk: Organizations in action.* Cambridge, U.K.: Polity.

Boje, D. M. (1991). Organizations as storytelling networks: A study of story performance in an office-supply firm. *Administrative Science Quarterly, 36,* 106–125.

Braverman, H. (1974). *Labor and monopoly capital: The degradation of work in the twentieth century.* New York: Monthly Review Press.

Bryson, J. M. & Crosby, B. C. (1992). Settings for exercising leadership: Forums, arenas, and courts. *Leadership for the common good* (pp. 81–117), San Francisco, CA: Jossey-Bass.

Cheney, G., & Christensen, L. T. (2001). Organizational identity. In F. M. Jablin and L. Putnam (Eds.), *The new handbook of organizational communication* (pp. 231–269). Thousand Oaks, CA: Sage.

Cohen, I. J. (1989). *Structuration theory: Anthony Giddens and the constitution of social life.* New York: St. Martin's Press.

Cooren, F. (2000). *The organizing property of communication.* Amsterdam/ Philadelphia: John Benjamins.

Cooren, F. (2004). The communicative achievement of collective minding: Analysis of board meeting excerpts. *Management Communication Quarterly, 17, 517–551, (4).*

Davies, B., & Harré, R. (1990). Positioning: The discursive construction of selves. *Journal for the Theory of Social Behavior, 20,* 43–63.

Emirbayer, M., & Mische, A. (1998). What is agency? *American Journal of Sociology, 103,* 962–1023.

Foster, C. (1969) *Building with men.* London: Tavistock.

Foucault, M. (1977). *Discipline & punish: The birth of the prison.* New York: Vintage Books.

Giddens, A. (1976). *New rules of sociological method.* Berkeley: U. of California Press.

Giddens, A. (1979). *Central problems in social theory: Action, structure, and contradiction in social analysis.* Berkeley: University of California Press.

Giddens, A. (1984). *The constitution of society: Outline of the theory of structure.* Berkeley: University of California Press.

Giddens, A. (1987a). Structuralism, post-structuralism and the production of culture. In A. Giddens, & J. Turner, (Eds.), *Social theory today.* Stanford, CA: Stanford University Press.

Giddens, A. (1987b). *Social theory and modern sociology.* Stanford, CA: Stanford University Press.

Hutchins, E. (1996). Organizing work by adaptation. In M. Cohen and L. Sproull (Eds.), *Organizational learning* (pp. 20–57). London: Sage. (Reprinted from *Organization Science,* 2(1), 14–39.)

Iverson, J. (2003). Knowing their place: Volunteers' knowing and identification in a community of practice. Ph.D. dissertation, Arizona State University.

Kramer, M. (2004). *Managing uncertainty in organizational communication.* Mahwah, NJ: Erlbaum.

Lippmann, W. (1937). *The good society.* London: G. Allen & Unwin.

McPhee, R. D. (1985). Formal structure and organizational communication. In R. McPhee, & P. Tompkins, (eds). *Organizational communication: Traditional themes and new directions* (pp. 149–177). Beverly Hills, CA: Sage.

McPhee, R. D. (1989). Organizational communication: A structurational exemplar. In B. Dervin, L. Grossberg, B. O'Keefe, and E. Wartella (Eds.) *Rethinking communication.* Vol. 2: Paradigm exemplars (pp. 199–212). Beverly Hills, CA: Sage.

McPhee, R. D. (1990). Organizational communication and hierarchy. Presented at the International Communication Association Convention, Dublin, Ireland.

McPhee, R. D. (1998). Giddens' conception of personal relationships and its relevance to communication theory. In R. Conville, & E. Rogers (Eds.), *The meaning of "relationship" in interpersonal communication* (pp. 83–106). Westport, CT: Praeger.

McPhee, R. D. (2004). Text, agency, and organization in the light of structuration theory. *Organization Studies, 11,* 355–371.

McPhee, R. D. & Iverson, J. (2002). Discourse systems structurate organizations and their discursive resources. Organizational Communication Division, National Communication Association Convention, New Orleans, November.

McPhee, R. D., & Poole, M. S. (1980). A theory of structuration: The perspective of Anthony Giddens and its relevance for contemporary communication Research. Paper presented to the Rhetorical and Communication Theory Division, Speech Communication Association Convention, New York, November.

McPhee, R. D., & Poole, M. S. (2001). Organizational structures and configurations. In F.M. Jablin & L.L. Putnam (Eds.). *The new handbook of organizational communication* (pp. 503–543). London: Sage.

McPhee, R. D., & Zaug, P. (2000). The communicative constitution of organizations: A framework for explanation. *Electronic Journal of Communication,* 10(1/2), www.cios.org/getfile/McPhee_V10n1200.

Miller, V. D., & Jablin, F. M. (1991). Information seeking during organizational entry: Influences, tactics, and a model of the process. *Academy of Management Review,* 16, 92–120.

Mintzberg, H. (1979). *The structuring of organizations.* London: Prentice Hall.

Orr, J. E. (1996). *Talking about machines: An ethnography of a modern job.* Ithaca, NY: ILP Press.

Parsons, T. (1951). *The social system.* New York: The Free Press.

Patriotta, G. (2003). *Organizational knowledge in the making: How firms create, use, and institutionalize knowledge.* New York: Oxford University Press.

Poole, M. S., Seibold, D. R., & McPhee, R. D. (1985a). A structurational approach to theory building in group decision making research. In R. Y. Hirokawa and M. S. Poole (Eds.), *Communication and group decision making* (pp. 237–264). Beverly Hills, CA: Sage.

Poole, M. S., Seibold, D. R., & McPhee, R. D. (1985b). Group decision-making as a structurational process. *Quarterly Journal of Speech, 71*, 74–102.

Robertson, T. (1997) Cooperative work and lived cognition: A taxonomy of embodied actions. In Marmolin, H., Sunblad, Y., and Schmidt, K (Eds.), *Proceedings of the Fifth European Conference on Computer-Supported Cooperative Work* (pp. 205–220). London: Kluwer Academic Publishers.

Searle, J. (1995). *The construction of social reality.* New York: Free Press.

Sheridan, T. (1988). *Where the dove calls.* Tucson: University of Arizona Press.

Sherry, J. (1995). Cooperation and power. In H. Marmolin, Y. Sundblad, and K. Schmidt (Eds.), *Proceedings of the fourth European conference on computer supported cooperative work* (pp. 67–82). London: Kluwer Academic Publishers.

Simmel, G. (1990). *The philosophy of money*, (2nd edition). London: Routledge.

Taylor, J. R. (2000). What is an organization? *Electronic Journal of Communication, 10*(1/2). www.cios.org/www.ejc/v10n200.htm.

Taylor, J. R., & Van Every, E. J. (2000). *The emergent organization: Communication as its site and surface.* Mahwah, NJ: Erlbaum.

Weick, K. E. (1979). *The social psychology of organizing.* New York: Random House.

Wittgenstein, L. (1953). *Philosophical investigations.* Trans. G. E. M. Anscombe, Oxford, U. K.: Blackwell.

4

CONSTITUTIVE COMPLEXITY

Military Entrepreneurs and the Synthetic Character of Communication Flows*

Larry D. Browning, Ronald Walter Greene, S. B. Sitkin, Kathleen M. Sutcliffe and David Obstfeld

Introduction

This chapter uses examples drawn from observation of an Air Force maintenance squadron to illustrate how communication occurs within and across organizations. We draw upon concepts introduced by Mitchell (constitutive complexity) and McPhee and Zaug (the four flows of communication) to reveal how the four flows model identifies communication behaviors and how these behaviors move through the organization to keep communication in dynamic motion. We find that the entrepreneurial action associated with the Air Force technicians we studied exemplified the blending or combination of communication flows in a variety of ways. Moreover, constitutive complexity emerges when two or more of these flows overlap.

We begin this chapter on the constitution of communication by first introducing Mitchell's (2003) concept of "constitutive complexity,"

* The authors gratefully acknowledge support from the National Science Foundation (Grant No. SBR-94–96229 and SBR-94–20461) and the United States Air Force (Grant No. USAF-F49642–97–P-0083) for the program of research on which this chapter is based. They would also like to thank the editors of this book for their contribution to this chapter.

which couples with dynamic complexity and evolved complexity to focus on and help explain the dynamic relationships within organizations. We specifically employ constitutive complexity because of its focus on the complexity that organisms display when many parts are organized in a non-random order (Mitchell, 2003, p. 4). Cells, organisms, insect colonies, and ecosystems are all examples of constructive complexity in nature. "In short, almost every level of the biological hierarchy is constitutively complex" (Plutynski, 2004). This chapter analyzes a human communication example of constitutive complexity and offers multi-theoretical explanations of it by using McPhee's four flows of constitutiveness: membership negotiation, reflexive self-structuring, activity coordination, and institutional positioning. We address the task of critiquing and extending the four flow version of the constitution of organizations by revisiting an earlier research example and examining the emergent complexity among the four flows as a guide for the analysis (Browning, Sitkin, Sutcliffe, Obstfeld & Greene, 2000). The chapter concludes by showing how the four flows demonstrate syncretic and synthetic capacities.

To build our case in this chapter, we first describe the parameters of McPhee's critique of constitutiveness. Next, we offer three examples from the Air Force maintenance squadron that show how different parings of the four flows merge into a single explanation. In the following discussion section, we tie constitutive complexity to the four flows by unpacking the idea of synthetic and syncretic forces. In this way we make a conceptual base for the pairings and show the value of integrative complexity for understanding self-organizing and entrepreneurial behavior (McGaffey & Christy, 1975). We conclude by analyzing the value of the four flows paradigm for understanding our example.

The theme of the story we use as an example can be stated briefly. We examined the process improvement practices used by the United States Air Force technicians in an aircraft maintenance squadron. They were good at developing tactics to save money by looking for efficient ways to maintain the fighter aircraft that were used to train pilots in advanced air-to-air combat skills. The technicians were challenged not only to find fixes for their planes, but to market and sell their solutions to other similar units across the Air Force. They were urged to treat the

Air Force repair process as an open market with material consequences. These specialists located and marketed their solutions through the use of new channels, both interpersonal and technical. As such, they became "military entrepreneurs," in their blending of traditional military roles with new economic imperatives to find new ways to extract monetary value from work place innovations.

Mitchell's Constitutive Complexity

Through the concept of constitutive complexity and the related concepts of dynamic complexity and evolved complexity, Mitchell seeks to articulate a middle ground between determinism and pluralism in the scientific world (2003). Mitchell's contention that multiple theories can co-exist regarding a particular subject or phenomenon has broad application. This idea is increasingly used as a point of departure for inquiries into the philosophy of science (Forber, 2005; Jamniczky, 2005; Machamer & Sytsma, 2007; Mitchell & Dietrich, 2006).

Constitutive complexity allows us to search for multiple dimensions that explain a particular question, rather than accepting one and only one "correct" answer. As dynamic relationships in organizations move from singular, to paired, to group processes, the concept of dynamic complexity emerges (p. 5). The third component, evolved complexity, accounts for units developing in different ways despite originating in quite similar circumstances. Mitchell observes that theory requires the same plurality that the structures being studied have, and calls for "models and theories deployed at multiple levels" (Plutynski, 2004, p. 1). This set of theories fits well with the four flows of communication first outlined by McPhee and Zaug (2000) and extended in later work. Applying the pluralistic approach to human communication, as we do here, extends both concepts further still.

McPhee's Four Communication Flows

McPhee and Iverson's (this volume, Chapter 3) focus on messages that flow in the interaction process draws our attention to the role of this discourse in making up organizational structure. Discourse is a medium for social interaction and a powerful force beyond the text

(Fairhurst & Putnam, 2004). In McPhee's formulation, the effect of any given message is important because organizations speak to several constituencies at once—including each other, a hierarchy, and external institutions.

The four flows set forth by McPhee and Zaug (2000) are defined as:

1. Membership negotiation, which includes socialization, identification, and self-positioning activities. Membership negotiation asks the question, "Who are we?"
2. Organizational self-structuring, which refers to reflexive structuring and control activities, especially managerial activities. Self-structuring asks the question, "What rules do we operate by?"
3. Activity coordination, meaning interactions that serve to "align or adjust local work activities" (p. 587). Activity coordination asks the question, "What work are we doing together?"
4. Institutional positioning, comprised primarily of external communication for the purpose of gaining "recognition and inclusion in the web of social transactions" (p. 588). Institutional positioning asks the question, "What external forces provide legitimacy, and what kinds of communication are necessary to please them?"

Our contention is that constitutive complexity emerges in instances where McPhee's communication flows overlap. We take this position based on the abstract of McPhee's article: "These four sorts of communication are analytically distinct, even though a single message can address more than one constitutive task; we need to recognize that complex organizations exist only in the relatedness of these four types of flow." The four flows are conceptually separate, but they drift quickly into each other's space when applied to a particular instance. We will build a case that says understanding the overlap in what any particular message addresses is a key to understanding the four flows. By re-analyzing data from our earlier structuration analysis, we will show that the flows emerge into constitutive complexity as they become *synergistic* (Sutcliffe, Sitkin, & Browning, 1997*)*, or in the terms of religious and cultural theory, *syncretic* to each other.

There are conceptual reasons to look for synthetic and complex ties among the four flows. For example, *membership negotiation*, which addresses, "Who am I in relation to you?" is historically linked in the social sciences to *activity coordination*, "What are we doing to complete the task?" In this chapter, we collapse McPhee's four flows in an effort to show how they come together for useful purposes. We will show that the four flows are reflexive and vary in power in any given instance.

Methodology and Data Collection

This analysis is drawn from a larger set of examples collected to examine process improvement methods across the United States. The United States Air Force was selected as a site for analysis because a panel of judges considered it to be among the best governmental efforts at implementing process improvement methods. We examined several sites across the United States and the aircraft repair program at Barmstorm Air Force Base (a pseudonym) agreed to make their program technicians available for interviews, observations, and a review of official documents about their work performance. The technicians were United States Air Force enlisted personnel, approximately one half of whom were men of color, in the rank of Sergeant. The technicians were aircraft repairmen who were assigned the mission of not only making the needed repairs, but also finding less expensive ways of completing them. Changes in repair protocol required approval by a civilian review board, also known as the Civilian Depot, which was charged with enforcing the Secretary of the U.S. Air Force's Technical Orders (TOs) for aircraft maintenance. One mechanism for getting repairs approved was the Repair Initiatives Conference—a public forum authorized by Air Force Instruction 21–123 for resolving differences between the Depot approvers and those initiating a change. The meeting was intended to "break any communication 'gridlock'" as well as provide opportunities for "cross-tells," new technology, and demonstrations of repair processes (AFI-21-123, p. 3). In the next section, we offer three examples that demonstrate how the overlapping communication flows result in a change in culture for Air Force repair methods.

Activity Coordination and Institutional Positioning

Our first example focuses on the relationship between the Air Force technicians who plan and complete repairs and the civilian review board at the Repairs Depot that monitored and controlled the legitimacy of any given repair protocol. The working relationship between these two groups, in effect, combines the flows of *activity coordination* and *institutional positioning*. The technicians were charged with the task of not only fixing their aircraft using the least resources possible, but getting new repair processes approved by the civilian review board so that their methods could be certified and marketed to other Air Force units (and allied units, such as the Singapore Air Force) that were addressing the same problems.

The technicians saw their relationship with the Civilian Review Board as contentious. The technicians regularly ran afoul of the Depot, because the Depot had sole responsibility for determining whether a U.S. Air Force unit could use solutions they devised internally and whether they could sell those same solutions to other U.S. Air Force units. The technicians imagined themselves as change agents engaged in the generation of entrepreneurial solutions to costly operating problems, and characterized the Depot as a bureaucratic block to the flow of innovation and communication between the technicians and other Air Force bases. These battles with the Depot over the most safe and efficient ways to repair aircraft were evident in many of the cases the technicians provided. As a result of these differences, the technicians viewed the Depot engineers as opponents and gave them careful scrutiny.

As one of the technicians said about the approval unit, "You know, what's funny about this business is the people who approve our initiatives are responsible for the status quo. So if they approve our idea, it actually ends up reflecting badly on them."

The self-constitution of the technicians as change agents and the Depot as defenders of the status quo mirrors the rhetorical character of how the "bureaucracy/enterprise dualism" is often deployed in public sector contexts (du Gay, 2004) and speaks to the technicians' adoption of a more entrepreneurial self (du Gay, 1996). The technicians' new identity as change agents rhetorically challenges the authority of the Depot in light of the new values required of Total Quality Management (TQM) at the same time as it highlights Llewellyn, Lewis, & Wood's (2007) findings about the uneven expansion of entrepreneurial values in the public sphere.

As one example of the interaction between the two groups, the technicians reported finding a cheaper source for an external instrumentation device (EID) that provides the aircraft's pilot data on the aircraft's performance. Because the EID device is exposed to outside air, its tips are often damaged from bug splatter. The technicians managed to find a company able to redo the tips at a considerable saving from standard replacement costs. The technicians judged the admittedly ambiguous testing data to demonstrate the repair's safety. The Civilian Depot, however, unconvinced that such a repair was truly safe, rejected the solution. The difference in interpretations of the performance data meant that the technicians' proposed method, rather than being permanently discarded, was held in abeyance over several months, until a third set of data could be collected.

Part of the civilian–military difference was over money. When the technicians at a base could not solve a particular problem, they had to pay for the Depot's engineers to come solve it for them. The technicians believed that the Depot engineers were careless with their expenses:

> We have to pay these guys to come down here, and we pay all their expenses. And what we find out is the people get here and then the tool was being used at Langley (another Air Force Base) and they have to wait for those guys to get done with it and ship it to Barnstorm U.S. Air Force Base. So these guys are here two, three or four days—a week—before the tool comes in.

In addition to the technicians' cost consciousness, the case shows the independence and superior status of the civilian group and a difference in priorities. The civilian-based Depot was only responsible for certifying the safety of any given solution. The expense money they "burned," according to the technicians, was of little concern to the depot personnel. The technicians, in contrast, worked longer hours for less money, and continually scouted for possible places to save money. Such a tension between priorities exemplifies the difficulty of integrating task and institutional requirements.

In other words, the AFI-21–123 asked technicians to move beyond their mechanical role; they were asked to be entrepreneurs responsible for stretching and producing resources. As such, the technicians began to embrace more entrepreneurial forms of organizing (du Gay, 1996) while the Civilian Depot wasted valuable resources. Thus the procedures begin to act upon the subjectivity of the technicians differently than the Depot. The interactive process between technicians and the Depot was a recognition on the part of the technicians that the Depot is institutionally outside of the mandate of the technicians. Activity coordination and institutional positioning emerge as a dynamic constitutive process in which inside and outside are formulated by the flow of communication associated with activity coordination. While the self-structuring of the Air Force regulation designed an interactive process between the technicians and Depot to guide the flow of repair innovations, a process that placed the technicians and Depot inside a communicative process, the entrepreneurial demands on the technicians increasingly constituted the Depot as an institution outside of the Air Force mandate.

We provide a deeper analysis of one side of the communication taking place—that of the technicians by identifying the communicative behaviors they used to get official approval for their newfound methods.[1] To make a change in the repair procedures, technicians were obligated to engage in communicative action to persuade the Civilian Depot of the need for organizational change. Our focus on these communicative actions highlights the recursive relationship between the technicians' task (activity coordination) and their relationship with and constitution of this important external audience (institutional positioning). This pairing draws together a powerful instance of these two concepts. They set up issues of independence, obligation, and, importantly, negotiation as their interaction informs us of the dynamic between the two. We briefly list the technicians' description of a complex series of communicative and organizational strategies that they used in the service of changing the TOs necessary to give them certified methods they could sell. Based on several interviews we determined that there were five steps crucial to negotiations with the Civilian Depot.

1. Get a request into queue. Technicians understood that many requests had to be formally processed and evaluated. Initiating a request began a strategic sequence. One interviewee gave the example of needing to get his superior to sign off on a request for a change even though he knew it would be rejected, in order to register the "turndown" that

allowed him to argue for a reversal of the Depot's decision in the next formal meeting.

2. Conform to internal standards. Technicians developed an internal standard, called the "six parts," that they ran all initiatives through to increase the possibility of Depot approval. This method assured that everything had been documented, which meant that all the internal supervisors had signed off, in advance, on any request going to the Depot.

3. Communicate with the long-term relationship with the Depot in mind. Technicians indicated the need for patience as gaining acceptance for a change took time. The technicians were conscious that certifying safety issues was a protracted process. The Depot required more evidence and took longer to evaluate and approve changes.

4. Integrate personal frustration with a concern for the task. The technicians were required to be aware that personal concerns influenced institutional decisions. As one technician said, "You've got a lot of personal issues involved—pride and ownership and all that stuff you got to deal with, too." For example, the technicians were aware that pressure on the Depot for approval could have a pushback and punishing component. One technician related how the aggressive pursuit of Depot approval for two change items at the same time backfired:

> We lost both battles just on this issue. And that other one wasn't even up for consideration. [The Depot engineer] said, "If you don't let this slide the way it is, then I will take this away, too."

5. Develop influential networks. Most importantly, the technicians were aware of the value of powerful alliances and made sure to keep stakeholders informed. For example, while one aircraft maintenance squadron worked on a training base, the technicians discovered that the most powerful argument involved the support of the actual air combat command. One interviewee indicated:

> We're a training base. Our major command is Air Education Training Command. However, the real power broker in the F-15 community is not AETC. It's Headquarters ACC [Air Combat Command] out

of Langley. Their F-15s, you know, have real missions as opposed to training missions. And if you convince them—they backed us on a lot of our other successes. And if they're not backing you, you can almost forget about it. You could look at Langley as a very strong ally. When ACC says it, they're speaking on behalf of front-line F-15 fighter units.

This series of practices that were designed to get rules changed and thus allow the technicians to accomplish their mission were inextricably connected to their relationship with the external audience made up of the civilians at the Depot. In addition, the strategies outlined above for getting the civilian Depot engineers to certify their methods included a variety of accompanying practices such as timing, patience, restraint, documentation, and networking. The array of practices the technicians used to get institutional approval (not to mention keeping their mouths shut when they saw the civilians acting capriciously) were prime examples of how activity coordination and institutional positioning come together to produce constitutive complexity.

Membership Negotiation and Activity Coordination

Our second example is briefer because it addresses a deeply structured and essentially silent pairing in this case. It is the relationship between the technicians and the pilots at Barnstorm Air Force Base that flew the planes they repaired. This pairing combines McPhee's two flows, *membership negotiation* ("Who are we?") and *activity coordination* ("What are we doing?"). Membership categories here include both the enlisted men who repaired the planes and the pilots who flew them, and it excludes the "civilians" at a distant site who, in their 40-hour-a-week jobs and better pay, were making decisions about safety. In this analysis, the civilians are the "other."

This analysis places both the technicians and pilots in the same organization despite their differences in rank because they are "blue-suiters" and are members of the same community on the same Air Force Base. They see each other throughout the duty day and are acutely aware that the quality of the repair work determines a major part of the risk the pilots take every time they fly a plane. This blending of membership and activity coordination, simultaneously defines the organization (in this case the Air Force) and generates an outside institution—the Civilian Depot. The structurational feature of simply being in the same physical space is the term Giddens (1984, p. 64), using Goffman's (1959) concept of "face," refers to as "co-presence," which means the communicators are in unmediated and direct face-to-face contact. No one wants to lose face.

The interdependence between the technicians and the pilots was best exemplified by the "Foreign Object Damage" (FOD) walk, which took place each morning. Every day, technicians, spaced a few feet apart, walked every inch of the flight line where the planes had been repaired the night before to assure that any object that might have been left behind during repairs or fell off the plane during landing was picked up before the jet engines were ignited. To guarantee the greatest impact, this walk took place each morning about two hours before the jets began to fly. The technicians looked under and around the planes, often using a magnet, to assure that nothing, not even the tiniest star washer, was left on the flight line that could be sucked into an aircraft engine. They also had continuous committee meetings to review FOD data and to look for ways to keep the error rate going down.

The FOD is an example of both *membership negotiation* and *activity coordination* because it provides a visual, spatial, and physical example of what the technicians do to protect the pilots. Each Air Force Base is considered to be and is promoted as a "family culture" that takes care of its own. The FOD walk, for example, displayed the support of one part of the community (the technicians) for another (the pilots). Seeing this walk meant not only that the repairs were finished, but also that the final step in safety had been taken. The perception was that technicians, despite the pressure to save money and do things cheaper, would never put a pilot at risk. Thus the technicians were freed to search for inexpensive solutions.

Activity coordination associated with the local dynamics of base culture built a shared sense of membership between the technicians and the pilots. The FOD built mutual trust among the technicians and pilots that the Air Force mandate to do things cheaper would not sacrifice mission readiness or the safety of the pilot.

While this research project lacks direct evidence, we might speculate that as the pilot trust in his/her technician increases, the more likely the pilot will find common ground with the technician in his/her encounters with the Depot and support the technicians' mandate to operate more efficiently. This may be so because of the ability of trusting relationships to generate social capital (Nooteboom, 2007). Since the pilots come to trust the technicians because they experience a higher sense of vulnerability than that experienced by the technicians, they augment the social networks in support of the decision-making of the technicians. In so doing, the new entrepreneurial subjectivity of the technicians is enhanced because their decision-making is valorized by those most directly affected by the technician's decisions (Casson & Della Guiusta, 2007).

Our research indicates that the flow of communication associated with membership negotiation and activity coordination coalesced in local forms that created new relationships of institutional positioning between the base, the Air Force, and the Depot. In other words, power relationships are partly the constitutive result of how communicative flows create local alliances within a complex organization. There exists an inherent power imbalance associated with the status of the pilots and technicians (officers and enlisted), but the interaction between membership negotiation and activity coordination pulls them together as a power block—a composite body, if you will, constitutively distinct from the Air Force's self-structuring assumptions about rank. However, more research is called for in this case because of the situational character of trust. The social capital produced by the technicians in the FOD walk may not yield a return for the technicians if the pilots privilege the competence and motives of the Depot over the technicians (Nooteboom, 2007).

Self-structuring and Activity Coordination

Our final example will be a more extensive one and it includes *self-structuring* ("What rules do we operate by?") and *activity coordination* ("How do we work together?") because it focuses on the rule structure the technicians were obligated to follow. This brief example focuses on the policy AFI-21–123, an "Air Force Instruction." An AFI is a non-binding directive as opposed to an Air Force Regulation (AFR), which would require compliance. The text of AFI-21–123 runs only four pages and provides only general guidance (Air Force Instruction, ND). The brief instruction is represented in a PERT (Program Evaluation and Review Technique) chart, which is a series of yes/no choices among eight step-wise criteria, and an outline for submitting a case to the Repair Initiatives Conference.

Our analysis suggests that the AFI's brevity accounts for the high level of innovation practiced by the technicians. After reading it, one would be hard-pressed to know what any actions based on the AFI-21–123 would look like. The instruction promotes bottom-up change and emphasizes the use of local resources. The document's lack of detail allowed each technician to interpret the document individually and fashion creative responses to the different problems they chose to address. The instruction is a prime example of self-structuring in that it provides a plan from the Air Force management that enables the technicians to undertake their own operational practices (a form of activity coordination).

In essence, AFI-21–123 directs technicians to experiment, to find unique solutions to maintenance and repair problems, and then to sell them. This instruction inaugurates the transformation of the technicians into entrepreneurial actors by rewarding innovation and encouraging the technicians to size up opportunities to earn a profit by selling their cost-saving solutions. While McPhee's four flows analytically represent the constitutive role of communication in the making of the organization, the self-structuring associated with the AFI-21–123 demonstrates a process of (re)constituting membership identity by changing the very work to be done. In this case, the stakes are high. They must sell repair solutions within the U.S. military maintenance community in order to fund the last 10 percent of their budget cycle each year.

The tightening of resources creates an incentive for changing the repair process. At the same time, this new incentive becomes part of the constitutive distinction between the technicians as entrepreneurial change agents and the Civilian Depot as the representatives of the status quo (bureaucratic actors).

The AFI-21–123 instruction empowers technicians to change rules due to their proximity to maintenance problems. The instruction takes advantage of this proximity to activate new entrepreneurial behaviors among the technicians that might lead to bottom-up change. The purpose is to break down constraints—but only useless ones. As such, AFI-21–123 broke down one control structure and replaced it with another, more flexible one. If a technician devises a faster, cheaper way to implement an aircraft repair, he writes up his proposal on one of the official suggestion-box forms and sends it to the Depot. A Depot approver must, if he/she is to approve it, override an existing, official procedure, which as mentioned above, was a TO given by the Secretary of the U.S. Air Force, which makes it the official legal guide for how to maintain the aircraft. However, since Whittle (2005) has identified how practicing and preaching flexibility can produce a subjectivity that must struggle with "contradiction, disaffection and cynicism", it is important to assess how communicative flows produce commitment and organizational integrity. One way of conceptualizing this mix of order and change is through the concept of integrative complexity.

Self-organizing and Integrative Complexity

AFI-21–123 is actually quite ingenious. It's an example of integrative complexity (Harvey, 1966; Maruyama, 1992, 1994; Suedfeld, Tetlock, & Streufert, 1992) because, though it focuses on rule-driven behavior, it also opposes rules for rules' sake, and directs technicians to test rules via action and experiments.

Integrative complexity is a body of research in strategic and interpersonal communication (Burleson & Samter, 1990; Delia, O'Keefe, & O'Keefe, 1982; Gruenfeld, Thomas-Hunt, & Kim, 1998), social psychology (Suedfeld and Tetlock, 1977), and conflict resolution and planning (Maruyama, 1992) that focuses on information processing and decision-making—especially on how fixed or flexible the interpretation of information is and how, once interpreted, information is connected to decision-making structures. An integratively complex system is both stable enough to remain safe from destabilizing while experimenting to invent systems that create opportunity (Holling, 2001). Integrative complexity was developed in the United States through research sponsored by the Office of Naval Research as a conceptual system applicable to individuals, groups, and organizations by Harvey and associates (Harvey, 1961; Harvey, Hunt, & Schroder, 1963; Schroder, Driver, and Streufert, 1967). The concept was developed in Japan by

Maruyama (1992, 1994) by accounting for the systemic features of decision-making behavior in the professions through a category system he called "mindscape types." Maruyama's concept of complexity is also applicable at the individual, group, or organizational level (Maruyama, 1992, 1994).

Integrative complexity has carried over to the next generation of social psychologists primarily through the work of Suedfeld and Tetlock (Suedfeld & Rank, 1976; Suedfeld & Tetlock, 1977; Tetlock, Armor, & Peterson, 1994). Their work is focused on decoding the levels of complexity in manuscripts of historical events (Bright & Tarrant, 2002; Tetlock, Armor & Peterson, 1994; Suedfeld & Rank, 1976; Suedfeld & Tetlock, 1977; Porter & Suedfeld, 1981; Tetlock, 1979, 1985; Tetlock, Bernzweig, & Gallant, 1985). Integrative complexity (Suedfeld, Tetlock, & Streufert, 1992) refers to the degree to which thinking and reasoning involve the recognition and integration of multiple perspectives and possibilities and their interrelated contingencies. As applied to this chapter, the concept attends to two features: (a) differentiation, which is the number of features of a problem situation recognized and taken into account in decision-making; and (b) integration which refers to the number of complex connections among the characteristics that have been differentiated (Walker & Watson, 1994). Integrative complexity focuses on the extent to which individuals make differentiations in their thinking and integrate them into coherent systems and solutions (Pratt, Diessner, Pratt, Hunsberger, & Prancer, 1996).

What follows is how the Air Force's instruction tries to activate integrative complexity at an organizational level (a kind of constitutive process and effect all in one). The focus is on the instruction rather than on whether particular individuals demonstrate integrative complexity or whether certain behavior or roles correspond to integrative complexity.

The AFI is integratively complex in this way: The instruction increases emphasis on local access to measurement (in integrative complexity terms, more information) that can be later monitored by independent reviews by the Depot approvers who sit far above the action (a complex connection among the characteristics). Because the military technicians have to apply to civilian controllers at a distant Depot, the instruction contains both control and action—another property of integrative complexity (Suedfeld, Tetlock, & Streufert, 1992). Once proposals are taken under review, they remain on the forum's agenda for a period of time until they are resolved. One of the precepts of integrative complexity is tolerance for uncertainty (Harvey, 1966). Having repair proposals before the forum over a period of months is in keeping with this idea, since it takes time for level heads to prevail. The AFI-21–123 process is public, with an agenda and a forum for speaking. Public behavior tends to increase the complexity of the arguments; when individuals make public commitments, they are more likely to be accomplished (Tetlock, 1985).

The regulation exists as a meta-rule allowing for the possibility of change in the operational rules of aircraft repair procedures. The interaction between meta-rules and operational rules is one place where a self-structuring communication flow re-organizes the work activities. The communicative process underwrites the instruction by creating a deliberative forum—the Repairs Initiative Conference—that it relies on to transform this organization at the level of work rules. This U.S. Air Force efficiency program grew out of a process improvement strategy that was negotiated in the early 1990s between the Air Force and defense-oversight groups in Congress to get funding for the next generation of technology, especially electronics, in exchange for the promise of achieving cost savings by effectively implementing process improvement methodologies.

The technicians also exemplify integrative complexity by adhering to rules, but not rules for rules' sake. Technicians were strikingly cavalier about adherence to prescribed procedures as stipulated in AFI-21–123. One technician said he did not follow the method at all. Others said they simply took from it the need to "look for the best way" to do the job and gave almost no details on the specific language of the method. They seemed to be following the details of the method, but they felt no need to affirm it in our interviews. But this relaxed attitude toward the process improvement method in fact foreshadowed a change in emphasis across the entire Air Force. These interview data were collected in 1995. When this study was updated in 2004, the Air Force had reduced the emphasis on the language of the TQM method and gave directions for major commands to supplement this instruction "to provide tailored guidance and procedures" and identified a waiver authority[2] for it and returned to other mission-related goals in their policy toward process improvement.

This approach is not uncommon when organizations initiate process improvement methods. Florida Power and Light, a utility that had a reputation for implanting process improvement methods, essentially said, "Once you learn to dance, you can take the painted footsteps up off the floor." Such a shift in strategy explains this theme in our data.

As our previous research shows, people tend to disregard the origins of rules once they have simplified and internalized them; they retain the spirit of the rule but drop the specific features of it (Browning, Sitkin, & Sutcliffe, 1998). The technicians were following the precepts of the AFI-21–123 rules and doing so in an improvisational, self-organizing, emergent, strategic, and individually driven way—which is what AFI-21–123 directed them to do. The question seems to be: What is the relationship between integrative complexity and learning to follow the spirit of the rule?

The interaction between the communicative flow of self-structuring (AFI-21–123) and the coordination of the way technicians work relies on a dynamic and reflexive interface. AFI-21–123 generates integrative complexity and transforms the self-structuring of Air Force technicians by changing the repair procedures. The Repairs Initiatives Conference becomes a deliberative forum that functions to re-route the initial pairing of communicative flows (self-structuring and activity coordination) either "upward"—changing the TOs of the Air Force manual for repairing damaged parts—or "downward"—back to the local base culture due to a rejection and/or further study. If the TO is changed, then a new flow of communication is generated between bases (constituting a new relationship of institutional positioning) in which one base becomes the buyer of services from another base. In this case, a market is formed so that the technicians might entreprenuerialize their innovation. A rather loose mandate to experiment becomes the starting point for the emergence of integrative complexity with the potential to re-constitute the very character of the organization. To fully appreciate the power of integrative complexity requires a more detailed examination of the synergistic consequences of communicative flows coming together in interactive pairs.

Synthetic and Syncretic Flows

We have built on McPhee's four flow formulation by showing how these streams of variables overlap. We interpret the three pairings of flows above as a complicated interplay causing the streams of variables to become "syncretized." That term, which is derived from the Greek term *sunkrtizein*, means "to unite" and was used specifically during the Hellenistic period to account for combining disparate religious beliefs from the Middle East into a single, if loose, system. More recently, it has been applied to a wide variety of settings, from software product strategy, to accounting for chemical interactions in pharmaceutical products (Keith, Zimmermann, Lehár, & Borisy 2004). In academic research the idea is represented as a distinctive, formal cognitive system and encompasses such topics as cultural linguistics, child language development, psychology, philosophy, industrial policy, and organizational design. We review them here to set up an explanation of our combinations of pairs of flows.

In these varied applications, syncretism is the process of "fusing diverse ideas into a single, general, inexact impression." This definition (*New Shorter Oxford English Dictionary*, p. 3188) fits what we see in the four examples of how the technicians implemented the process improvement program.

The term "syncretic" as it is broadly used is reflected in the following examples: In linguistics, syncreticism occurs when speakers must traverse language shifts between each other's natural preferences and still manage to make sense of what's being said. Another example is how the term is used as a framework for analyzing how diverse cultural practices inform the organization of literacy activities in an ethnic community in Los Angeles. The report details the story of a six-year-old boy and how his family switches between the public school English the child uses to study math and the Samoan his family uses to help him complete his assignments. Alessandro & Ochs (1996) saw three essential activities at play, including reinvention, integration, and prioritization. In basic language development another kind of syncretism occurs. Vygotsky (1962) postulated a theory of meaning by observing children on the playground. For him, meaning begins with the existence of syncretic images produced by Kantian action—that is, what pre-schoolers learn by doing. Their syncretic images are temporary and playful, and they draw no generalizations from them, since they are only vague impressions. But using these syncretic images, a child learns the tacit rules of etiquette until a more complex understanding can be acquired. As such, language develops from the social group back to the individual rather than the other way around.

Jung's (1948) psychological use of syncretism comes from his assertion that if serial events, however dissimilar, occur in the same unit of time, they will be assigned significance by the individual. As such, he posits a kind of temporal logic, the kind that shows up in narratives as powerful forces in the relationship among technology, consequences, and actions. For these reasons, narrative therapy that addresses such simultaneity is a commonly used method for helping clients change their thinking and behavior that results from past events.

McNamara's (2002) analysis of the means of production in Korea shows that the country operates under "syncretic capitalism," which is an arrangement of an odd combination of trust and limited corruption between the nation-state and conglomerates. Letting some errors pass while exerting a modicum of control over others allows the Korean industrial economy a mix of looseness and tightness in which to operate. Staker (2001) asserts that organizational problem-solving models are ineffective when addressing changing circumstances and thus require a combination of programs that, if each were considered alone, could be fairly opposite in their purpose and design. He refers to this as a "syncretic method" that combines particular features into a heuristic practice. Syncretic can be seen as the opposite of discrete; syncretic means that processes are still linked together, while discrete means that they can be separated without doing damage to either concept.

This section offers a perspective on continuous improvement methods and syncreticism under the rubric of "synergistic process," which was developed by Sutcliffe, Sitkin, & Browning in an earlier report from this research project (1997). Process improvement methods necessarily combine methods of controlling structures to produce a reliable outcome with variation to produce new information and learning. As such, the combination of control and learning in projects and organizations is a syncretic achievement. As we applied this scheme to the cases presented above, we showed how accomplishing different pairings of McPhee's essentials were synergistic.

In the three examples from this chapter, flows are combined to account for the compelling forces that explain how the technicians operated, usually very effectively, in finding more efficient ways to maintain fighter aircraft for readiness. The result of this syncretic encounter between communication flows was also the creation of a new entrepreneurial self. This entrepreneurial technician learns to take initiative to solve repair problems and sell the innovations to other bases. In so doing, the technicians become responsible for their own funding. The entrepreneurial characteristics of initiative, risk-taking, and self-reliance create distinctions between the technicians and the Civilian Depot at the same time as their identity as technicians responsible for the care of fighter planes and pilots re-enforces their military identity and allegiance to base culture. The syncretic character of the communication flows also re-orients the very identity of the technician in syncretic ways—blending military, technical, and economic characteristics together to produce a new ideal type of Air Force technician.

Synergistic Processes

The Air Force technicians' case is synergistic for several reasons. First, it is a good example of *joint optimization* of both the processes of control and learning. The technicians felt the urgency of finding new solutions because of the budgetary constrains. But their interviews on this topic showed a particularly energetic tone. Rather than lamenting the short budget, they saw it as a reality and a challenge. They seemed to like the game of finding ways to perform and meet these new requirements. Rather than being frustrated by this barrier, they enjoyed the search for efficient means and the ability to produce surprise and marvel in the face of others when they produced a solution. Our evidence indicates a general desire on the part of the technicians to be creative and innovative. The budgetary constraints and the search for solutions were *mutually reinforcing*—the increase in structural constraints caused an increase in communication, both over the Internet in the worldwide search for parts in the U.S. material system and with allies. At its best, the new instruction generated complimentarity between the limits placed on the solution search by the distant and all powerful civilians and the freedom to come up with any solution that passed muster with these same evaluators. They were *complimentary and interdependent* on the task of improvement in that the overwhelming influence of either one alone could have been disastrous for the project, but powerful when structurally combined. Finally, the technicians had *resilience* in their sensing and coping abilities in that they continuously searched both for information and for strategic ways to get solutions passed by the civilian evaluators.

Summary and Conclusion

What can we say about the four flows of constitutiveness from this analysis? First, the three pairings of stories from the Air Force interviews show that the four flows are all-encompassing. This theoretically driven interpretation makes a finer distinction (than Giddens alone gives) about constitutiveness without reducing the conceptual space covered. It is necessary to complete a task (activity coordination) by a standard (self-organizing), to work out a relationship with each other, to relate to a superior or other external authority, and all of these, more or less, require doing. McPhee would probably not use the term, but they are "essentials" or "requirements." As such our focus on the technician as a change agent makes visible how the communication flows couple together to unleash new entrepreneurial characteristics: experimentation, innovation, and risk-taking among the technicians.

Second, the theory parcels out constitutiveness in such a way that it directs us to search for specific examples to match the four categories. In that sense, the theory increases theoretical specificity. In this chapter, this is achieved by McPhee's use of narrative as the site of the enactment of constitutiveness (McPhee and Zaug, 2000). Our analysis confirms that constitutiveness exists in micro examples that make up a story. The theory allows for theoretical efficiency; it allows us to reduce what is necessary to say about a narrative yet leave the story intact. Entrepreneurial dynamics and integrative complexity are played out here via the discourse that takes place among these major players.

Third, McPhee's four features show, in varying ways, the essentials for survival, and that a weakness in one area is likely to be offset by some overwhelming strength somewhere else to remain viable. For example, the technicians had a structural weakness (they were paid much less), were more controlled (subject to both civil laws and the Uniform Code of Military Justice), and had less education (the Civilian Review Board were professional engineers), but the technicians had the front-line fighting command structure backing them on decisions. Despite this, we do not see a skewed relationship among the four flows. To a substantial degree, they all seem important here.

Fourth, the case analysis acts as a caution to us about how global and powerful any one of these four categories is in any given instance and how likely they are to remain that way. The best examples of the four flows idea will come from what they mean, operationally, over time, but also, how they look when they are "flowing" in some kind of directional motion.

But how might these flows dry up or surge in their relative power? For example, our original analysis, completed in 1995, shows probably the strongest feature of the technicians is how they worked together (we have no data on whether that is the same or remains the same). The second most influential flow is the self-organizing that occurred as a result of the process improvement program. Surprisingly, they were doing quite well but showing little attention to the features of it. Many of the technicians declared no allegiance to and/or showed *no* emphasis on official Air Force philosophy. They appear to have received the word to get the job done and only use TQM dimensions, in DeSanctis' terms at the "spirit level" (DeSanctis, Snyder, & Poole, 1994). Process improvement methods emphasized a few basics—keep your mind on the goal, use the best information possible, and "look for better ways of doing things."

What to make of this inconsistent data? One explanation is that a side issue shaped the stories. While we have only observational rather than interview data to support the following contention, the technicians kept a distance that bordered on disrespect for the "civilian" that ran the process improvement program at the base. They didn't seem to like him (even during the brief time we were there for the research interviews, he broke into a tirade about the abortionists killing all those children) and were reluctant to give any credit to his process improvement contribution to their effort. That personal dynamic alone may account for a considerable part of the differences in the technicians' reports of the technique.

Fifth, and in conclusion, the theory with our example broadens our definition of self-organizing. We usually equate the idea with an inside-out variable (something organizes itself) or a bottom-up variable (micro-political processes and arrangements tell us a lot about how structures come to be as they are). McPhee's conceptualization is different from these; self-organizing can occur at any level with any amount of force, which is in keeping with the Foucauldian notion of power—it can come from anywhere. At the same time, consistent with Foucault (1977), power relationships can form that re-define how different individuals and elements interact with one another. As our case demonstrates, these power relationships are partly a result of the constitutive dynamics generated by the syncretic flow of communication, for example, membership identity (blue-suiters vs. civilian depot) and activity coordination. In other words, new power relationships can emerge between different organizational elements; an inside/outside emerges and local power blocks form as the constitutive effect of the blending of communication flows.

The best example of self-organizing is the work of the technicians as they negotiated their work relationship with each other. Each had a lot of knowledge about what the others were doing; they were willing to take risks in their own area because they were certain there was a check to their actions in another functional area. The technicians made up ways of doing things quite improvisationally (Weick, 1998) that seemed to work. In addition to looking out for each other's back, they accepted the military reality that you had to "suck up" not only to get by, but also to be effective.

What emerges from integrative complexity launched by the pairing of communicative flows is a newly syncretic identity that blends military, technical, and entrepreneurial characteristics to create a new membership type for the Air Force. The constitution of this "military entrepreneur" is the result of the unification of communicative flows that dynamically relies on the entrepreneurial technician as a change agent capable of re-constituting the organizational structure of the U.S. Air Force.

Notes

1 The 2000 paper by Browning, Sutcliffe, Sitkin, Obstfeld, & Greene was read by a former Depot civilian who worked with the technicians during the same time this data were being collected. He said while factually accurate, our analysis was decidedly from the Air Force technicians' point of view.
2 www.e-publishing.af.mil/pubs/info.asp?shorttitle=AFI21-123.

References

Air Force Instruction AFI-21-123 (ND). www.e-publishing.af.mil/pubs/info.asp?shorttitle=AFI21-123.

Alessandro, D., & Ochs, E. (1996). Syncretic literacy: Multiculturalism in Samoan American families, University of California, Los Angeles, Research Report: 16, www.ncela.gwu.edu/pubs/ncrcdsll/rr16/.

Bright, A. D., & Tarrant, M. A. (2002). Effect of environment-based coursework on the nature of attitudes toward the endangered species act. *Journal of Environmental Education, 33* (4), 10–19.

Browning, L. D., Sitkin, S. B., & Sutcliffe, K. M. (1998). A structuration analysis of control and learning in TQM using organizations: The presence of feature and spirit in the reports of the use of procedures. A paper of the Organizational Communication Division, presented to the annual meeting of the International Communication Association, Jerusalem, Israel.

Browning, L. D., Obstfeld, D., Sitkin, S., Sutcliffe, K. M., & Greene, R. (2000). Keep 'em flying: The constitutive dynamics of an organizational change in the U.S. Air Force. *Electronic Journal of Communication,*10(1/2).

Burleson, B., & Samter, W. (1990). Effects of cognitive complexity on the perceived importance of communication skills in friends. *Communication Research, 17,* 165–182.

Casson, M., & Della Guiusta, M. (2007). Entrepreneurship and social capital: Analysing the impact of social networks on entrepreneurial activity from a rational action perspective. *International Small Business Journal, 25*(3), 220–244.

Delia, J. G., O'Keefe, B. J., & O'Keefe, D. J. (1982). The constructivist approach to communication. In F. E. X. Dance (Ed.), *Human Communication Theory* (pp. 147–191). New York: Harper & Row.

DeSanctis, G., Snyder, J. R., & Poole, M. S. (1994). The meaning of the interface: A functional and holistic evaluation of a meeting software system. *Decision Support Systems: The International Journal, 11,* 319–335.

DeSanctis, G., & Poole, M. S. (1994). Capturing the complexity in advanced technology use: adaptive structuration theory. *Organization Science, 5* (2), 121–147.

du Gay, P. (1996). Organizing identity: Entrepreneurial governance and public management. In S. Hall, & P. du Gay (Eds.), *Questions of cultural identity* (pp. 151–169). London: Sage Publications.

du Gay, P. (2004). Against "Enterprise" (but not against "enterprise," for that would make no sense). *Organization, 11* (1), 37–57.

Fairhurst, G. T. (1993). Echoes of the vision: When the rest of the organization talks quality. *Management Communication Quarterly 6*(4), 331–371.

Fairhurst, G. T., & Putnam, L. (2004). Organizations as discursive constructions. *Communication Theory, 14*(1), 5–26.

Fairhurst, G. T., & Wendt, R. F. (1993). The gap in total quality. *Management Communication Quarterly*, 6(4), 441–451.

Forber, P. (2005). Biological complexity and integrative pluralism. *Biology & Philosophy, 20*(4), 913–924.

Foucault, M. (1977). *Discipline and punish: The birth of the prison.* Trans. Alan Sheridan. New York: Pantheon Books.

Giddens, A. (1984). *The constitution of society: Outline of a theory of structuration.* Berkeley: University of California Press.

Goffman, E. (1959). *The presentation of self in everyday life.* New York: Doubleday.

Gruenfeld, D. H., Thomas-Hunt, M. C., & Kim, P. H. (1998). Cognitive flexibility, communication strategy, and integrative complexity in groups: Public versus private reactions to majority and minority status. *Journal of Experimental Social Psychology, 34,* 202–226.

Harvey, O. J. (1966). *Experience, structure and adaptability.* New York: Springer Pub. Co.

Harvey, O. J. (Ed.). (1961). *Conceptual systems and personality organization.* New York: Wiley.

Harvey, O. J., Hunt, D. E., & Schroder, H. M. (1963). *Motivation and social interaction: Cognitive determinants.* New York: Ronald Press Co.

Holling, C. S. (2001). Understanding the complexity of economic, ecological and social systems. *Ecosystems 4*(5), 390–405.

Jamniczky, H. A. (2005). Biological pluralism and homology. *Philosophy of Science, 5,* 687–698.

Jung, C. G. (1948). *Preface to the anonymous I Ching: Collected Works,* Vol.11. London: Routledge.

Keith, C. T., Zimmermann, G. R., Lehár, J., Borisy, A. A., (2004, September 14). CombinatoRx, Inc. Polypharmacology: Single vs. combination drug. www.sbsonline.org/04conf/talks/S40514174924.htm.

Llewellyn, N., Lewis, P., & Woods, A. (2007). Public management and the expansion of an entrepreneurial ethos? *Public Management Review, 9*(2), 253–267.

Machamer, P., & Sytsma, J. (2007). Neuroscience and theoretical psychology: What's to worry about? *Theory and Psychology, 17*(2), 199–216.

Maruyama , M. (1994). *Mindscapes in management: Use of individual differences in multicultural management.* Aldershot, U.K.; Brookfield, VT: Dartmouth Pub. Co.

Maruyama, M. (Ed.). (1992). *Context and complexity: Cultivating contextual understanding.* New York: Springer-Verlag.

McGaffey, T. N., & Christy, R. (1975). Information processing capability as a predictor of entrepreneurial effectiveness. *Academy of Management Journal, 18*(4) 857–863.

McNamara, D. (2002). *Market and society in Korea: Interest institution in the textile industry.* New York: Routledge.

McPhee, R. D., & Iverson, J. (2008). Agents of constitution in comunicad: Constitutive process of the communication in organizations. Chapter 3, this volume.

Mitchell, S. D. (2003). *Biological complexity and integrative pluralism.* Cambridge, U.K.: Cambridge University Press.

Mitchell S. D., & Dietrich, M. R. (2006). Integration without unification: An argument for pluralism in the biological sciences. *American Naturalist, 168*(6), 73–79.

Neuberg, S. L., & Newsom, J. T. (1993). Personal need for structure: Individual differences in the desire for simple structure. *Journal of Personality and Social Psychology, 65,* 113–131.

New Shorter Oxford English Dictionary: On historical principles. Vol. 1, A-M (1993). Oxford: Clarendon Press.

Nooteboom, B. (2007). Social capital, institutions and trust. *Review of Social Economy, 65*(1), 29–53.

Pancer, S. M., Pratt, M., Hunsberger, B., & Gallant, M. (2000). Thinking ahead: Complexity of expectations and the transition to parenthood. *Journal of Personality, 68*(2), 253–280.

Plutynski, A. (2004). A book review of Mitchell, S. (2003). *Biological complexity and integrative pluralism,* Cambridge. *Notre Dame Philosophical Reviews, 4,* (03). http://ndpr.nd.edu/review.cfm?id=1423.

Porter, C. A., & Suedfeld, P. (1981). Integrative complexity in the corresponding of literary figures: Effects of personal and societal stress. *Journal of Personality and Social Psychology, 40*(2), 321–330.

Pratt, M. W., Diessner, R., Pratt, A., Hunsberger, B., & Prancer, S. M. (1996). Moral and social reasoning and perspective taking in later life: A longitudinal study. *Psychology and Aging, 11* (1), 66–73.

Pratt, M. W., Pancer, M. Hunsberger, B. & Manchester, J. (1990). Reasoning about the self and relationships in maturity: An integrative complexity analysis of individual differences. *Journal of Personality and Social Psychology, 59,* 575–581.

Schroder, H. M., Driver, M. J., & Streufert, S. (1967). *Human information processing: Individuals and groups functioning in complex social situations.* New York: Holt, Rinehart & Winston.

Staker, R. (2001). Towards a syncretic method for complex systems-of-systems problems. In the proceedings of the Systems in Management 7th Annual ANZSYS Conference 2001, The Relevance of Systems Thinking in the Contemporary World, Perth, Western Australia, November, 27–28 pp. 201–208.

Suedfeld, P., & Leighton, D. C. (2002). Early communications in the war against terrorism: An integrative complexity analysis. *Political Psychology, 23*(3), 585–599.

Suedfeld, P., & Rank, A. D. (1976). Revolutionary leaders: Long-term success as a function of changes in conceptual complexity. *Journal of Personality and Social Psychology, 34,* 169–178.

Suedfeld, P., & Tetlock, P. (1977). Integrative complexity of communications in international crises. *Journal of Conflict Resolution, 21,* 169–184.

Suedfeld, P., Tetlock, P. E., & Streufert, S. (1992). *Motivation and personality: Handbook of thematic content.* Cambridge, U.K.: Cambridge University Press.

Sutcliffe, K. M., Sitkin, S. B., & Browning, L. D. (1997). Perspectives on process management: Implications for research on twenty-first century organizations. In C. L. Cooper, & S. Jackson (Eds.), *Handbook of Organizational Behavior* (pp. 207–22). New York: John Wiley.

Tetlock, P. E. (1985). Accountability: A social check on the fundamental attribution error. *Social Psychology Quarterly, 48,* 227–236.

Tetlock, P. E. (1979). Identifying victims of groupthink from public statements of decision makers. *Journal of Personality and Social Psychology, 37,* 1314–1324.

Tetlock, P. E. Armor, D., & Peterson, R. S. (1994). The slavery debate in antebellum America: Cognitive style, value conflict, and the limits of compromise. *Journal of Personality and Social Psychology, 66,* 115–126.

Tetlock, P. E., Bernzweig, J., & Gallant, J. L. (1985). Supreme court decision making: Cognitive style as a predictor of ideological consistency of voting. *Journal of Personality and Social Psychology, 48,* 127–139.

Vygotsky, L. S. (1962). *Thought and language*. Cambridge MA: MIT Press.

Walker, S. G., & Watson, G. L. (1994). Integrative complexity and British decisions during the Munich and Polish crises. *Journal of Conflict Resolution*, *38*, 2–23.

Weick, K. E. (1998). Improvisation as a mindset for organizational analysis. *Organization Science, 9*(5) 543–555 (1976).

Whittle, A. (2005). Preaching and practicing "flexibility": Implications for theories of subjectivity at work. *Human Relations, 58* (10) 1301–1322.

5

Dislocation and Stabilization:

How to Scale Up from Interactions to Organization

François Cooren and Gail T. Fairhurst

In this chapter, we address a crucial and recurrent question encountered in the field of organizational communication: How can we describe and analyze the details of interactions while demonstrating that they literally contribute to the constitution of an organization? In other words, how can we bridge the gap that seems to exist between communication, which always appears to be micro and local, and structures, which always appear to be global and macro? While this issue is hardly new to communication or sociological inquiry,[1] it is our hope that our answer will prove to be original.

In order to address the question of the communicative constitution of organization (CCO), we should first ask ourselves what we mean by the term "constitution." Though Taylor (1993) and Taylor and Van Every (2000) certainly are the communication scholars who have addressed this question most systematically, an original attempt to address this issue has also recently been proposed by McPhee and Zaug (2000). In their essay on the CCO, they write:

> As agents behave, they constitute interaction and its meaningful units because meanings, communicative acts, and episodes are what they are only due to the knowledgable, empowered, contextually positioned action that implicates them. ... a pattern or array of types of interaction

117

constitutes organizations insofar as they make organizations what they are, and insofar as basic features of the organization are implicated in the system of interaction. (p. 4, emphasis added)

The question of the CCO thus implies, according to McPhee and Zaug, that human agents' behaviors constitute meaningful interactions, which can in turn constitute organizations under specific conditions to be determined. Following the social ontology proposed by Giddens (1984) in *The Constitution of Society*, the starting point of their reflection explicitly is the "conscious, capable agent" (p. 5) who can reflexively make sense of his/her environment in interactional situations.

McPhee and Zaug (2000) also rightly point out that all communication is not necessarily organizational. For instance, they note that a casual conversation between acquaintances can be said to constitute an interactional system, but not an "organization."[2] In other words, only some specific types of communication qualify as "organizational," which McPhee and Zaug define according to four different communicative flows. These flows are presented as "interactive communicative episode[s]" (p. 7) through which the *organization* is said to enact and maintain relations:

1. to its members (membership negotiation),
2. to itself (self-structuring),
3. to its internal subgroups and processes (activity coordination),
4. to other organizations (institutional positioning) (cf. p. 7).

According to these authors, communication can thus be said to be "organizational" only to the extent that it contributes to these four flows that constitute what an organization should be all about.

McPhee and Zaug (2000) state that an adequate theory of constitution must be highly general, analogous to the nature and growth of whole organs and bodies, so as to allow organizations to occur in a variety of ways. Hence, they offer up the four flows as larger, more general units of analysis. They reject bottom-up or inductive answers to the constitution question, offered by the likes of Boden (1994) and Taylor and Van Every (2000), because they have limited ability to distinguish and explain the complex social form "organization." In their view, inductive approaches may show how organizing is manifest in communication or help in the discursive analysis of texts, but ultimately a deductive approach provides a more satisfying answer to the constitution question.

We take issue with this position for two reasons. First, although McPhee and Zaug's analytical starting point is the human being and his/her reflexive capacity, it is noteworthy that their description of the communicative flows tends to vacillate between human and organizational agency. While in some accounts, they do not hesitate to speak about how "*organizations* require distinct types of relations to four audiences" (p. 1, emphasis added), i.e., their members, themselves, their internal subgroups and other organizations (cf. also p. 7); in other accounts, agency is ascribed to humans, as in their conclusion where they sum up what the four flows are all about:

> The first recounts the struggle of *individuals* to master or influence their member roles, statuses, and relations to the organization. The second articulates how *organizational leaders* design, implement, and suffer problems with decision and control mechanisms. The third focuses on *members* engaging in interdependent work or deviating from pure collaborative engagement. The fourth describes the organization as a partner, often *anthropomorphized*, in exchange and other social relations with other organizations. (p. 12, emphasis added)

This "vacillation" between two forms of agency (human vs. organizational) is not unusual, but has been denounced by Taylor and Van Every (2000) in their critique of Weick's (1979; Daft & Weick, 1984; Weick & Daft, 1983) model of organizations as interpretive systems. Like many authors before them, McPhee and Zaug (2000) seem to have problems "scaling up" from members' interactions (micro) to the organization (macro), a problem that leads them, like Weick, to oscillate between human and organizational agency without truly explaining how we can analytically or practically pass from one to the other.

Second, by deducing the pattern or array of types of interaction in the form of the four flows that constitute the "organization," McPhee and Zaug (2000) give short shrift to the organizing properties of communication that enable it to constitute in the first place. Regarding the properties of communication that enable it to constitute, one might ask: Which is the more fundamental constitution question, an approach that focuses on the complex social form "organization" or one that emphasizes the processes of organizing? In contrast to the position taken by McPhee and Zaug, we argue that the issue is largely undecidable because both approaches are necessary for an adequate theory of constitution. Consequently, the constitution question should not only be approached deductively by starting from the position of an assumed whole and reasoning downward, but also inductively by starting from the position of a set of component parts and reasoning upward. We agree with McPhee and Zaug that despite its many merits, an organizing emphasis alone is an unsatisfactory answer to the constitution question. But it would be a mistake to suggest that all scholars with an organizing emphasis are unconcerned with how one moves from micro organizing processes to macro organizational form. As we will show, several scholars address this dilemma, although real differences exist among them. To lump these scholars together, as McPhee and Zaug (2000) seem to do, is quite unfortunate.

Inductive Answers to the Constitution Question

One early solution to bridging the gap between macro and micro levels of analysis can be illustrated by the *aggregation thesis*, i.e., the social ontology according to which the macro or interactional system emerges over repeated human interactions (Cicourel & Knorr-Cetina, 1981). While micro-analyses enable aggregation proponents to identify *patterns* by which organizational members position themselves throughout their interactions, thus fighting against the "container metaphor" (Fairhurst & Putnam, 2004; Putnam & Fairhurst, 2001; Smith, 1993; Taylor, Cooren, Giroux, & Robichaud, 1996), it appears that such identification is insufficient to exhaust analytically what truly constitutes an organization. For example, interaction analysts show that communicative acts in a social system constrain future acts in unique and recognizable structured sequences and that redundancy or predictability of these recurring patterns defines the structure of the system (Fairhurst, 2004, 2007; Putnam & Fairhurst, 2001). However, even if they seem to scale up as they test for interactional regularity, the question remains as to what extent this *regularity* is sufficient to account for what composes an organization.

Following Weick (1979), these organizational communication analysts tend to focus on what is "organizing" in these interactions; however, our point is that organizing by itself *does not* seem to exhaust what constitutes an organization. Even if we recognize that the focus on the organizing properties of discourse historically constituted a theoretical breakthrough (especially in its reaction to positivist reifications of organization), identifying organizational patterns does not seem to be enough. For example, a group of individuals can organize themselves to accomplish a common objective (for example, moving) and develop some patterns of interaction, but this does not necessarily mean that this group constitutes a formal organization (for example, a moving company). They could just be a bunch of friends trying to help one of them to move.

This difficulty in "scaling up" (a term we borrow from Taylor and Van Every, 2000) thus seems to play in favor of the structuro-functionalists and critical scholars who take structure as their starting point to explain what constitutes an organization or a society. Rules, statuses, norms of behavior, protocols, ideologies, organizational charts, allocation of resources, discretionary power all constitute this *source of order* that appears to transcend the "here and now" of interactions (McPhee, 1985, 1989). Not surprisingly, while micro-oriented scholars tend to analyze the details of interactions, macro-oriented scholars typically skip this type of analysis, judging them either futile (micro-oriented scholars are accused of focusing on insignificant details of interactions while the real game would be in the "big picture") or, even worse, naive (by not acknowledging this "big picture," they tend to neglect effects of domination and ideologies). Given that interactions appear to be dictated by structures, there is, properly speaking, very little to be found there.

Using Deetz (1992) as an example, Taylor and Van Every (2000) note that he, like other prominent critical scholars (Clegg, 1989; Mumby, D., 1988; Mumby, D., 2001; Mumby, D. K., 1997), rarely describes organizational interactions because such analyses would tend to neglect what makes such interactions *possible* in the first place (cf. p. 29). In other words, while more micro-oriented scholars tend to focus on the "here and now" of interactions (what could also be called the "actual," "local," or "situational"), macro-oriented scholars tend to analyze the "there and then" of structures (what could be called the "potential," the "global," or the "trans-situational"), which are supposed to *exceed* the local.[3]

Other micro-analysts have proposed interesting solutions to respond to this issue. For example, Boden (1994), borrowing a concept from Goffman (1974), speaks in terms of lamination of conversations to explain how specific decisions, events, or topics pertaining to a given meeting can be referred or oriented to during subsequent encounters. In the case of organizational rationality, she convincingly shows how actors pull from what appears to be overarching organizational rationalities that which is relevant in a local situation and made relevant in the immediate discourse at hand to form what she calls "local logics." As organizational rationales, topics, agendas, past events, etc. are made locally relevant, they laminate or layer one upon the other as conversation unfolds. Through this *lamination thesis*, which significantly differs from the social ontology proposed by the aggregation thesis, we would thus have a way to pinpoint how the local can be transcended: just as the relevancies of the past are oriented to as needs dictate in the present, the relevancies of the present will be oriented to in the future as future needs dictate. Thus, what happened during a meeting, a conversation, or a discussion can be *taken up* in subsequent interactions, which might then explain how the "interactional ordering [of meetings] structures the organization from within" (Boden, 1994, p. 106). But is it really enough? Can we truly reduce the constitution of an organization to its interactions, even laminated? Can we agree with Boden when she writes:

> It is in the closed internal times and spaces of meetings, as well as in the many phone calls that link people, topics and tasks, that the actual structure of the organization is created and recreated. The interaction order contains its own autonomous logic and, reflexively, encapsulates the organizational domain. (1994, p. 106)

Taylor and Van Every's (2000) response is clearly "no." What is lacking from this picture is the organization's *identity* and *agency*. As they suggest, neither conversations nor meetings have the capacity to act. They are *not* agents. If laminated interactions or interactional regularity truly constituted what an organization is, we would be still wondering how organizations could be *doing* anything, i.e., could display agency (cf. p. 299). By doing things, we not only mean designing or producing goods and products (e.g., when we say that Microsoft *designs* or *produces* operating systems), but also saying or deciding things (e.g., when we say that Microsoft *decided* to go to court or *claimed* it was innocent).

But again, is it enough? Is agency sufficient to identify what an organization is? Going back to our previous example, we could again compare a group of friends moving to an apartment and a moving company accomplishing the same tasks. We can surely say that in both cases they do the same thing, i.e., moving. Thus, agency can be ascribed to both because there appears to be a way to delineate their identity: a group of friends in one case, a company in the other case. Similarly, somebody in both cases can set him/herself up as speaking or, more generally, acting on behalf of the group or the company. But here is where we start to see a difference: while there could be some negotiations between the friends about who is allowed to do that for the group, such a negotiation would hardly occur for the company. Each crew representing the moving company is supposed to have a formal leader, who is authorized to assign specific tasks to the members and speak on its behalf. A *stabilization* effect thus seems to occur, which appears to transcend the here and now of the moving. Throughout the different moving operations, specific roles, rights, and duties will remain stable, and it is this *source of stability* that needs to be unveiled.

Instead of maintaining the reflection solely at the theoretical level, we undertake this analysis using a concrete interaction to illustrate how "scaling up" occurs through actions that first appear to be locally performed. To do so, we will first present a third social ontology, called the *association thesis*, by introducing concepts that have been developed by Bruno Latour (1986, 1994, 1996, 1999) to depict and analyze how *non-human entities* tend to not only dislocate interactions, but also stabilize them. This bottom-up perspective will then enable us to show that interactions are *never* completely local. Instead, they are what we call, using a neologism, "dis-local," that is, their local achievement is always mobilizing a variety of entities—documents, rules, protocols, architectural elements, machines, technological devices—that dislocate, i.e., "put out of place" (*Webster's New Encyclopedic Dictionary*, p. 289) what initially appeared to be "in place," i.e., local.

Since we contend that there never is such thing as a purely local interaction, we propose that organizational communication be reconceptualized in such a way that the effects of transportation in time and space—what we called elsewhere "timing" and "spacing" (Cooren & Fairhurst, 2004)—be acknowledged. Our analyses will show that the "here and now," which is traditionally privileged in the micro-analyses of organizational interactions, is always contaminated by the "there and then" (whether in the past or future). However, and this is the main point of our argument, this "there and then" *was* or *will be* another "here and now." We *never* leave the level of events and actions even as these events and actions become linked to one another through space and time. Paraphrasing Latour (1993) while giving it a Derridian flavor, we could say that the immanent (micro) is *also always already* transcendent (macro).

Instead of starting from an overarching organizational structure that would dictate, from top down, how interactions function, we show, using Taylor and Van Every's (2000) term, that we never leave the "site" of dislocated interactions. Like the ethnomethodologists and the conversation analysts, we focus on how and what people do things locally, but we extend this action-oriented approach to entities that have been traditionally neglected by our analyses, namely what Latour calls *non-human actors*. As we will show, it is by extending a form of agency (to be defined) to non-humans that we can expect to identify the properties of communication that enable it to constitute organizations.

The Bottom-Up Perspective

Though the micro–macro debate has been especially lively since the 1970s, given the growing success of conversation analysis, ethnomethodology, and symbolic interactionism, its starting point can actually be first identified in a heated argument that took place at the end of the nineteenth century between Gabriel Tarde and Emile Durkheim. Though Tarde has been completely forgotten by most social thinkers,[4] his ideas have been recently rediscovered through the republication of his most important texts (Tarde 1999a; 1999b; 1999c; Tarde, 1999d). Following Latour (2002), we note that Tarde was one of the first sociologists to adopt a bottom-up perspective, that is, a perspective that consists of starting from the details of interactions to explain social order. Here is, for example, what he says in *Les lois sociales*:

> [I]t is always the same mistake that comes to light: the one that consists of believing that in order to see the regularity, order, logical pattern progressively appearing in the social facts, one needs to extract oneself from their essentially irregular details and rise up very high until one embraces vast landscapes panoramically; that the principle and source of all social coordination lies in some very general fact from where it goes down by degree to the particular facts, while getting radically weaker; and that, all in all, man agitates himself while a law of evolution leads him. I believe exactly the opposite. (1999b, p.114, our translation)

Instead of starting, like his contemporaries, Herbert Spencer, Emile Durkheim, or Auguste Comte, with what appears to *transcend* our interactions (whether under the form of a force, a law, a principle, or a structure), Tarde insists that it is only in the details of social life that we can find the source of its order and harmony. The latter should never be considered *given*, by some a priori and overarching structures, but rather be analyzed as the *product* of infinite interactions in which disorder and chaos also have chances to emerge. For Tarde, scholars like Spencer, Durkheim, or Comte (but we could today add Marx, Parsons, or even, to a certain extent explained later, Giddens) tend to believe in these overarching laws and structures because they first observe harmony and order, which makes them think that these must come from some transcendental phenomena. In one of his most insightful comments, Tarde (1999b) notes,

> It is precisely because everything, in the world of facts, goes from the small to the big, that, in the world of ideas, inverted mirror of the first, everything goes from the big to the small and, by progress of analysis, lastly reaches the elementary facts, which are truly explicative. (p. 92, our translation)

Caught in the world of ideas, structuro-functionalists and systems theorists thus approach problems by starting from the big to explain the small, an approach that Tarde kept rejecting throughout his career. For him, the source of order (whether social, biological, or physical) has to be found in the details, in the "small," never in the "big." But if Tarde is right, there remains to explain the mechanisms by which order and stability are produced from these micro-actions, an explanation that might ultimately lead us to what constitutes the wholes that we call societies and organizations.

Ethnomethodologists and conversation analysts have, for example, convincingly shown that people are not "judgmental dopes" (Garfinkel, 1967, p. 68). As sensemaking creatures, they constantly orient to—and position themselves vis-à-vis—specific norms, rules, procedures, and values while interacting with each other. Thanks to these scholars, we now know that what seems to transcend the here and now of interaction is not something that *dictates*—from top down—social actors' behavior. Borrowing Giddens' (1984) vocabulary, these "structures" are, on the contrary, resources and constraints that people decide to use or discard given what they consider to be the nature of the situation at hand (McPhee, 1985, 1989; McPhee & Poole, 2001). In this regard, Pomerantz and Fehr (1997) write that the central focus of conversation analysts is "the organization of the meaningful conduct of people in society, that is, how people in society produce their activities and make sense of the world around them" (p. 65).

By concentrating on these sensemaking activities, most ethnomethodologists and conversation analysts even end up questioning the relevance of the term "structure" because of its lack of explanatory power. As Hilbert (1990) notes, even if these scholars regularly refer to structures as they describe members' orientations to them, we can actually speak about a general "indifference to structure at any level" (pp. 794 and 798) from their part. Given that their analysis is focused on the *ethnomethods* used by social actors to make sense and produce their activities, structure, whether micro or macro, is a term that is basically eliminated from their concerns. Accordingly, Hilbert writes,

> [Social structures] are produced from within the settings they supposedly regulate. The fact that members may experience their force as originating elsewhere, for example, from an independent structural or prescriptive order, or the fact that members may experience mutually accomplished constraint as an independent force exercising itself on members collectively, attests to the artfulness of their techniques. Indeed it is precisely such impressions that ethnomethodologists suspend faith in, including the structural imagery they conjure up. (p. 796)

In other words, the concept of "ethnomethods" is supposed to replace the one of "structures." Though they do not, according to Hilbert, transcend human activity (otherwise they would qualify as structures), ethnomethods are deemed to be standing "outside each individual" (p. 796), which gives them the characteristic of exteriority, "constraining on each individual's participation in that very activity" (p. 796), which qualifies them as constraints.

For ethnomethodologists, as for conversation analysts, the micro–macro debate therefore is a wrong debate. Given their "suspension of faith," they argue that structures are relevant as long as they are *oriented to* in the micro-details of their locally situated interactions. If a member orients in his/her discourse to a specific rule or procedure, or to the specific status, social class, or gender of his/her interlocutor, these "structures" will be considered relevant by the analyst at this specific moment of the conversation. But as long as they are not *problematized* or characterized by the participants, social analysts should not focus on them or even bother about them.

It is noteworthy that this suspension of faith confirms and illustrates the phenomenological origin of ethnomethodology and conversation analysis. Like Edmund Husserl (1964) and his disciple Alfred Schutz (1966, 1973), a form of phenomenological reduction (*epochè*) is operating, which consists of focusing on members' accounts, perceptions, or orientations while "bracketing out" what is—but especially what *is not*—accounted and oriented to. Though ethnomethodologists and conversation analysts clearly are some of the most empirically-oriented analysts of social life (a fact that should immediately disqualify any accusation of solipsism), their primary focus on members' orientations apparently leaves them ill-equipped to address questions related to the constitution of an organization or the origin of organizational order. Though they might reply that such questions are irrelevant, we cannot help asking ourselves if such indifference comes from some theoretical misconceptions.[5]

Even Giddens (1984), who does not hesitate to address this very question, tends to reduce "structures" to something very similar to the ethnomethodological position. In a famous passage from *The Constitution of Society*, he writes:

Structure thus refers, in social analysis, to the structuring properties allowing the "binding" of time–space in social systems, the properties which make it possible for discernibly similar social practices to exist across varying spans of time and space and which lend them "systemic" form. To say that structure is a "virtual order" of transformative relations means that social systems, as reproduced social practices, do not have "structures" but rather exhibit "structural properties" and that structure exists, as time–space presence, only in its *instantiations in such practices* and as *memory traces orienting the conduct of knowledgable human agents.* (p. 17, emphasis added)

Though he mentions the binding of space and time—what he also calls "distanciation" (Giddens, 1981, p. 30), i.e., the embedment of social systems in time and space—as an essential structural effect, the source of this binding, i.e., what Giddens calls "structure," has to be found in the very practices and memory traces of the social members. Similar to ethnomethodologists and conversation analysts, Giddens' focus appears to be on social actors and their mutual orientations as opposed to what they orient to (for more details, see McPhee, 1985, 1989, as well as McPhee and Poole, 2001).

Can such a reduction be truly performed? If the bottom-up perspective appears indeed to be the right starting point, can we still reduce, using Tarde's (1999b) terminology, "the big" to members' actions, accounts, perceptions, and orientations? In other words, is it acceptable to operate an indirect form of epochè, which consists of reducing structures to what people problematize or address in their interactions? Can "the big" be really shrunken away to this? After all, isn't it the case that procedures, protocols, rules, policies, values, as well as other forms of technological devices have specific forms of existence outside members' accounts and orientations? If we really want to adopt a bottom-up perspective, isn't it time to account for all these non-human entities, which appear to fill our world?

Latour's Symmetrical Stance: The Association Thesis

Fortunately for us, this filling of the world—what Garfinkel (1988) problematizes under the term "plenum"—has already been recognized for more than 20 years by a group of scholars belonging to the field of social studies of science and technology. Initiated by Latour and Woolgar's (1979) landmark book titled *Laboratory Life: The Social Construction of Scientific Facts*,[6] this movement called *Actor Network Theory* (Law & Hassard, 1999) has produced a series of empirical studies aimed at illustrating the role non-human actors play in the constitution of what they call "collectives" (Latour, 1993). If the filiation with ethnomethodology is explicitly acknowledged (Latour, 1994, 1996, 2005), actor network theorists radically distance themselves from the reduction we denounced earlier. For example, Latour (1996) does not hesitate to critique what he considered to be a recurrent omission in social sciences in general, and ethnomethodology in particular, i.e., the tendency to neglect the fact that "objects" actively contribute to the stabilization and structuration of our world. Actor network theorists thus invite us to extend *agency* to entities that were initially "bracketed out" by social scientists, whether micro- or macro-oriented.

An ethnographic work conducted by the first author of this chapter can be used to illustrate this controversial thesis. This fieldwork, which lasted from January 13–15, 2003, consisted of shadowing with a video camera the general manager of a 60-story building in Manhattan in order to better understand the daily routine of his work. What was particularly striking was the role that certain texts and technological devices played in the general management of the building. For instance, at the entrance of the building, a new device was installed after the events of September 11, 2001. Each tenant is supposed to be equipped with a security card that has to be swiped in a machine upon entering the building. If the card is not recognized (either because the card has not been swiped correctly or because the card is not valid), a signal warns the personnel, who is then supposed to intervene (by asking the tenant to swipe the card again or by checking her identity). As for the visitors (who are by definition not equipped with such a card), a sign posted in the lobby invites them to check in and informs them that the building is under TV surveillance.

How would an ethnomethodologist or interpretive scholar analyze what happens when a visitor enters the building and goes to check in at the front desk? We could imagine that the attitude would be to focus on the visitor's orientation to the sign, an approach that would consist of showing that, to the visitor, it is recognized as a device specifically designed to invite the visitor to check in and to inform him/her about the TV surveillance of the building. In addition, the visitor might also recognize the security system, a device that can be oriented as a potential obstacle preventing him/her from accessing the building without proper identification, as well as the front desk, which can be positioned as the place to check in. The combination of the sign, the front desk, the security system and past experiences (or simple knowledge) is usually enough to create the following practical syllogism:

- There is a sign indicating that I need to check in
- I know that normally I cannot go through a security system without proper identification (past experience or simple knowledge)
- I know that the front desk is the place where visitors usually check in (past experience or simple knowledge)
- I should check in at the front desk.

This sensemaking activity thus explains why most visitors decide to check in upon entering the building, a behavior that was repeatedly observed as we were watching people entering the building. Interestingly enough, this analysis is perfectly congruent with Pomerantz and Fehr's (1997) previously quoted explanation of the focus of conversation analysis, i.e., "the organization of the meaningful conduct of people in society, that is, how people in society produce their activities and make sense of the world around them" (p. 65). Upon entering the building, the visitors make sense of the situation by associating the sign and the security system to an invitation to follow a specific pathway, which then explains why the decision to check in at the front desk is usually made.[7]

However, another analysis, perfectly compatible with the last one (and we want to insist on this compatibility), can be proposed. Nothing indeed prevents us from focusing on the two other "actors"[8] of the story, i.e., the sign and the security system. Why speak in terms of agency here? Using Giddens' (1984) own definition (a definition strategically chosen because Giddens cannot certainly be accused of animism!), we could say that there is an "action" to the extent that,

> [a]ction depends upon the capability of the individual to "make a difference" to a pre-existing state of affairs or course of events. An agent

ceases to be such if he or she loses the capability to "make a difference," that is, to exercise some sort of power. (p. 14)

If we (shamefully!) substitute "sign" or "security device" for "individual" and "it" for "he or she," we have a definition of what "action" could be for a non-human entity. The sign and the security device do something (or acts) to the extent that they *make a difference* in this situation. By the same token, they would cease to be agents should they lose their capability to make a difference. To be sure, our idea is not to ascribe any intention to these devices (as far as we know, the sign and the security device are made of inert materials and have no intention to do anything); however, our point is that this lack of will or intention does not disqualify them from making a difference.[9]

But what do the sign and the security system do in this situation? Based on repeated observations during the three-day fieldwork, we can confidently say that the sign usually *invites* visitors to check in at the front desk while the security system *dissuades* them from entering without having been identified. To be sure, these two actions *do* necessitate not only the presence of a visitor (one can only invite a human being and dissuade an animal in general), but also his/her reasoning. As we saw, for most visitors, the security system is *known* to be a potential obstacle, i.e., they can *infer* that unwanted consequences will ensue from going through it without swiping an identification card. According to this (ethnomethodological) analysis of the situation, the visitor can be said to be deterred by his/her own reasoning and knowledge. This analysis is absolutely valid, and we do *not* question it. However, nothing a priori should prevent us from *also* ascribing to the sign and security system a capacity to make a difference. After all, without their presence, the visitor's reasoning would not have been triggered.

Deterring or dissuading actually corresponds to what Austin (1962) calls "perlocutionary acts," that is, acts like "convincing" or "persuading" whose completion necessitates a *reaction* from an interlocutor. As for inviting, it corresponds to an "illocutionary act," i.e., acts whose completion also necessitates the uptake from an interlocutor, what Searle (1979) calls an "illocutionary effect" (for more details, see Cooren, 2000). For example, when it is said that X persuaded Y to stay calm or that X informed Y that the end was near, we have no problem acknowledging that X *made a difference* by providing arguments and some information to Y; however, we *also* recognize that Y played a role in this action *attributed* to X (Y has to be convinced by X's arguments and understand the information, two actions that require sensemaking activities, i.e., reasoning). As we see, this analysis has the advantage of *not* "bracketing out" the contribution of the human actor while recognizing the participation of a non-human entity in a given situation. By just focusing on what humans do, ethnomethodologists and conversation analysts tend to neglect what triggers the members' sensemaking activities and it is, as we will try to demonstrate, this negligence that leads them to this so-called "indifference to structure."

But where are we going with such reasoning? To what extent does it help us understand the micro–macro conundrum, the source of social order, or the communicative constitution of organizations? First, we can note that the analysis proposed by Actor Network Theory enables us to address specific questions that were raised in our introduction. For example, it is easy to see that the sign and the security system display characteristics that, for instance, a security guard does not have: while a security guard is physically *unable* to stay in the lobby 24 hours a day, 7 days a week, to check the ID and inform visitors of the TV surveillance, this is something that the security device and the sign can easily do by the very way they are designed. Like many non-human entities, they have the capacity to *stay*, to *remain*, to *last*. In other words, their capacity to make a difference, i.e., to communicate something, appears to *transcend* time. Though we have not left "terra firma," i.e., the level of actions, we start to realize that the "here and now," which is the traditional focus of ethnomethodologists, conversational analysts, and phenomenologists in general, is already contaminated by the "then and there." As Latour (1994, 1996) shows in many of his insightful analyses, the involvement of non-humans in our daily life appears to *dislocate* our interactions.

But what is the "there and then" in this situation? To answer this question, we can transport ourselves in space and time to find out some tenants calling down to the building manager to voice their concerns about the general security of the building a few days after the events of September 11.[10] Aware that they need to improve the control of the access to the building, the ownership then decides to study the possibility of installing a new security system. The building manager organizes a series of meetings with the tenants (one with the low-rise tenants, one with the middle-rise ones, and one with the high-rise ones) in which security systems are discussed and proposed. While a big majority of the 130 tenants seem comfortable with the idea of installing security card readers for all their employees (around 2,500 come and go daily in the building), a more controversial issue is the question of the visitors.

Many visitors enter the building every day for many different purposes: from delivering packages and lunch to dealing with business issues like signing contracts or meeting with a new client. While some of them are regular visitors, others are more occasional ones. To deal with this source of security hazard, the classical solution usually is to ask for the visitors' picture ID and have them sign in a book at the front desk. But with more than 2,000 visitors coming and going in the building every day, this solution is considered very cumbersome, ineffective, and time-consuming by the building manager. Having some knowledge in computer technology, he has the idea of creating his own security system for the visitors. He buys an 80 GB computer, a digital video camera and installs the new set at the front desk. From now on, each time a visitor enters the building a sign invites him/her to check in at the front desk. Following a strict procedure implemented by the building manager, the concierge then asks the visitor what company he/she is coming to see, a piece of information that leads to the opening up of the corresponding tenant file in the computer. Once the file is opened by the concierge, the person is then invited to identify him/herself while his/her face and voice are video recorded and stored as a video clip for 30 days in the tenant file. With this new device, important information can be obtained and stored without impeding the fluidity of the circulation in the building.

As we see in this example, what was decided and implemented six years ago continues to make a difference—that is, to *act*—today. The security card system, the sign, the procedure, and the video-recording device continue to make a difference each time a visitor or tenant enter the building. Note also that any reference to "structures" is completely *useless* to explain what is happening in this specific situation. What we have is a *string of associations* linking the tenants, the ownership representatives, the building manager, the procedure, the concierge and the security device, that is, a series of actors whose contribution to the present situation appears to transcend space and time. Note also that some actors appear to speak on behalf of others: some tenants set themselves up as speaking on behalf of other tenants, the ownership representative speaks on behalf of the owner's interests, the sign invites the visitors to check in in the name of the company. In keeping with the bottom-up perspective, we see that collective action actually is the product of associations. For instance, it is because the sign was designed and installed by the company that it can do something on its behalf. What we have thus appears to be a series of actions that *associate* actors with each other. In other words, this analysis shows that the origin and attribution of action is definitely problematized.

In effect, who can be said to be at the origin of the channeling of the tenants and visitors at the building entrance? The tenants themselves who first voiced their concerns? The ownership, which ultimately made the decision to invest in a security system? The contractor who was hired to install the security card readers? The building manager who came up with the idea of the video-recording system and installed it? The whole security device itself? In a way, we could answer "all of them," depending on the starting point we want to take in our analysis. Through a series of delegations, we see a (representative?) sample of the tenants voicing their concerns to the building manager, who then communicates these worries to the ownership, which then proposes to invest in a security system, which is partly built by a contractor (for the security card readers) and partly operationalized by the building manager (for the video-recording system). Note that *each* of these actors can be said to be at least *partly* responsible for the channeling of the tenants and visitors. Under this form of analysis, we also see that we can remain at the level of *actions* while still acknowledging how these actions transcend space and time. In other words, we here have a clear way to *scale up* in space and time: interactions that took place in the past can continue to have very tangible effects today.

Moreover, this example illustrates the phenomenon Latour (1993) termed "hybrid action," that is, action whose origin is problematized because it involves the *association* of many different actors who appear to participate in what is happening. For instance, "controlling who is entering the building" involves "hybridicity" to the extent that this action attributed to the security system can also be ascribed to the tenants themselves, to the ownership, the building manager or his employees. Each of these actors contributes to the control and it is for this reason that each of them can *appropriate* (or be associated with) the difference that is made after the security system is finally built.[11]

Though always locally produced, action thus appears in its "dislocality"—its capacity to produce effects from a distance, i.e., throughout space—and its "mediacy"—its capacity to produce effects from a past period, i.e., throughout time. As Latour (1994) notes,

> Of course, ethnomethodologists are right to criticize traditional sociology with its fanciful macro level, but they are wrong to conclude that there is such a thing as an absolutely local interaction. No human relationship exists in a framework homogeneous as to space, time, and actants. However, the error that traditional sociology makes is as great, when it forgets to ask how a difference of scale is obtained, how power is exerted, irreversibility sets in, and roles and functions are distributed. Everything in the definition of macro social order is due to the enrollment of nonhumans—that is, to technical mediation. Even the simple effect of duration, of long-lasting social force, cannot be obtained without the durability of nonhumans to which human local interactions have been shifted. (p. 51)

Though Latour recognizes his intellectual debt to ethnomethodologists, he thus criticizes their tendency to solely focus on human contributions and sensemaking activities, while neglecting all the technologies and devices that these same humans contribute to create. As he convincingly shows, it is precisely through these non-human contributions and associations, sources of hybridicity, that we can expect to "fill the gap" between the micro and the macro order.

Discussion

As we see in this analysis, ascribing agency to non-human entities *does not* force us to retrieve any agency from the human beings. On the contrary, and this is the most crucial lesson drawn from ethnomethodologists and conversational analysts, human beings can decide to *disregard* the contribution of rules, procedures, documents, or machines at specific moments of their interaction (see also McPhee, 1985, especially p. 159).

In other words, the agency that was attributed to the sign and the security system does *not* make the visitors or tenants "judgmental dopes." As any agent, they can also "make a difference" and not follow injunctions or disregard information, as we noticed many times when we observed their behaviors upon entering the building. Though our analysis is not incompatible with what ethnomethodologists and conversation analysts propose, we think it offers a "bigger picture," in which agency, i.e., the capacity to make a difference, is not restricted to a human property.

With this notable amendment, we can finally understand why organizational order (or, more generally, social order) cannot truly be reduced to interactional patterns (the aggregation thesis) or layers of conversations (the lamination thesis). Though these theses do help us understand interactional redundancies and local logics/relevancies, what is missing in these two pictures of the social/organizational world is what non-human entities are contributing, whether under the form of texts, artifacts, or machines.[12] As we saw in our previous analyses—and as it has already been theoretically developed elsewhere (Cooren, 2000, 2004, 2006; Cooren, Taylor, & Van Every, 2006; Cooren, Thompson, Canestraro, & Bodor, 2006; Taylor & Van Every, 2000)—texts or machines have this wonderful property that consists of *lasting, remaining, staying*, what Derrida (1988) identified under the neologism "restance," i.e., staying capacity. By just focusing on members' orientations and sensemaking activities, everything happens as though one was cutting oneself off from the lasting effects of these artifacts, which then would explain why sociologists and organizational communication scholars keep worrying about the so-called *micro–macro gap*.

According to the *association thesis*, and in accordance with the bottom-up perspective advocated by Tarde more than 100 years ago, we indeed never truly leave the terra firma of interactions, but we then need to broaden the extension of the concept of agency and communication by acknowledging that it covers not only the differences made by humans, but also the ones made by non-humans. Having recognized this, we can then overcome the ethnomethodological indifference to structures by showing that the term "structure" is a conceptual hodgepodge that does not really explain anything. As we show in our analysis, there are *no* overarching structures transcending the local interactions of the visitors and the building personnel. What actually transcends the local interactions of these human actors are non-human entities that *might*—but also *might not*—make a difference in the given circumstances. These non-human entities can have *textual forms* like statuses, rules, titles, procedures, protocols, messages (whether under the form of documents or memory traces), but they can also be simple artifacts devoid of any textuality (like a monitoring device, a uniform, or an architectural element).

More importantly, these things are not truly structures to the extent that they are *part* of the situations we strive to describe. For example, even if a procedure *does have* lasting effects, which can be identified in the way members talk throughout their interactions, it should first be considered as what it is, that is, *a text* that defines how people should proceed in many different circumstances. Whether under the form of memory traces or documents, this text can be defined as an actor whose injunctions are supposed to be repeatedly complied with. The difference with what human beings can do mostly has to be found in the fact that procedures, once they are defined orally or in writing, have the capacity to *do the same things at any time* (however, they are not truly permanent to the extent that they can be amended or even cancelled also at any time). In other words, their agency is *almost*[13] omnipresent.

We think that it is precisely this quasi-omnipresence that gives the illusion of a structure. There is no structure overarching human interactions to the extent that what makes human actors do things (which is usually what we have in mind when we use the term "structure") is nothing but *other human or non-human actors*. A foreman who supervises workers in an assembly line certainly makes them do things: his/her simple presence and his/her panoptical gaze tend to *dissuade* them from slowing down, taking a break, or being dilettante. Similarly, if the foreman is replaced by a camera, its mere presence and panoptical gaze will also tend to *dissuade* workers from slowing down, taking a break, or being dilettante.[14] Again, recognizing this *does not* make us skip over the workers' contributions to the situation. It is *also* because the workers orient to the foreman and the camera that they decide to adopt specific behaviors. Ascribing agency to *what* or *who* makes them do things *does not* amount to neglecting their own agency or sensemaking activities. On the contrary, we precisely saw that it is most of the time through people's own agencies and sensemaking activities that other non-human or human agents can be said to make them do things. As Latour notes, agency is always a *hybrid* accomplishment, made of human and non-human contributions and associations.

If we all agree that the foreman is not a structure, but an agent, why should not we be authorized to do the same thing with a monitoring device? The camera has agency to the extent that *its presence makes workers do things that they would not do otherwise*. To be sure, if the workers stop orienting to the camera, this non-human agency disappears, but the *same thing* can be said about the foreman. If tomorrow the workers decide not to orient to her presence anymore, the foreman will be said to have lost her capacity to make a difference, i.e., her agency (at least vis-à-vis the workers' attitudes and behaviors).

Instead of referring to social or organizational structures, we would thus do better as analysts to acknowledge non-human agency, an analytical position that would then allow us to solve many theoretical and empirical problems in our field. For example, we might start to show how interpretivists' and critical scholars' perspectives could be, to a certain extent, reconciled. Recognizing that the presence of cameras usually contributes to workers' behavior on an assembly line is *not* incompatible with acknowledging that the way workers orient to this monitoring devices does matter. On the contrary, we just saw that the cameras can contribute to the situation to the extent that the workers orient to them as a possible threat. Recognizing the *effects* of micro-technologies, procedures, policies, or statuses on organizational members' behaviors and attitudes (which traditionally constitute the focus of critical research) thus appears to be perfectly congruent with recognizing their sensemaking activities and orientations.[15]

The main difference between the two research orientations is actually to be found in the focus of their respective analyses. Typically, critical scholars and structuro-functionalists will center their analyses on what *pre-exists* organizational members' interactions, which then explains why they tend not to dwell on empirical occurrences of *talk-in-interaction*. But what pre-exists organizational members' interactions? The response is *non-human entities*, which, as we saw earlier, can be technological devices, memory traces, architectural elements, or simple documents. In other words, using the term "structure" (whether deep or surface structures) to identify what precedes and constrains talk in interaction is misleading, since this "cover-all" concept does not truly explain anything. The strength of the association thesis is to demonstrate that it is theoretically and analytically more productive to reveal the role played by all the non-human entities that fill our everyday world.[16]

On the other side, we can note that the opposite bias consists of essentially focusing on what is occurring in human interactions, which is traditionally what ethnomethodologists, conversation analysts, and interpretivists tend to do. To be sure, the role of the context is very often acknowledged in these studies, but we also saw that, because of their phenomenological origins, these approaches tend to neglect what is *not* problematized or oriented to by the participants (hence, the indifference to structure, noted earlier). Against the "almighty structure" of the critical scholars, these approaches set the "almighty sensemakers" who are always portrayed at the *origin* of what is taking place in the interaction. What we have been trying to show is that such an opposition not only is fruitless, but also reinforces the so-called gap between the macro and micro. As our analysis illustrates, and as Latour (1986, 1987, 1991, 1993, 1996, 1999) or Derrida (1985, 1986, 1988, 1992a, 1992b) have been saying throughout their numerous essays and analyses, *there is no true origin to action*. Human participants are *acted upon* as much as they are *acting*. We live in a plenum, a world full of human and non-human entities that can at any moment make a difference in a given situation (Cooren, 2006).

Now that we have recognized the contributions of procedures, documents, machines, computers, and architectural elements in organizational life, we might be well-equipped to answer the question that was opening this chapter, i.e., how can we describe and analyze the details of interactions while showing that they literally contribute to the constitution of an organization? Given what has been said before, it should be no surprise that our response pleads for an extended version of the concepts of interaction and communication, i.e., a version that acknowledges the interactions between entities with variable ontologies (textual, physical, technological, animal, and, of course, human). As advocated by the association thesis, it is *to this extent* that we can re-establish the link between communication and organization.

For example, it is essentially through the contribution of non-human entities that an organization usually can be de-fined, i.e., circumscribed.

As we saw in our example, the security system has a crucial role in delimiting who is *in* and who is *outside* the building. Similarly, we could acknowledge the role of walls, floors, ceilings, doors, fences, gates, and other forms of enclosures in the de-finition of the organizational space. By their staying capacity, i.e., their restance, these architectural elements interactively contribute to the demarcation of a space: they prevent some people from accessing specific areas, they enable others to work far from prying eyes, they demarcate departmental territories, they communicate what kind of behaviors should be undertaken, etc. Note that this analysis even holds for what we call "virtual organization," since even these forms of organization are at least delineated by the channels that enable the coordination of the activities. Furthermore, this analysis *by no means* reifies the organization. Though it definitely shows that things like walls, radio networks, and fences do *contribute* to the constitution of an organization, it does not *reduce* the organization to these contributions. As our analysis shows, an organization actually resembles what Callon and Latour (1981) had already described years ago as a Leviathan, a sort of monster[17] made of machines, enclosures, documents, and humans associated with each other to form a collective (Cooren, Fox, Robichaud, & Talih, 2005). So, if an organization is made of things, it, of course, cannot be reduced to them.

So what else do we need to put in the organizational equation? We just saw that an organization usually is delimited through the contribution of non-human entities. However, it is not enough to have an organization. For instance, if a shepherd builds a fence to delineate the space within which his sheep can move, we cannot properly say that an organization was just created. We just have a flock of sheep surrounded by barbed wire. What is missing is other sources of order: statuses, contracts, responsibilities, rights, knowledge, procedures, rules, policies, protocols, programs, organizational charts, that is, a series of texts that contribute to the resistance of specific schemas of action. It is to these texts, whether under the form of memory traces or documents, that human actors orient to, and it is through their contribution that order can be said to emerge. These texts not only have a specific form of existence—they are, to a certain extent, *autonomous* by being severed from their human origin—but they also contribute to the *stabilization* of specific schemas of action and the *coordination* of activities. We think that it is to this extent that we can speak about an organization, that is, a collective that appears to be organized, i.e., *written in advance*. If members can orient to these texts, it is because these very texts have a specific mode of existence, which we might call "symbolic," that tightly or loosely defines what, how, or why something needs to be done and in what circumstances.

But doesn't this reasoning bring us backward? Aren't we losing Weick's (1979) central contribution to the field when he taught us to focus on the organizing instead of the organization? Worse, aren't we going back to the "container metaphor" with our reflection on the demarcation? We think not. To recognize that every organization is, *to a certain extent*, written in advance (programmed) does not compel us to reduce its mode of existence to its textual dimension. Though the organization is made of texts, but also of machines and architectural elements, its mode of existence, of course, *also* depends on the contribution of humans—what Taylor and Van Every (2000) refer to as "conversation." Our objective is not to neglect their contributions (for example, their capacity to design and redesign the organization, to coordinate their activities, to improvise new schema of actions, or to disregard rules and policies when they think these are obtrusive), but to propose an alternative to the reduction of an organization to its members' sensemaking activities. An organization always is *in process*—this is the "organizing" Weick (1979) is talking about—but this process always is the product of various contributions, from texts, machines, artifacts, and humans.

As we just saw, scaling up from interactions to organization thus requires a broader conception of what "communication" means. The association thesis basically constitutes a form of *radical constructivism*, to the extent that we contend that the organizational (and social) world always is *in construction* and *constructed*. However, we are not speaking here about the so-called "social construction of reality" à la Berger and Luckmann (1966), with its phenomenological flavor, but about a world literally *made of* non-human and human contributions and associations. It is through this hybrid agency that organized forms and organizing take place. As Latour (1994) says,

> Society is the outcome of local construction, but we are not alone at the construction site, since there we also mobilize the many non-humans

through which the order of space and time has been reshuffled. To be human requires sharing with non-humans. (p. 51)

By substituting the term "organization" for "society," we thus have a way to understand what truly constitutes these social forms and how scaling up occurs.

If the idea of the communicative constitution of organization makes any sense, it is for us on the sole condition that the concept of "communication" is extended to what non-humans do. For instance, this means that we need to acknowledge that the sign indeed *tells* visitors what behaviors has to be adopted upon entering the building, that the security system *dissuades* visitors from squeezing in without checking in at the front desk, or that the procedure *leads* the concierge to ask visitors specific questions. Only if these contributions are acknowledged can we expect to find in communication and interaction the building blocks of organization. Going back to the four flows identified by McPhee and Zaug (2000), we can then adopt a bottom-up perspective and translate them to show that they are the product of these micro-associations between humans and non-humans.

Membership negotiations, identified as the flow by which the organization maintains relations to its members, become the interactions by which members problematize, orient to, or even question their statuses, rights, and responsibilities, that is, a series of texts that are supposed to make a difference in organizational situations. These membership categorization devices, as the conversation analysts call them, are not just oriented to in conversation. They also are what *authorize* or *enjoin* members to adopt some specific behaviors. For instance, his/her status *literally* authorizes and enjoins the concierge to prevent unidentified visitors from entering the building. Certainly, this authority could be questioned by a visitor and even be the object of negotiation, but it is to the *agency* of this status and the rights and responsibilities that come with it that both the visitors and the concierge orient if a controversy occurs. In other words, membership negotiation certainly constitutes a flow, but only if we precisely recognize to what extents membership categories *do something* in organizational situations.

As for "self structuring," identified as the flow by which the organization maintains relations to itself, it can be translated into the strain of associations by which humans and non-humans contribute to the structure of the organization. Instead of adopting the top-down worldview of systems implicit in the term "self-structuring," the bottom-up approach advocated by the association thesis shows that any structuring effect is the result of micro-interactions between humans and non-humans. For instance, we saw how the post 9/11 security system enables the ownership, the building manager, the tenants and the concierge to control from a distance who is entering the building. This structuring effect, which channels the visitors' behaviors, was only possible through the contributions of texts (procedures), machines (security card system) and humans (the manager, the concierge, the tenants, the ownership).

Concerning what McPhee and Zaug call "activity coordination," identified as the flow by which the organization maintains relations to its internal subgroup and processes, we see again that such a coordination cannot be expected to be maintained without the contributions of non-humans (documents or technological devices). Instead of having a top-down (systemic) explanation of the third flow, our bottom-up approach shows that any coordinative activity should be considered the result of different types of agency: from the memo, which spreads information among the tenants to the work order that indicates to the employees what needs to be done (Cooren, 2004). Instead of analyzing the situation as an organization maintaining relations to its internal subgroups and process, we see a building manager who, in the name of the organization and its ownership, keeps mobilizing documents and technological devices to assure the coordination of activities. This does not mean that "the organization" or "the groups" do not exist; this means that accounting for their functioning consists of showing *who* or *what* is acting on their behalf.

This paves the way to "institutional positioning," the fourth flow identified by McPhee and Zaug (2000), by which the organization maintains its relations to other organizations. Against this top-down description, our bottom-up approach shows that such a flow can only exist through the different humans and non-humans that speak or act on behalf of collectives. Far from preventing us from scaling up, we saw that it is precisely through the strain of associations that collectives like organizations can be said to position themselves. For instance, we saw how ownership was positioned vis-à-vis the tenants through the representatives who participated in the meetings organized by the building manager. Similarly, some tenants spoke in the name of their employees and sometimes even in the name of other tenants. It is always through a local interaction that something apparently more global (a company, a department, even a country) can be said to talk or do something. Interaction and communication never are purely local or purely global, they are dislocal.

As we see, the association thesis enables us to account for the four flows without resorting to a deductive, top-down approach, which ends up contributing to the broadening of the micro–macro gap. Speaking meaningfully of the communicative constitution of organizations implies that we start from an extended view of agency, a form of agency in which humans, but also things, machines, and texts can be said to communicate. It is by recognizing how our world is filled by all these agencies that we can hope to understand the source of order and organizing.

Notes

1 For more details on this issue, see Cicourel and Knorr-Cetina (1981), Putnam and Pacanowsky (1983), McPhee (1985, 1989), McPhee and Poole (2001), and Taylor and Van Every (2000).

2 In their essay, they propose the following definition for the concept of "organization": "a social interaction system, influenced by prevailing economic and legal institutional practices, and including coordinated action and interaction within and across a social constructed boundary, manifestly directed toward a privileged set of outcomes" (p. 5).

3 Note however that more and more critical studies are devoted to the empirical exploration of organizational interactions. For some illuminating examples, see Murphy (1998), Rosen (1988) and Tracy (2000).

4 One exception is the English translation of a collection of his papers, symptomatically titled *On Communication and Social Influence* (Tarde, 1969).

5 In this regard, Boden (1994) makes a point of saying that her focus always is on the nature of organizing and on the temporal and sequential details of organiza*tion* rather than organiza*tions* as theoretical or empirical objects. As she writes, "[E]thnomethodologists never 'study organizations' in the conventional sense. They are not interested in organizations, but in organization, which is to say that they are animated by a curiosity for

the organization of experience and the 'extraordinary organization of the ordinary'" (p. 31). Our focus precisely is to focus on organizations.

6 Symptomatically, the term "social" was omitted from the second edition (Latour & Woolgar, 1986).

7 Of course, we also observed some visitors who were directly going through the security device without checking in, a behavior that inevitably triggered the alarm. Whether this was an attempt to avoid checking in or was the result of their inattention, it is clear that visitors' behaviors were never completely programmed and determined by the security device.

8 Instead of the term "actor," Callon and Latour (1981) sometimes use the term "actant," which they directly borrow from Greimas (1987), to express the agency displayed by nonhumans. As for Taylor and Van Every (2000) who take up this idea, they prefer to use the term "agent" to insist on the delegative nature of objects: nonhumans tend to function as agents for principals (humans) who appropriate their contribution. In this chapter, we use these three terms—actor, actant, and agent—synonymously to express agency in general.

9 To be clear, we understand that Latour's position (and ours!) consists of questioning more than 2,500 years of philosophical reflection, which has always requested the imperative presence of an intention or will to speak in terms of "action," "agent," and "actors." According to this quasi-universal conception, we can speak of an action if the individual has some intent to accomplish it. From Searle (1979) who reduces speech acts to intentional acts to Burke (1961) who creates a clear distinction between motion and action, the consensus seems: "no intention, no action." Even if we were ready to respect such a conceptual purification, it would remain to be known how to call these "events" where nonhuman entities seem to make a difference. For instance, when an ATM machine tells us to type our PIN number, a request to which we respond by typing our code on the keyboard, how can we call what the ATM "does"? Some people propose the terms "motion" or "event," but this is not a motion (the ATM machine does not move!) and the term "event" appears too vague to really capture what is happening. We have nothing against calling that "doing," a term that would make the ATM a doer. However, we go back to the initial reaction: shouldn't "doing," like action, be used only to qualify what human beings "do"? As we see, everything happens as though the language we use could be accused of being segregationist: no word seems acceptable to qualify the difference nonhuman entities make, as though human beings did not want to recognize nonhuman entities' contributions. For lack of better terms, action and doing still seem to be the most appropriate to describe what is happening when nonhumans make a difference.

10 This event has been reconstructed from an interview with the building manager.

11 Similarly, we could say that we can *attribute* to each of them the difference made after the security system is built. Attribution and appropriation are two "mirror terms" that deconstruct the immediate and local characters of action.

12 Interestingly enough, Derrida does not hesitate to compare texts to machines. In *Signature Event Context*, the text he initially wrote in 1971 for a philosophy conference devoted to communication (Derrida & Ricoeur, 1973), we can read, "To write is to produce a mark that will constitute a sort of machine which is productive in turn, and which my future disappearance will not, in principle, hinder in its functioning, offering things and itself to be read and to be rewritten" (Derrida, 1988, p. 8). Following Derrida's point, we could thus identify any kind of text to a machine. A text or a writing is a machine to the extent that "it must continue to 'act' and to be readable even when what is called the author of the writing no longer answers for what he has written, for what he seems to have signed, be it because of a temporary absence, because he is dead or, more generally, because he has not employed his absolutely actual and present intention or attention, the plenitude of his desire to say what he means, in order to sustain what seems to be written 'in his name'" (p. 8).

13 We say "almost," because "omnipresent" means "present in all places at all times" (Webster's dictionary), which is, of course, too strong to describe a procedure's agency. We should rather speak in terms of "limited omnipresence" (which is almost an oxymoron), given that the procedural agency is always de-fined, that is finite.

14 Some might retort that it is only because workers orient to the possible presence of a human being "behind the camera" that specific behaviors are adopted. To this argument, we could respond that it is, in fact, because the workers *first* orient to the camera that they can *then* orient to the human monitor who might *possibly* be behind. It is *not* the presence of a human being behind the camera that actually makes a difference. As Foucault (1979) so wonderfully demonstrated in *Discipline and Punish: The Birth of the Prison*, the effectiveness of any panoptical device does not come from the presence of a human monitor, but from his/her *possible* presence behind the panopticum. This demonstrates that, before orienting to this possible human presence, it is to the *monitoring device* that the inmates orient. Though we haven't acknowledge Michel Foucault's contribution so far, it should be clear by now that most of the reflection we try to develop here owes a lot to his writings devoted to the micro-technologies of power. See also McPhee and Poole (2001), especially pp. 522–523.

15 To a certain extent, this compatibility between the interpretive and critical traditions was recognized some 20 years ago by Putnam (1983) as well as Deetz and Kersten (1983). However, it is no surprise that Deetz and Kersten (1983) write that "[n]aturalistic [i.e., interpretive] and critical research perspectives separate most radically in their interest in the forces

that direct organizational construction. ... The critical school views the systems of meaning that exist at the surface or participant level as resulting from deep social and material forces" (p. 160). What this chapter tries to show is that such "deep social and material forces" actually are texts, machines, and artifacts. For more recent developments on this debate, see also Deetz (2001), and Deetz and Mumby (1990).

16 This is what Foucault (1979) started to do in his reflection on the role micro-technologies plays in the "normalization" of human behavior. Note that our point is *not* that the emancipative agenda of critical research is misled or wrong. On the contrary, what we propose is that effects of domination, segregation, or manipulation could be better acknowledged and revealed by starting from the micro-details of human and nonhuman agencies. If the *source of order* has to be found, as Tarde contends, in the small, it is, we think, also *in the small* that we might find the best resources to denounce the abuse of power.

17 Interestingly enough, McPhee (1985) wrote in his classical essay on structure, "Are organizations the social-scientific equivalent of the monster? I mean this question (perhaps it should be phrased a bit less emotionally) seriously—Is Structure, in principle, an ill?" (p. 160). Though the term "monster" is used differently by Callon and Latour (1981), it is still striking to see the equivalence established by McPhee between organization, structure, and monstrosity.

References

Austin, J. L. (1962). *How to do things with words*. Cambridge, MA: Harvard University Press.

Berger, P. L., & Luckmann, T. (1966). *The social construction of reality: A treatise in the sociology of knowledge*. New York: Irvington Publishers.

Boden, D. (1994). *The business of talk: Organizations in action*. Cambridge, U.K.: Polity Press.

Burke, K. (1961). *The rhetoric of religion: Studies in logology*. Los Angeles: University of California Press.

Callon, M., & Latour, B. (1981). Unscrewing the big leviathan: How actors macro-structure reality and how sociologists help them to do so. In A. V. Cicourel & K. Knorr-Cetina (Eds.), *Advances in social theory and methodology: Towards an integration of micro- and macro-sociologies* (pp. 277–303). Boston, MA: Routledge & Kegan Paul.

Cicourel, A. V., & Knorr-Cetina, K. (1981). *Advances in social theory and methodology: Towards an integration of micro- and macro-sociologies*. Boston. MA: Routledge & Kegan Paul.

Clegg, S. (1989). *Frameworks of power*. Newbury Park, CA: Sage.

Cooren, F. (2000). *The organizing property of communication.* Amsterdam/ Philadelphia: John Benjamins.

Cooren, F. (2004). Textual agency: How texts do things in organizational settings. *Organization, 11*(3), 373–393.

Cooren, F. (2006). The organizational world as a plenum of agencies. In F. Cooren, J. R. Taylor, & E. J. Van Every (Eds.), *Communication as organizing: Empirical and theoretical explorations in the dynamic of text and conversation* (pp. 81–100). Mahwah, NJ: Lawrence Erlbaum.

Cooren, F., & Fairhurst, G. T. (2004). Speech timing and spacing: The phenomenon of organizational closure. *Organization, 11*(6), 793–824.

Cooren, F., Fox, S., Robichaud, D., & Talih, N. (2005). Arguments for a plurified view of the social world: Spacing and timing as hybrid achievements. *Time & Society, 14*(2/3), 263–280.

Cooren, F., Taylor, J. R., & Van Every, E. J. (Eds.). (2006). *Communication as organizing: Empirical and theoretical explorations in the dynamic of text and conversation.* Mahwah, NJ: Lawrence Erlbaum.

Cooren, F., Thompson, F., Canestraro, D., & Bodor, T. (2006). From agency to structure: Analysis of an episode in a facilitation process. *Human Relations, 59*(4), 533–565.

Daft, R. L., & Weick, K. E. (1984). Toward a model of organizations as interpretation systems. *Academy of Management Review, 9*(2), 284–295.

Deetz, S. (1992). *Democracy in an age of corporate colonization: Developments in communication and the politics of everyday life.* Albany: State University of New York Press.

Deetz, S. (2001). Conceptual foundations. In F. M. Jablin, & L. L. Putnam (Eds.), *The new handbook of organizational communication: Advances in theory, research, and methods* (pp. 3–46). Thousand Oaks, CA: Sage.

Deetz, S., & Kersten, A. (1983). Critical models of interpretive research. In L. L. Putnam & M. E. Pacanowsky (Eds.), *Communication and organizations: An interpretive approach* (pp. 147–171). Newbury Park, CA: Sage.

Deetz, S., & Mumby, D. (1990). Power, discourse and the workplace: Reclaiming the critical tradition. In J. A. Anderson (Ed.), *Communication Yearbook 13* (pp. 18–47). Newbury Park, CA: Sage.

Derrida, J. (1985). *Post card: From Socrates to Freud & beyond.* Chicago: University of Chicago Press.

Derrida, J. (1986). Declarations of independence. *New Political Science, 15,* 7–15.

Derrida, J. (1988). *Limited inc.* Evanston, IL: Northwestern University Press.

Derrida, J. (1992a). Force of law. In D. Cornell, M. Rosenfeld, & D. C. Carlson (Eds.), *Deconstruction and the possibility of justice.* New York/ London: Routledge.

Derrida, J. (1992b). *Given time. I, Counterfeit money* (Peggy Kamuf, Trans.). Chicago: University of Chicago Press.

Derrida, J. (1993). *Spectres de Marx: l'état de la dette, le travail du deuil et la nouvelle internationale.* Paris: Galilée.

Derrida, J., & Ricoeur, P. (1973). Philosophie et communication. In V. Cauchy (Ed.), *La communication. Actes du XVe Congrès de l'Association des Sociétés de Philosophie de Langue Française. Université de Montreal. 1971* (Vol. 2, pp. 393–431). Montréal: Montmorency.

Fairhurst, G. T. (2001). Dualisms in leadership research. In F. M. Jablin, & L. L. Putnam (Eds.), *The new handbook of organizational communication: Advances in theory, research, and methods.* Thousand Oaks, CA: Sage.

Fairhurst, G. T. (2004). Text, context and agency in interaction analysis. *Organization, 11*(3), 335–353.

Fairhurst, G. T. (2007). *Discursive leadership: In conversation with leadership psychology.* Thousand Oaks, CA: Sage.

Fairhurst, G. T., & Putnam, L. L. (2004). Organizations as discursive constructions. *Communication Theory, 14*(1), 5–26.

Foucault, M. (1979). *Discipline and punish: The birth of the prison.* Alan Sheridan, New York: Vintage Books.

Garfinkel, H. (1967). *Studies in ethnomethodology.* Englewood Cliffs, NJ: Prentice Hall.

Garfinkel, H. (1988). Evidence for locally produced, naturally accountable phenomena of order, logic, reason, meaning, method, etc. In and as of the essential quiddity of immortal society (I of IV): An announcement of studies. *Sociological Theory, 6*(1), 103–109.

Giddens, A. (1981). *A contemporary critique of historical materialism.* London: Macmillan.

Giddens, A. (1984). *The constitution of society.* Cambridge, U. K.: Polity Press.

Goffman, E. (1974). *Frame analysis: An essay on the organization of experience.* New York: Harper & Row.

Greimas, A. J. (1987). *On meaning. Selected writings in semiotic theory.* Trans Paul J. Perron, & Frank H. Collins. London: Frances Pinter.

Hilbert, R. A. (1990). Ethnomethodology and the micro-macro order. *American Sociological Review, 55*, 794–808.

Husserl, E. (1964). *The idea of phenomenology.* The Hague: Martinus Nijhoff.

Latour, B. (1986). The powers of association. In J. Law (Ed.), *Power, action and belief: A new sociology of knowledge?* (pp. 264–280). London, Boston, & Henley: Routledge & Kegan Paul.

Latour, B. (1987). *Science in action: How to follow scientists and engineers through society.* Cambridge, MA: Harvard University Press.

Latour, B. (1991). The impact of science studies on political philosophy. *Science, Technology, & Human Values, 16*(1), 3–19.

Latour, B. (1993). *We have never been modern*. Trans. Catherine Porter. Cambridge, MA: Harvard University Press.

Latour, B. (1994). On technical mediation—philosophy, sociology, genealogy. *Common Knowledge, 3*(2), 29–64.

Latour, B. (1996). On interobjectivity. *Mind, Culture, and Activity, 3*(4), 228–245.

Latour, B. (1999). *Pandora's hope: Essays on the reality of science studies*. Cambridge, CA: Harvard University Press.

Latour, B. (2002). Gabriel Tarde and the end of the social. In P. Joyce (Ed.), *The social in question: New bearings in history and the social sciences* (pp. 117–133). London: Routledge.

Latour, B. (2005). *Reassembling the social: An introduction to Actor-Network Theory*. London: Oxford University Press.

Latour, B., & Woolgar, S. (1979). *Laboratory life: The social construction of scientific facts*. Beverly Hills, CA: Sage.

Latour, B., & Woolgar, S. (1986). *Laboratory life: The construction of scientific facts*. Princeton, NJ: Princeton University Press.

Law, J., & Hassard, J. (Eds.). (1999). *Actor Network Theory and After*. Malden, MA: Blackwell.

McPhee, R. D. (1985). Formal structure and organizational communication. In R. D. McPhee, & P. K. Tompkins (Eds.), *Organizational communication: Traditional themes and new directions* (pp. 149–177). Beverly Hills, CA: Sage.

McPhee, R. D. (1989). Organizational communication: A structurational exemplar. In B. Dervin, L. Grossberg, B. J. O'Keefe, & E. Wartella (Eds.), *Rethinking communication* (Vol. 2, pp. 199–212). Newbury Park, CA: Sage.

McPhee, R. D., & Poole, M. S. (2001). Organizational structures and configurations. In F. M. Jablin, & L. L. Putnam (Eds.), *The new handbook of organizational communication: Advances in theory, research and methods* (pp. 503–543). Thousand Oaks, CA: Sage.

McPhee, R. D. & Zaug, P. (2000). The communicative constitution of organizations: A framework for explanation. *The Electronic Journal of Communication, 10*(1/2), 1–16

Mumby, D. (1988). *Communication and power in organizations: Discourse, ideology, and domination*. Norwood, NJ: Ablex.

Mumby, D. (2001). Power and politics. In F. M. Jablin & L. L. Putnam (Eds.), *The new handbook of organizational communication: Advances in theory, research and methods* (pp. 585–623). Thousand Oaks, CA: Sage.

Mumby, D. K. (1997). Modernism, postmodernism, and communication studies: A rereading of an ongoing debate. *Communication Theory, 7*(1), 1–28.

Murphy, A. G. (1998). Hidden transcripts of flight attendant resistance. *Management Communication Quarterly, 11*(4), 499–535.

Pomerantz, A., & Fehr, B. J. (1997). Conversation analysis: An approach to the study of social action as sense making practices. In T. A. V. Dijk (Ed.), *Discourse as social interaction* (pp. 64–91). London: Sage.

Putnam, L. L. (1983). The interpretive perspective: An alternative to functionalism. In L. L. Putnam, & P. E. Pacanowsky (Eds.), *Communication and organizations: An interpretive approach.* Newbury Park, CA: Sage.

Putnam, L. L., & Fairhurst, G. T. (2001). Discourse analysis in organizations: Issues and concerns. In F. M. Jablin & L. L. Putnam (Eds.), *The new handbook of organizational communication* (pp. 78–136). Thousand Oaks, CA: Sage.

Putnam, L. L., & Pacanowsky, M. E. (1983). *Communication and organizations. An interpretive approach.* Newbury Park, CA: Sage.

Rosen, M. (1988). You asked for it: Christmas at the bosses' expense. *Journal of Management Studies, 25*(5), 463–480.

Schutz, A. (1966). *Collected papers III: Studies in phenomenological philosophy.* The Hague: Martinus Nijhoff.

Schutz, A. (1973). *Collected papers I: The problem of social reality.* The Hague: Martinus Nijhoff.

Searle, J. R. (1979). *Meaning and expression: Studies in the theory of speech acts.* Cambridge, U.K.: Cambridge University Press.

Smith, R. C. (1993). Images of organizational communication: Root-metaphors of the organization–communication relation. Paper presented at the International Communication Association Annual Conference, Washington DC.

Tarde, G. (1969). *On communication and social influence: Selected papers.* Chicago: University of Chicago Press.

Tarde, G. (1999a). *La logique sociale.* Paris: Les empêcheurs de penser en rond.

Tarde, G. (1999b). *Les lois sociales.* Paris: Les empêcheurs de penser en rond.

Tarde, G. (1999c). *L'opposition universelle.* Paris: Les empêcheurs de penser en rond.

Tarde, G. (1999d). *Monadologie et sociologie.* Paris: Les empêcheurs de penser en rond.

Taylor, J. R. (1993). *Rethinking the theory of organizational communication: How to read an organization.* Norwood, NJ: Ablex.

Taylor, J. R., Cooren, F., Giroux, N., & Robichaud, D. (1996). The communicational basis of organization: Between the conversation and the text. *Communication Theory*, *6*(1), 1–39.

Taylor, J. R., & Van Every, E. J. (2000). *The emergent organization: Communication as site and surface*. Hillsdale, NJ: Lawrence Erlbaum Associates.

Tracy, S. (2000). Becoming a character for commerce. *Management Communication Quarterly*, *14*(1), 90–128.

Webster's New Encyclopedic Dictionary (1993). New York: Black Dog & Leventhal.

Weick, K. E. (1979). *The social psychology of organizing*. New York: Random House.

Weick, K. E., & Daft, R. L. (1983). The effectiveness of interpretation systems. In K. S. Cameron, & D. A. Whetton (Eds.), *Organizational effectiveness: A comparison of multiple models* (pp. 71–93). New York: Academy Press.

6

ORGANIZING FROM THE BOTTOM UP?

Reflections on the Constitution of Organization in Communication

James R. Taylor

> Language occurs only in the flow of coordination of recursive consensual actions between organisms caught up in continuing interaction.
>
> (Maturana, 1997, p. 54)

In an important contribution to the communicative theory of the constitution of organization, McPhee and Zaug (2000, reproduced as Chapter 2 of this book; see also McPhee & Iverson, Chapter 3 of this book) argue that "organizations are constituted in four constitutive flows" (McPhee & Zaug, p. 21). In each flow, they propose "a sort of social structure is generated through interaction." The flows are, however, analytically, not practically, distinct in that "a single message can and often does make more than one type of contribution." The "flows" identified by the authors are those which can be seen as:

1. linking the organization to its members (membership negotiation),
2. to itself reflexively (self-structuring),
3. to the environment (institutional positioning),
4. to adapting interdependent activity to specific work situations and problems (activity coordination).

Each flow is, they say, "actually a kind of interactive communication episode, usually amounting to multi-way conversation whether or not mediated by texting, typically involving reproduction of as well as resistance to the rules and resources of the organization."

I am in agreement with McPhee and Zaug in believing that an adequate communicative theory of the constitution of organization must explain how communication activities interface with practical problems of dealing with a material world in the usual contexts of work, how members relate to each other and to their organization, how organizations come to have apparent characteristics of (relative) permanence and structure, and how they are positioned within the larger sphere of many other organizations. I perceive, in fact, that McPhee and Zaug have identified a set of criteria by which to assess the adequacy of any communication theory which aims to explain how organizations come to be constituted in the first place, and then maintain their status as organizations.

What is missing in their account, however, is an explanation of *which* communication theory would correspond to such a set of requirements. To describe a "flow" as "a kind of interactive communication episode," or a "multi-way conversation or text passage," does not offer much guidance to the properties of communication that would explain *how* organization is generated in interaction. What exactly is a "flow," for example: a sequence of communication interactions or episodes? A pattern of activities? A history? And what are the properties of flow that explain the genesis of organization?

Weick (1985; Orton & Weick, 1990) distinguished between tightly and loosely coupled interaction. Does the concept of flow that applies to the patterns of interaction of small working groups whose members are in frequent and intense interaction with each other (tightly coupled) apply with equal force to the global and sporadic (i.e., loosely coupled) interactions of the organization as a whole? Is there a model of flow that would illuminate these two aspects of organization or do we need to distinguish different kinds of flow?

While I am in agreement with McPhee and Zaug on the issue of criteria I believe that their program of research needs to be supplemented with a more precise theory of communication that has as its objective to trace the genesis and grounding of organizational form and process in the communication event. My purpose in this chapter is to outline a theory that I believe clarifies the issues that they raise. In doing so I will group their proposed flows in a rather different way than they do, in that I first emphasize activity and membership as it emerges in tightly coupled environments. I then turn to the more loosely coupled interactions within which the organization emerges as an identity distinct from that of any of its members, and is thus able to relate to its members and to others outside the organizational boundaries. The resulting flows need to be distinguished even though I will argue that they conform to a general model of communication I will propose.

My response to the challenge McPhee and Zaug have presented us with is organized in two main parts. In the first, I consider issues of activity coordination and membership negotiation. I believe that the constitution of organization is a *self*-organizing process, grounded in practical activities that have definable (and often quite concrete) outcomes and that are mediated by language. Language plays many functions in social life but one of them, as Wittgenstein observed, is to empower people to work together to accomplish practical things. One of the components of this self-organizing is an interpersonal negotiation of roles and responsibilities. Dealing simultaneously with a world of objects and relating to others in the act of doing so are thus, from my perspective, intrinsic to the very idea of organizational communication.

The explanation I develop in this first part of the chapter is constructed on a conception of communication as *coorientation*. Coorientation implies a simultaneous relationship to something to be done, and to others with whom one is doing it. The unit of communication thus takes the form of a triad that links, at a minimum, two communicators to a common object or objects. I claim this to be a flexible and productive unit of analysis in that it not only describes the basic communication relationship, but also explains more complex associational configurations and how they tend to become structured over time as people repeatedly interact with each other in regular ways, in dealing with their joint environment, to produce an emerging structure that I call *imbrication*.

In the second half of the chapter I describe the mechanism by which a collective identity emerges that is distinct from that of the communities who make it up. One of the cumulative consequences of some group of people doing some kind of common activity in a regular pattern is that they come to form a distinct community—a "community of practice" (Wenger, 1998). In the special ways they use language to support their work such communities develop patterns of sensemaking that are special to them, and different from those of other communities: distinct *rationalities*, in other words (Taylor, 2001a). Such communities are not only different; they may (and often do) develop a mutual antagonism to each other. Because they perceive the world in ways that demarcate them from neighboring communities, communication between different communities of practice is problematical. Coorientation is thus not a phenomenon restricted to the negotiation of member roles and responsibilities; it also applies to the bridging of inter-related communities of activity and sensemaking. The bridging is itself a crucial activity.

The product of inter-community coorientation—the "bridging"—is the organization itself. Coorientation is thus a recursive mechanism in that the process that generates organization (what I call "closure") is isomorphic to that which creates inter-personal relationships. The organization is a composite identity that legitimates and sanctions those who are its members.

It is the necessity for inter-community coorientation that motivates and justifies management. Management, because it too is a community of practice and sensemaking, forms a kind of "cognitive domain" or rationality that reflects in varying degrees the rationalities of the organization's constituent communities of practice. Some become dominant; others do not. I discuss briefly the implications of this bias. Finally I note that the organization relates in two different ways to other agencies within its external environment: through the activities of its members, or as a corporate agent supported by, and in competition with, a variety of other collective actors, including government.

Activity Coordination and Membership Negotiation: Communication at the Level of the Working Group

My theoretical investigation of the constitution of organization in communication is predicated on one basic assumption, that human communication is primarily mediated by language. This is not to downplay the considerable role played by non-verbal and para-linguistic signals, nor by artifacts, as everyday as the way workspaces are configured and as elaborate as the architecture of a whole city. Nevertheless, by far and away the most important (and flexible) of all the means we possess to communicate is language. I thus believe that the primary task of organizational communication theory is to investigate two questions: (1) what communicators do *with* language, and (2) what language does *in*, and *to*, communication.

To look at what *people* do with language means to take account of human motive and intention. It also means placing the uses of language within the context of purposeful action in which people are typically engaged. Context comes into play, in other words, and it is typically a context of situatedness in a mixed material and social world. To look at what *language* does means to explore the communicative properties of language as a medium, or instrument that people put to work within contexts of interaction (as distinct from the strictly grammatical properties of language, which is the province of formal linguistics). Language incorporates also its own agencies. It too is capable of "acting" (Cooren, 2006).

I begin by considering the first of these themes: what people do with language.

Language as a Resource

Language is a facility for the accomplishment of two tasks: (1) establishing interaction between people, and (2) expressing individual thought. Obviously, both these activities are reflected in the most ordinary uses of language. Nevertheless, these respective "affordances" (Gibson, 1979) of language may also be thought of as corresponding to two manifestations of communication: *conversation*, or the to-and-fro construction of a collaborative fabrication of shared talk, and *text*, or forms of communication that may be extended in time and space beyond the bounds of a single time/space setting: what Ricoeur (1981, 1991) calls "distantiated" (Taylor, Cooren, Giroux, & Robichaud, 1996).

The difference between a text that is *in* conversation and one that is not visibly situated within an immediate conversational context is, however, one of degree, not of kind. As Halliday and Hasan (1985) point out, even verbal expressions, in a conversational context, are in fact texts. Similarly, as the Internet illustrates, people may feel themselves to be in a conversation, even though it is mediated in time and space by written text. *All* communication—face-to-face or otherwise—is mediated. What differs are the *extensions of mediation* in time and space that different language vehicles make possible (not that this is a trivial distinction, empirically speaking). To the extent that we are *in* communication we are always engaged in both expressing ideas and interacting through language. What varies is the emphasis on conversation (which we sometimes define as face-to-face interaction, and is thus overtly interpersonal) or on text (which we tend to think of as abstracted from situations of interaction, and thus more as individual expression than interpersonal interaction).

Let us first consider synchronous communication (that which occurs within a single time/space nexus), or in other words face-to-face conversation. Maturana (1997, p. 50), like McPhee and Zaug, uses the term "flow" but he does so by relating it to language. As he observes, "languaging" (a neologism he introduces both in English, Maturana, 1991, and in Spanish, *lenguajear*, Maturana, 1997) is a self-organizing "flow" (*flujo* in Spanish). "Language occurs," he goes on, "in the domain of participants' coordination of their actions." From the beginning, in other words, language use is about coordination, and the "conservation of organization" (p. 51). To cite Maturana at greater length (the translation is my own):

> To the extent that a structurally determined system retains its organization while interacting in a certain medium, and continues to flow in the sequence of structural changes that these interactions trigger in it, then that system is conserving its structural correspondence or adaptation in this medium; otherwise it disintegrates. (p. 51)

The languaging-as-flow perspective is a key, I believe, to understanding the first of McPhee and Zaug's flows: activity coordination.

Activity Coordination

Face-to-face interaction occurs not just as an exchange of messages; it is an organizing in language. It is in the flow of conversation that people coordinate their activities. For one thing, coordination involves arriving at a common focus of attention on some ongoing activity (otherwise, why "coordinate"?). Let us designate this shared object of focus X. (I need to clarify one point here. I understand "object" in a way similar to that outlined by Engeström, 1990, less as a goal than as a project under construction, one that emerges as individuals interact with each other, and with their environment of work. It has to do with anticipation, projection, transformation, and achievement. It is not a fixed target. It serves to direct people's attention to what needs to be dealt with.)

For another, coordination, implicating as it does at least two persons, supposes the establishment of a relationship between the ones who are interacting. Let us designate this A–B. But since the relationship has a shared object of focus, the relationship is more properly thought of as a triad, namely A–B–X. Coordination implies, in other words, more than the couple relating to each other. It is the synchronization of their joint beliefs and/or actions *with respect to X* that make it an instance of coordination. This basic unit of communication, which is responsive to McPhee et al.'s criterion of activity coordination, is thus composed of an association, to use a term employed by Cooren and Fairhurst (Chapter 5 of this book), of three *actants*, two human subjects and one object.

I term this triad, following Newcomb (1953), a unit of coorientation (Taylor, 2000, 2001b, 2005; Taylor & Robichaud, 2004). It is, from my perspective, the building block enabling the analyst to climb the scale of complexity, rung by rung, to arrive at a characterization of complex organizations of the kind we who live in modernity have become accustomed to. Nor are the people who play the role of agents in a system of activity static points of established identity. One of the properties of the A–B–X model that intrigues me most is that the triadic relationship is not just a configuration of separate dyads; it is a genuinely triadic system, in which X is a construction that depends on the A–B state, but in which the A and B states are emergent as well, and depend on X, as well as on each other (Weick, 1979). Identity is constructed in communication—not merely what they bring to it. As Giddens (1984) observes, people are not "docile bodies" (p. 16); they are nodes of intentional action. Nor is the world outside, material or otherwise, just "there." It is in continual change, and it incorporates its own agencies and needs to be attended to. A–B–X must be *enacted* and, as Weick (1979) points out, that is a dynamic process of continuing adaptation.

A's identity emerges in the context of a relationship with B–X, but the same is true for B and X. Since each node of the triad is itself under construction, so is the triadic relationship; it remains permanently open-ended (Lave & Wenger, 1991). To use Weick's felicitous term, it is an ongoing *organizing*.

Newcomb calls an A–B–X occurrence a "communicative act" and he further claims that "group properties are predetermined by the conditions and consequences of communicative acts" (1953, p. 402) He may well be right (if we substitute the word "organization" for "group" this is the hypothesis that underpins the present book), but it still remains to show *how* properties of communication constitute the genesis of organization as being, as McPhee and Zaug put it, "multi-way." In reaching this goal, Newcomb's formulation offers three advantages over other competing models: flexibility, productivity and imbrication.

Flexibility.

The A–B–X model is adaptable to a variety of communication situations. It applies equally well to a two-way transaction (selling and buying), an offer ("Why don't I pick you up after work?"), a request ("Do you mind driving?"), an order ("Get back in line!"), a plea, such as Cooren and Fairhurst's chapter illustrates ("I need help!"), a joint effort ("You lift that end and I'll lift this!"), or any of a variety of other human interactions. It is not simply about one person addressing another person (as some of these examples might suggest); it is about coordinating the actions of two (or more) people with respect to a shared object. It is a consequence of conversation, not of any single speech act.

The essence of Newcomb's idea is this: people are positively cooriented when their respective attitudes or intentions are aligned (not identical, but compatible). How the alignment is arrived at is not the issue. It may happen through a simple question–reply sequence (first person: "Are you coming?"; second person: "Yeah"), or in a more elaborate sequence in which several people are involved in resolving a problem that has arisen that can only be dealt with by coordinated action. When several people are involved, however, the overall sequence is typically decomposable into articulated two-person exchanges (Cooren, 2000) that exhibit an A–B–X form, as I will shortly illustrate.

Productivity

A–B–X interactions do not necessarily, or even usually, occur in isolation. They are normally chained to each other and embedded one within the other to produce more complex sequences of interaction. For example, a request such as "Pick up some bread on the way home, would you?" engenders another action involving the buying of the bread: one action is chained to another. The availability of bread to be bought, in turn, implies a prior sequence of action leading to the making of the bread, and this in turn supposes other previous transactions: milling flour, growing and selling grain (Latour, 1994). If the person to whom the request was addressed is able to prevail upon a colleague or friend to pick up a loaf of bread over lunchtime then we have one unit of communication embedded within another. Embeddings of this kind are of particular significance in the context of the study of organization because they occur where delegation of responsibility for the performance of an action is involved. In my imaginary bread-buying sequence A has delegated to B responsibility for object X (buying bread and bringing it home) and B in turn delegates responsibility to a colleague or subordinate B' (buying the bread). The acts forming the sequence are both chained and embedded.

Imbrication

Because organizational communication is anchored in practice, and occurs in environments of work involving many of the same people performing many of the same activities together, it tends to become *imbricated*. In any ongoing context of work the routine tends to take over, since it corresponds to an elementary principle of economy of effort. The object becomes clear, and roles are not for the moment up for negotiation. This is all I mean by imbrication.

To summarize, the coordination of activities produces coordinated organized action at the level of practice. But coorientation also involves, from the beginning, McPhee and Zaug's criterion of membership negotiation.

Membership Negotiation

Transactions in which one person delegates responsibility for the performance of an action to an agent, such as I have described, are referred to by Watzlawick, Beavin, and Jackson (1967) as *complementary* (as contrasted with *symmetric*). Such transactions initiate a particular kind of relationship, where each person or agent plays a distinct role, and where roles entail responsibilities as well as privileges (Labov & Fanshel, 1977). They also illustrate a point made by Giddens (1984) as he writes, "action logically involves power in the sense of transformative capacity" (p. 15). But as he also points out, "All forms of dependence offer some resources whereby those who are subordinate can influence the activities of their superiors. This is what I call the *dialectic of control* in social systems" (p. 16). The coordination of organizational activities that I describe as flowing from the negotiation of an A–B–X relationship in communication is my interpretation of a dialectic of control (although we might want to use a softer term such as "mutual attempts at influence" in some contexts). I assume its outcomes are forever re-negotiable; as Sigman (1995) puts it, communication is *consequential*: it matters because it is more than the playing out of a pre-ordained script. Sometimes the worm turns!

I need, perhaps, to interject a cautionary note here on the method I am following. I think of the coorientational unit proposed by Newcomb, A–B–X, as a model: an analytic device. To me, a model has a role somewhat analogous to an architectural drawing: useful until the building is done, but something to be consigned to a shelf to collect dust afterwards. People do not experience themselves as As, or Bs, nor do they think of themselves as oriented to an X: these are all attributions I am making as an analyst. What people experience is the organization. They perceive themselves to be in a situation that they are more or less familiar with, and they react to that situation using whatever acquired knowledge and intuitions they possess to make sense of it.

To illustrate, consider a situation described by Suchman (1996). The context is the Operations Room of an airline, located in a smallish airport. There are five people in the room: a supervisor and four others each with his/her own specific assignment (passenger service and baggage planning, monitoring incoming flights, coordinating with an affiliate airline). The episode filmed by Suchman's crew is initiated when a set of ramp stairs breaks down and an incoming plane is unable to disembark its passengers. The team in the Operations Room is mobilized to alert ground crews, contact other airlines for a possible loan of stairs, and to update the plane on what is happening. Everyone in the room is at least peripherally implicated in the incident, and aware of others' activities, even if they have no direct role to play in them. They don't merely relate to their own responsibility in the team; they experience the crisis as an episode with organizational meaning, defining pragmatically who they are, both individually and collectively, who they interface with (ground crew, pilot, baggage handlers), and who they work for (one airline, as opposed to another). It is also clear, and Suchman is insistent on this point, that the configuration of the operations room is itself an active agency in dealing with the situation. As Cooren and Fairhurst point out in Chapter 5, facilities like television monitors, telephones, and radio are very much part of the complex of agents that is responding to the crisis.

Although the Operations Room team respond as a unit, nevertheless, when Suchman turns to analyze the recorded communications in the Ops Room, she finds that they immediately break down, on closer inspection, into a sequence of dialogic interactions. In these components of the overall organization of the room couples of workers step through the activities that such a dilemma calls for, each time one on one: pilot to Ops A (the person responsible for monitoring incoming flights), Ops A to PP (passenger planner), PP to ground crew, Supervisor to PP, Supervisor to BP (baggage planner), and so on. Technology, of course, plays its own role at every step. Even though the occurrence may be experienced as a holistic episode, the communication it generates is realized as a sequence of coorientational adjustments, one on one. Eventually the problem is resolved and things return to "normal."

Fairhurst and Cooren's (2004) analysis of the Cincinnati Police emergency has the same characteristics: the episode is perceived holistically, even though it is executed dialogically.

How Language Enters to Play a Role in Membership Negotiation

Up until now I have been taking the perspective of people who use various technologies to resolve practical problems and in the process manage to coordinate their own activities. Language figures in this perspective as one of the technologies they use. I now want to turn to look at the set of properties of language that make it an effective agent in coordinating activities and negotiating membership identities. I will be considering, in other words, not what people do in coorientation, but what language does: its role as an agent.

The alignment of attitudes or intentions on which the A–B–X model is predicated is made possible by a specific property of language. As Austin (1962) observed in his famous William James Lectures at Harvard in 1955, to say something is not merely to convey information; it is also to *do* something—to act. In order to explain the facility of language that accounts for its ability to serve as an agent mediating an interaction, Austin made an analytical distinction between language as *locution* and as *illocution*. As a locution, an expression of language can be read as having a corresponding external referent ("The grass is quite dry now" is true if and only if the grass is actually quite dry now). It is this facility of language that explains its capacity to inform (as, for example, Shannon's 1948 model of communication does, since it interprets A–B–X as sender→message→receiver, and message means a locution). But utterances are not just "locutions", nor do they refer uniquely to the world of external reference of the communicators. The illocutionary reference of an utterance (a dimension of *every* utterance), as Austin defines it, is not *outside* the communicative situation, a message conveying information about a state of the world, but *within* the situation itself, since it refers to the actors themselves in their orientations to the world. That which is in focus is not X but, reflexively, A and/or B, *in their connection to* X. Those markers of language which express the speaker's attitude/intention, and potentially impose on the listener's attitude/intention, go beyond the simple conveyance of information (message content) to become the affordance of language that communicators use to coorient, or align their respective attitudes/intentions in order to arrive at coordinated activity (Habermas, 1998).

Since Austin's time, developments in contemporary linguistics obviate the use of the concept of illocution, since it is now clear that the expression of attitude and the ability to influence others' attitudes is a feature of language that is present in every utterance, known as *modality* (for discussion, see Taylor & Van Every, 2000). Epistemic modality expresses "the degree of a speaker's commitment to the truth of the proposition contained in an utterance" (Bybee & Fleischman, 1995, p. 4). It is *explicitly* expressed by sentences components such as "I believe that...," "I doubt that..." (or even by a shrug of the shoulders), or, *implicitly*, just by making a flat statement of fact. Deontic modality, in contrast, "focuses on the notions of obligation and permission" (p. 4). Deontic modality gets expressed by phrases such as "Would you mind...?" or "I would hope that...," or "I warn you...," "Stand still!," but it is just as often expressed non-verbally (pointing, for example). It may indeed be implicit: most of us understand that when someone says "I'm uncomfortable" they really mean "Do something."

I do not want to over-simplify the phenomenon of expressing one's own, and reading other's, intentions: as Goffman (1959) observed, there is always an information game going on, since people may not always express their attitudes in so many words, for fear of offending (Labov & Fanshel, 1977), or for some other reason, such as the risk of reprisal or to disguise their intentions: people are sometimes deliberately misleading as to their real motives. Modality is thus as often tacitly understood as it is overtly manifested.

Modality, in both of its manifestations, epistemic and deontic, is a feature of language that allows communicators to negotiate coorientation by establishing a common perception of the situation and what is to be done about it. There is, however, an important difference between the earlier theory of speech acts and current studies of modality: modality is no longer understood to be a property of the single act of speech. Modal functions, in real communicative situations, in many cases "surface only in face-to-face interaction" (Bybee & Fleischman, 1995 p. 8), and depend "not just on a monologic speaker" but on "a dialogic speaker-addressee interaction" (p. 8). As Bybee and Fleischman put it, "modals can be viewed as strategic linguistic tools for the construction of social reality" (p. 8). Much of the work in Conversation Analysis, especially with respect to repair sequences, may, in fact, be seen as exploring the uses of language in constructing social reality (Schegloff, 1991; Boden, 1994).

So when people interact using language, it is the strings of language they utter that express their perceptions and intentions. Language functions, however, as more than an indispensable resource to make their attitudes known. As it becomes their agent in interacting with others, it establishes in spoken and written form—text—the character of their relationship to each other, in the context of their joint relationship to common objects. It *materializes* their relationship, even as it serves as the instrument they use to negotiate it. Language is thus more than a simple means; it is a construction of that relationship in text that may now be used as rule and resource (Giddens, 1984). It builds a framework for subsequent interaction, and stabilizes it. Organization is created in the organizing.

I'll have more to say about this later. Now I want to turn to a quite different issue: collective identity. This is how the organization as a whole manages to develop an identity (self-structuring) and, by itself becoming an actor, how it can subsequently negotiate a relationship with its members (membership negotiation in a different mode) and outsiders (positions itself institutionally).

Linking the Organization to Itself Reflexively: Self-Structuring, Negotiating with Members and with the Environment

So far I have concentrated my attention on the constitution of organization at the level of the working group (Weick's tight coupling). But organizations are configurations of many different worlds of work, each characterized by its own culture and modes of sensemaking. Coorientation, in this more loosely coupled interaction, implies more than the coordination of individual member's respective actions and intentions. It implies what we usually think of as management: integrating many areas of specialization into some kind of coherent pattern. This will succeed only if the organization is somehow recognized by people as being *itself* an actor. In this section, I am thus turning to consider how the organization as a whole gets to be structured, or at least given the appearance of functioning as a coherent unit of action and intention, whatever its multiple "invisible" contradictions (Suchman, 1995).

In this new context the concept of coorientation must be broadened to include not just inter-individual coordination, but the negotiation of working relations involving many communities of practice, each having its own character and interests. If an organization is composed of many communities of practice, or what Krippendorff (1998) thinks of as an ecology of communities, then the question is how to coordinate them. This is the problem of management. Yet the communities to be "managed" typically do not share the same practice, or even the same modes of making sense of their world.

Communities of Practice

Communication occurs in a context. I have argued that it is, for most people working in organizations, a context that involves recurrent patterns of interaction among a stable set of agents (both people and technology), with respect to objects that equally tend to be recurrent. We spend most of our time, in other words, in communities of practice where we are most comfortable because they are peopled by others who share our concerns and seem to understand us when we talk about them (Heaton & Taylor, 2002).

The concept of a *community of practice* has received its most explicit formulation in the work of Lave and Wenger (1991; Lave, 1988; Wenger, 1998). A community of practice comes into existence when a certain grouping of people find themselves regularly focused on a common object, or objects. Such contexts favor learning how to do certain things in certain patterned ways and involve certain people. These are what Lave and Wenger (1991, p. 50) call "an evolving, continuously renewed set of relations." As they put it, "a theory of social practice emphasizes the relational interdependency of agent and world, activity, meaning, cognition, learning, and knowing. It emphasizes the inherently socially negotiated character of meaning and the interested, concerned character of the thought and action of persons-in-activity" (pp. 50–51). Out of this activity "the world and its experienced forms" are mutually constituted (p. 51).

Work, in other words, is normally embedded in social practice—a practice that has to be learned, and once learned gives meaning to people's experience (Lave & Wenger, 1991). It is the reading of what others say in the context of a shared experience of relating to each other and to a common external world that allows people to align their attitudes and intentions: to be cooriented. As Garfinkel (1967) and other ethnomethodologists have pointed out, all communication that depends on the use of language is *indexical.* The sense of any linguistic expression whatsoever needs a context for it to be understood at all (even *mis*understood). It follows that to be an effective participant in any ongoing community, the individual must establish his/her credentials to function within it, as a fully accredited member of the community possessing the background knowledge to both understand others, and to make sense and be understood as doing so. To be a member of a community, and to be recognized as such, one must have mastered not just its practices, but also its modes of sensemaking, and be able to demonstrate concretely than one has done so (Heaton & Taylor, 2002). One has to know how to use the language of the community correctly.

Each community thus develops its own special kind of rationality. There is no universal standard of rationality rooted in what Maturana (1997) terms a *transcendent* objectivity. There are only what he calls *constitutive* rationalities, each of which is "objective" only within the context of its own taken-for-granted assumptions about the world. These are assumptions that are grounded in the experience of a particular community such, for example, as the one Suchman was describing (or in science, for Maturana). Our authority to be heard and be paid attention to as legitimate sensemakers depends on our capacity to meet the criteria established by a community of similar sensemakers (which is, by definition, a community of practice). Maturana (1997) calls these communities of shared rationality "cognitive domains" (p. 29). They take, he argues, the form of a framework of explanations, which "specify a domain of legitimate actions in the life practices (*la praxis del vivir*) of the observer" (p. 29). Since different fields of practice privilege different premises and operational preferences, there is no universal principle of objectivity; there is instead a *multiverse* of rationalities (p. 26). What one knows is tied to what one does, and who one does it with, and since people do different things with different partners they know different things.

Language as Itself a Practice

We constitute organization by participating in dialogues with others: through conversations with them. But language is itself a practice, and its rules are established, and regulated, within a community of practice. Modes of sensemaking reflect the community, not just the individual. To the extent that an organization is formed of communities, each characterized by its own practices, organization must also be thought of as a patchwork of cognitive domains, each privileging its own premises (unexamined assumptions) and modes of justifying belief: its own language. The construction of a *transcendent* rationality, associated with the organization as a whole, is thus inherently problematical. Browning, Sitkin, Sutcliffe, Obstfeld, & Greene (2000), for example, document the encounter of two different communities of practice and cognition: maintenance technicians who daily resolve problems by recourse to pragmatic strategies of adaptation, on the one hand, and the engineers who work in the Civilian Depot, and establish standards to which the technicians are obliged to conform, on the other. As Browning et al., 2000, put it "The technicians describe their relationship with the Depot engineers as contentious—and designed to be so."

The "contention" needs theoretical unpacking. Once again we need to take account of the structuring role of language, now no longer in how it shapes interpersonal interaction, but in how it serves to bridge communities. We need to see how the narrative basis of sensemaking becomes the key agency in forming the coorientational patterns of organization in the large.

Sensemaking as Generative of Antagonism: Language as Agent

It is now generally accepted in discourse-based research that the natural medium of sensemaking in organizational life is narrative (Boje, 1991, 1995, 2001; Boje, Alvarez & Schooling, 2001; Czarniawska, 1997, 1998, 1999; Fisher, 1987; Weick, 1995; Weick & Browning, 1986; Zilber, 2002). As Orr (1996) has pointed out, people doing specialized tasks use story-telling as a way of informing, even teaching, each other about the problems they face and ways to resolve them.

A narrative typically begins with a problem that has cropped up, or something that is awry and needs to be fixed. The first function of the narrative is thus to establish a common basis of understanding of the situation and what is wrong about it. This is equivalent to what I called earlier the epistemic modality of language. Establishing the facts of the situation may occur simply as something the story-teller does, or it may be negotiated interactively (Zilber, 2002). The second phase of narrative is establishing what is to be done and who is to do it. This is equivalent to what I called the deontic modality of language, and again it may simply form part of an account, or may be developed in conversation. The third phase of narrative is simply what happened, when, where, and who was involved in doing what. The fourth and final phase deals with how the situation ended up, and who was rewarded or punished—sanctioned—because of their roles in the episode.

Narrative, however, is told from a point of view. Because it is about action, and who participated in it, the actors who enter into the chronicle do so either as protagonists, helpers, and sponsors, on the one hand, or as antagonists, opponents, and behind-the-scene manipulators on the other. Stories are ways by which closure is established: how a resolution was brought to a problem, but also who was a friend or ally and who was not. Narrative is how we construct sense where human motive and action is involved. As Bruner (1991) observes, telling a story is not just recounting a sequence of events; a story has to conform to a patterning that we intuitively recognize as good narrative structure. It is both specific and generic.

We are accustomed to thinking of rhetoric as the skill of the speaker. But language, because it imposes the form of narrative, is itself an agency—an agency that divides the world into cooperators and competitors.

Sensemaking, however, is a collective, not merely an individual, accomplishment. It is the basis of a community's rationality: how it construes experience, collectively. But as the stories accumulate (Bruner, 1991) they instantiate a narrative account that people in the community share of who in the organization has to be dealt with as helpers, who as opponents. It becomes for people in the community their "map" of the organization (Taylor & Van Every, 2000). Communities are thus not simply different from each other in how they make sense; because of story-telling, some may be construed narratively as oppositional or antagonistic. Coorientation linking different communities thus means finding a meta-story within which everyone feels part of the same community (Robichaud, Giroux, & Taylor, 2004): differences sufficiently reconciled to support a common response. Management involves a good deal more than just coordinating people's activities within a unified cognitive frame of reference: a single interaction (Giroux & Taylor, 2002).

With this clarification in mind, I now turn to the key issue I am raising in this section: how the organization emerges to become itself an actor.

The Organization as Actor

I began this chapter by treating the agencies that figure in the coorientational dynamic as either individuals or artifacts that incorporate a human intention (or are interpreted as doing so). But McPhee and Zaug's analysis supposes a conceptualization of the organization as *itself* an agent: an "agent" that is linked relationally to its members, to elements in its environment, and to itself, reflexively. In what sense can an abstraction called "organization" be an agent, capable of establishing relationships on the same plane of interaction as its members, or other actors, corporate or otherwise, outside the organization? And if we admit organization to be an actor in its own right, how do we explain the genesis of this identity-as-actor and its power to act? What *is* an organization, in the sense that McPhee and Zaug use the word? If, for example, two organizations merge, or one takes over the other, do they stop being two organizations and become one, even if one is then managed as a quasi-autonomous subsidiary of the other? What is the criterion of "organization-ness" that applies here?

The concept of an organization as an actor has always seemed to me arcane—a great mystery. In this section, however, I offer my own account of the phenomenon (see also Cooren & Taylor, 1997; Taylor & Cooren, 1997; Taylor, 1999, 2000).

First, it is worth noting that the word "organization" is ambiguous in English (and in other European languages with which I am familiar: *organisation*, in French, *organización*, in Spanish, *organização* in Portuguese, *organisierung* or *organisation*, in German, *organisatie*, in Dutch). It means, on the one hand, "an organizing or being organized," and, on the other, "any unified group or systematized whole" (*Webster's New World Dictionary*, 1964). Until now, our discussion has focused on the first meaning: organization as "an organizing or being organized." But if we are to see how an organization may take on agency status, as an independent actor, we will have to consider how groups become "unified" (transformed from many into one) and wholes become "systematized" (endowed with a single structure of operations). I claim that the factor that explains how unification takes place, and a collective identity emerges, is *closure*. I then consider a second factor: *recursivity*.

My way of attacking the meaning and consequences of closure and recursivity is the same as before: I consider the question as one of (no doubt over-) simplified modeling. I then extend the analysis to more complex contexts, that I hope will strike the reader as having a greater bearing on reality.

Closure

The finality of coorientation is action (this is why modality is deontic, as well as epistemic: not just "messaging"). A secondary effect of coorientation is to instantiate some actor (or actant) as *qualified* to act, because the actor now incorporates an agency—the ability and authority to act. He, she or it must now be acting *for* someone or something: not just for him, her or itself, since in that case no attribution of coorientation nor of organization would be implied. It is this delegation of responsibility to act that confers legitimacy on the action. If, however, to qualify as an "agent," one must be *acting for* someone or something, the logical result would seem to be an infinite regress of successive delegations since the person or thing one is acting for must in turn, following the logic of coorientation, have earned agency status. That there is not an indefinite succession of delegations on delegations is a consequence of a little-investigated property of all human communication: *closure*.

Consider the elementary A–B–X unit. Suppose the negotiation process leading to a relationship of agency, or delegation of responsibility to act, begins as a suggestion or a request by A addressed to B to do something. Then, conversationally speaking, A assumes an "I" role; B, the person being addressed is constituted as a "you"; and X is an "it" (that which is to be done). If B goes along with A's solicitation, the exchange closes and the human actors of the A–B–X triad are transformed into a "we," or A/B. The pair of actors now form a couple united by a similar purpose with respect to X. At this point the couple is transfigured from one agent "I" addressing another one, a "you" (through making a request, giving an order, hinting, suggesting, passing a judgment, etc.) into a "we," a coupled agent. They are jointly cooriented with respect to X. A simple community has formed. They are now, figuratively speaking, "married." They could now enter *as a couple* into a relationship with yet another actor, let us say C (individual or collective).

Once a transfer of affiliation from the level of the individual to that of the collectivity is effected, the source agency is no longer, psychologically speaking, A, but A/B, and either A or B (or both) may be designated agents who perform the actual deed that defines the collective unit A/B(X) in its intentionality. Either A or B (or both) may in turn assume the role of A/B spokesperson. A/B becomes, by implication, an impersonal entity to whom both partners to the exchange may owe their loyalty since they have transformed themselves into a single node of agency, for which they as individuals may act and speak. The naked A–B power relationship (Giddens, 1984, pp. 14–16), in which one person gives orders (requests, suggestions, etc.) to another, is subtly cushioned by the shift in attribution of the source agency, from A to A/B. A's authority to issue a request is in turn legitimized (and neutralized) by its having become an expression of the intention of A/B. B is simultaneously transformed into a legitimated actor, authorized to act on the part of A/B, whose existence is thereby predicated. But the source of A/B authority, as we have seen, is itself a tacit delegation of agency on the part of A and B to the thus constituted social unit. The system is circular: closed.

A television producer (to draw on my own experience) may be obliged to report *to* a supervising producer, but he/she does not work *for* the latter. The producer works for the corporate broadcaster. The supervising producer may be authorized to speak for the corporation in dealing with producers, but the agency of origin resides elsewhere, in the corporation itself. But, seen from the alternative perspective, it is the association of them all that constitutes the organization for which they all work.

What we commonly think of as "organization" (as a unified group, or systematized whole) amounts to just this circularity. It sounds like a trick of language but the roots are more profound (Taylor & Cooren, 1997).

The rationale is, however, clear enough: it is a logic of association (Latour, 1987, 1984; Cooren, 2000; Cooren & Taylor, 2000; Cooren & Fairhurst, Chapter 5 in this book). Association adds weight to agency, and explains the authority of individual actors to act, since they do so as legitimated agents of a larger community. Companies such as Microsoft, for example, developed their weight through a succession of associations of smaller agencies, and as they did so their power to influence the actions and policies of others increased. The people who work for such companies, in turn, enjoyed enhanced prestige, influence, and authority. It is a logic that works beautifully, unless of course the company does an Enron, in which case the associational links break down and the company is in trouble.

This is what I mean by "closure." But, recalling our earlier discussion of narrative as the basis of sensemaking, closure means more than self-inclusion (A and B transformed into an A/B); it also means other-exclusion. A construction, through interaction, of "I," "you," and "we" identities implies, *necessarily* (although not always stated explicitly), a co-construction of a "he," "she," and "they." I say "necessarily" because a set of pronouns, as a property of language, forms a *paradigmatic system*. The meaning of "I," "you," and "we" originates in what Saussure thought of as a network of associations, where no term has a positive meaning in the absence of a set of contrasts, or negatives. To be a "we," then, logically implies a "they" (as well as an "I" and a "you"). Communication thus effectively creates selves, A(X), B(X), and A/B(X), in the simplest case (and whole organizations in more complicated cases), but it does so by simultaneously creating others, let us say C(Y)s (where Y may contradict X, giving to communication what Greimas, 1987, calls its "polemic" character).

There is no self-ness in the absence of other-ness. On the other hand, self-ness and other-ness are not restricted to individual human actors: collective identities are constituted in the same way—not just "I," "you" (singular), "he," and "she," but also "we," "you" (plural), and "they."

Some of those "theys" can be others with whom one is engaged in amicable relationships of exchange: clients, customers, patients, citizens, etc. Other "theys" are competitors, rivals, enemies—what Greimas (1987) calls "anti-subjects." There are "theys" who are not strictly part of the community of practice but who occupy a position of authority with respect to it, either as its investors, its regulators, or its judges. And finally, of course, there are the "theys" of other communities of practice in the same organization. Here the relationship is more ambiguous, since they are "theys" for some purposes (in competing for resources) and "wes" in others (as complementary partners within the same organization).

Organization as an "organizing," or "being organized," occurs simply as a result of the interaction of coorienting individuals, caught up in a conversation which has a practical focus: an orientation to an X. Organization-as-entity, however, can only be explained as a consequence of what Giddens (1984) calls "reflexive monitoring" and Weick (1995) calls "retrospective sensemaking" (p. 24). We become "wes" by *coorienting*. We only become *aware* that we are a "we," however, by reflexively and retrospectively *knowing* what and who we are. The organization thus emerges in two distinct ways, depending on the dimension of language we emphasize: interaction or sensemaking. By interacting we become an organization; by observing and expressing our experience—sensemaking—we create the organization as an object of discourse. Once we *know* that we are a "we," it follows, we can give ourselves a name, and our newly-minted identity allows us to enter into the conversational stream in a new guise, as a collective actor: a *we* (as in "we build cars" or "we take milk with our coffee"). The organization-as-actor has been born.

Recursivity

To be recursive simply means that the structure of a whole emerges in the same way as the structure of the parts. I have no doubt that many species have sophisticated systems of communication (whales and dolphins, for example, even bees and ants). But the language used by humans is, I believe, unique precisely in its recursivity: its ability to function both as the matter and framework of communication (Robichaud, Giroux, & Taylor, 2004). I believe that organization is recursive in just this way. Not only is it structured locally in the act of co-orienting, the same principle holds for the organization as a whole: coorientation links whole communities. Furthermore, as we saw for the local organization, language plays a key role in establishing the identity of the collective actor, whether community of practice or organization as a whole.

Consider again Suchman's case study. The pilot has participated in a conversation within the plane, where he has learned of a problem. When he calls Operations he does so as the legitimate representative of the crew, which is itself an exemplar of a community of practice: a "*we*." He reaches Operations, a collective "*you*" for him, even though he talks to only one person in it, Ops A. But Operations is itself an instance of a community of practice, or a virtual "*we*", and, as such, it in turn addresses other collective "*yous*" (such as ground crew), always, though, through the inter-mediation of some individual who becomes the spokesperson for the "*we*" (and who may even use precisely that word in speaking to others). Both individual and collective identities are thus confirmed in each of the exchanges. And all of these exchanges are expressing, without ever explicitly doing so, the background identity of the airline: the organization that the aircrew and the people in Operations collectively work for—all of the exchanges, that is, with one exception. The exception arises when the Supervisor instructs an assistant to contact another airline that uses the same airport: a "*they*." This action instantiates a double relationship: that of the employee to his/her own company, but also that of one airline to another: a "*them*."

Because language is simultaneously an interactive medium of organizing, and of individual expression, it is also the means by which people become, at one and the same time, participants in organization and observers of it. Organization is constituted as an actor in just this way: it is both a construction that emerges out of the sensemaking activities of people, and subsequently an active participant in those activities as a real actor.

Inter-community Communication

To summarize the points I have just been making:

• Any large organization is composed of many "cognitive communities." An organization, from this perspective, is a "multiverse" of activity-driven conversations, each "rational" within its own ambit.

- Because such communities each constitute a basis of knowing, and a rationality that is specific to them, and not just a projection of a generic "objectivity," they are, each separately, domains of knowledge. But their knowledge is grounded in practice—operational (Orr, 1996). As Brown and Duguid (2000) point out, knowledge is situated, not context-free.
- What sounds rational in one community may have little resonance in another. If the practices and the modes of making sense in their respective conversations are different (and they typically are) there is no single rationality that encompasses them all.
- There is, nevertheless, communication between communities and their conversations, and the question is now posed: how does that work?

Maturana (1997) supplies what I believe to be the answer to this question (wherever he uses the term "observer" substitute "sensemaker"):

> We human beings live in cognitive communities, each defined by the criterion of acceptability of what constitutes satisfactory actions or behaviors on the part of members. As such, cognitive domains are domains of consensus as to the life practices of observers. Because this is so, to be a member in whatever community is operationally determined: whoever satisfies the criterion of acceptability of being a member in whatever human community, is a member of it. ... As a consequence of its manner of constitution, cognitive domains are operationally closed domains: an observer cannot leave a cognitive domain while operating within it. Similarly, an observer cannot observe a cognitive domain while operating within it. An observer can leave a cognitive domain, and observe it, only through the recursive consensuality of language which specifies consensually another cognitive domain in which the first is an object of consensual distinctions. (p. 79)

You can't in effect be making sense simultaneously within the frameworks of rationality of two different communities whose taken-for-granted premises about the world are different, and who narrativize their organizational world in different and incompatible ways.

But Maturana argues that coorientation between communities is enabled when there are agents who, in effect, "speak the language" of both (although obviously not at the same time, or within the same communities). To some extent, because we all participate in more than one community of practice (the office versus the home, for example), we are all "bilingual." It is consequently *we*, as individual agents, who mediate the inter-community interaction of the organization. We are the crossing points between communities of practice and sensemaking: we are "boundary spanners" (Stohl, 1995). We become an "observer" (to use Maturana's term) in what he calls a life practice (and thus we have learned to be a sensemaker within the bounds of a specific "cognitive community"). But, through our participation in *more than one* conversational domain, or community, we may, in our persons, become in some sense both in and out of each community. We may alternate. We become bridges between communities, and their conversations (Robichaud, Giroux, & Taylor, 2004).

The catch is that an organization is not just a congeries of disjointed practices: it is itself a community of practice or "cognitive domain." It is, however, one within which other organizational communities figure as, to use Maturana's term, an "object of consensual distinctions." The people who participate in the trans-community conversation of management routinely pass judgment on these other communities. In other words, managerial sensemaking has as its object, X, all the communities of practice that make up the organization. When, to use Browning et al.'s research, the Air Force adopts Quality Management as a corporate strategy it intervenes in every separate community of practice to impose a common practice on them. (Small wonder then that the technicians followed the program's precepts, since it made sense to them, but as they did they claimed they were not. Otherwise, they would have to admit their own lack of sensemaking autonomy.)

For those who are privileged to participate in the managerial conversation, because they claim or are accorded the capability of speaking for their respective communities of practice, the result is an enhancement of their authority, and their power. Representative voices—people who claim to be both observers *in* a community and *of* it as passing judgment on it—presume to speak for one community while participating in another. Think of the union speaking for the workers in contract negotiations with management, the department head representing members of the department to the Dean or the Provost, the diplomat negotiating inter-state agreements for his/her country. Each is a case of what Maturana describes as "an observer who has left one cognitive domain" and is now constituted as a member of "another cognitive domain in which the first becomes an object of consensual distinctions."

Complex organization, I propose, emerges in a superordinate meta-conversation where all the conversations of the organization's members, including its own, have become *its* object of focus (Robichaud, Giroux, & Taylor, 2004). For example, Browning et al.'s research describes how the Air Force, as a corporate entity, adopted Quality Management as its stated policy. I have no idea how they arrived at that policy, but I have no doubt it was preceded by meetings, briefings, and conversations with consultants, and so on: multiple conversations, all focused, it would have been understood, on how to improve the performance of the work groups of the organization. That intention, once formulated as a text, was circulated to employees, including the repair mechanics. By doing so, the organization entered into a coorientational relation with its employees, with a rather loosely defined object (quality) in view, and with implications for the practices of the mechanics that the latter interpreted in their own manner, as Browning et al. describe. As a consequence the technicians found themselves in a dialogue with the engineers of the Civilian Depot who now acted as agents responsible for making sure the policy was carried out. But, since the quality movement originated outside the management of the Air Force, its members had already been in conversation with representatives of other organizations (Giroux & Taylor, 2002). It linked to its members, but it also was linked to an environment, in which it was positioning itself institutionally by its choices and activities.

This is how the intention of the organization is constituted, through an ongoing coorientational negotiation. Meetings at one site and time link up with meetings at another site and time. Each committee generates a report that provides the fodder for some other committee to meet and discuss what to do next. Each meeting justifies the designation of spokespersons who cross the boundary between different ongoing conversations, always representing one conversation to another. There is what Boden (1994) calls a "lamination" of conversations. Eventually, a level is reached where it is understood that the text that is now generated constitutes the intention of the organization. The person designated to enunciate that intention, by the usual convention, is the head of the organization. The process closes and the identity of the organization emerges, whether it is expressed by the official head of the organization, or by one of many other individual agents who are either designated to represent the organization or who take it upon themselves to do so. Not only is the organizational intention made manifest to its employees, and itself; the organization also is now able to "present itself" (Goffman, 1959) to others who make up its environment. As McPhee and Zaug observe, the same flow is capable of realizing more than one link: to the members of the organization and to those outside the organization. The Air Force is presenting itself simultaneously to its members and its homologues and sponsors.

I don't want to suggest, by the way, that with closure total unanimity has in some way been reached, nor that the organization is ever characterized by a single intention, or rationality. On the contrary, what emerges as the meta-text of the organization need not be representative of all the members of the organization or even a majority of them. The negotiation of an organizational intention, and the closing of its identity, does not obliterate the identities of its constituent communities of practice. Nor does it make the political games that characterize many meta-conversations vanish. On the contrary, as Browning et al.'s study illustrates, tensions remain. The managerial conversation is a bridge which creates an appearance of linkage, but in fact leaves the respective communities divided: some, like the repair technicians, pragmatically focused on the resolution of concrete problems, and others, like the higher levels of Air Force command, focused on the more abstract issues of policy. They may both use the same word "quality" but, as Browning et al. found, they don't mean the same thing. The rationalities are too different. The logics are not really compatible. The texts that the management conversation generates reflect its preoccupations and orientations, not necessarily those of the communities to which such texts are addressed.

Managerial sensemaking reflects in very different degrees the many rationalities that compose the cognitive patchwork of a large organization. The capacity to influence the construction in conversation and text of the intentionality of the organization as a unity is thus a source of power. It is also an incentive to an inter-community dynamic that might reasonably be said to have an ideological edge (where "ideology" means any rationality that is foreign to the usual sensemaking practices of some community).

Once an organization has been constituted as an agent with its own identity and orientation it is then in a position to interact with its own members, and other agents who people its environment. It has been instantiated as an agent within the larger institutional context of the society in which it is located.

Conclusion

McPhee and Zaug (2000) have proposed a set of criteria that provide a means to assess the adequacy of any theory of the constitution of organization in communication. What I have tried to accomplish in this chapter is to expand on some of the conceptual steps that we, as a community of scholars devoted to the study of organizational communication, might have to take to satisfy these criteria. I have argued that it will be by taking account of the properties of language, and the practices of language-users, that we will advance. Language is both how people relate to each other, and how they express their understandings of such relating. Interaction mediated by language is thus reflexive, and retrospective, as both Giddens and Weick have pointed out, in that people monitor the interaction they are caught up in and make sense of it in retrospect. It is this reflective-*cum*-retrospective capability that gives rise to the recursive property of communication and thus generates, not just meta-communication, but (crucially for organizational studies), a meta-conversation, out of which emerge meta-texts (Katambwe & Taylor, 2006). It is, furthermore, in this recursive/retrospective dynamic that the identities of objects, individuals, technologies, communities and, finally, the organization itself are born.

Finally, I have argued that identities that transcend those of the individual logically suppose closure. Closure is itself an instance of how language works, and how people use language, since the merging of individual intentions to produce a collective identity is both a real phenomenon (the cooperative performance of tasks) and a discursive phenomenon (the naming of a collaborative unit). Once constituted in fact and in language, the actor is enabled to enter other dialogues (a recursion), where he, she, or it is treated as an agent characterized by a single intention, and attitude. In this way, the organization is, as Boden (1994) puts, literally talked into existence, not uniquely as a function of language, but as a result of coorientation, in the context of a collective commitment to activity. But, of course, the organization is already present in every conversation, and informs its outcomes at every step. The loop, however, never arrives at a point of equilibrium. The dance is never quite over. Non-linear, not linear processes: closure is never quite reached; organization is not an "it" but a becoming.

References

Austin, J. L. (1962). *How to do things with words.* Oxford: Oxford University Press.

Boden, D. (1994). *The business of talk: Organizations in action.* Cambridge, U.K.: Polity Press.

Boje, D. M. (1991). The storytelling organization: A study of story performance in an office-supply firm. *Administrative Science Quarterly, 36,* 106–126.

Boje, D. M. (1995). Stories of the storytelling organization: A postmodern analysis of Disney as "Tamara-land." *Academy of Management Journal, 38*: 997–1035.

Boje, D. M. (2001). *Narrative methods for organizational and communication research.* Thousand Oaks, CA: Sage.

Boje, D. M., Alvarez, R. C., & Schooling, B. (2001). Reclaiming stories in organization: Narratologies and action sciences. In S. Linstead, & R. Westwood (Eds.), *The language of organization* (pp. 132–175). London: Sage.

Brown, J. S., & Duguid, P. (2000). *The social life of information.* Boston: Harvard Business School Press.

Browning, L. D., Sitkin, S. B., Sutcliffe, K. M., Obstfeld, D., & Greene, R. W. (2000). Keep'em flying: The constitutive dynamic of an organizational change in the U.S. Air Force. *Electronic Journal of Communication, 10*(1/2), www.cios.org/www.ejc/v10n200.htm.

Browning, L. D., et al. (chapter 4, this book). In A. Nicotera, & L. Putnam (Eds.), *The communicative constitution of organization: Centering organizational communication.* Mahwah, NJ: Lawrence Erlbaum.

Bruner, J. (1991). The narrative construction of reality. *Critical Inquiry* (Autumn), 1–21.

Bybee, J., & Fleischman, S. (1995). *Modality in grammar and discourse.* Amsterdam/Philadelphia: John Benjamins.

Cooren, F. (2000). *The organizing property of communication.* Amsterdam/Philadelphia: John Benjamins.

Cooren, F. (2006). The organizational world as a plenum of agencies: Ontological stances and empirical illustrations. In F. Cooren, J. Taylor, and E. Van Every (Eds.), *Communication as organizing: Approaches to research into the dynamic of text and conversation* (pp. 81–100). Mahwah, NJ: Lawrence Erlbaum.

Cooren, F., & Fairhurst, G. T. (chapter 5, this book). Speech timing and spacing: The phenomenon of organizational closure. In A. Nicotera, & L. Putnam (Eds.), *The communicative constitution of organization: Centering organizational communication.* Mahwah, NJ: Lawrence Erlbaum.

Cooren, F., & Taylor, J. R. (1997). Organization as an effect of mediation: Redefining the link between organization and communication. *Communication Theory, 7.*

Cooren, F. & Taylor, J. R. (2000). Association and dissociation in an ecological controversy: The Great Whale case. In N. W. Coppola, & W. Karis (Eds.), *Connections and directions: Technical communication, deliberative rhetoric, and environmental discourse* (pp. 171–190). Norwood, NJ: Ablex.

Czarniawska, B. (1997). *Narrating the organization: Dramas of institutional identity.* Chicago: University of Chicago Press.

Czarniawska, B. (1998). *A narrative approach in organization studies.* Thousand Oaks, CA: Sage Publications.

Czarniawska, B. (1999). *Writing management: Organization theory as a literary genre.* Oxford: Oxford University Press.

Engestrom, Y. (1990). *Learning, working and imagining.* Helsinki: Orienta-Konsultit Oy.

Fairhurst, G. T., & Cooren, F. (2004). Organizational language-in-use: Interaction analysis, conversation analysis and speech act semantics. In D. Grant, C. Hardy, C. Oswick, N. Phillips, & L. Putnam (Eds.), *The Sage handbook of organizational discourse* (pp.131–152). London: Sage.

Fisher, W. R. (1987). *Human communication as narration: Toward a philosophy of reason, value, and action.* Columbia: University of South Carolina Press.

Garfinkel, H. (1967). *Studies in ethnomethodology.* Englewood Cliffs, NJ: Prentice-Hall.

Gibson, J. J. (1979). *The ecological approach to visual perception.* Boston: Houghton Mifflin.

Giddens, A. (1984). *The constitution of society: Outline of the theory of structuration.* Cambridge, U.K.: Polity.

Giroux, H., & Taylor, J. R. (2002). The justification of knowledge: Tracking the translations of quality. *Management Learning, 33*(4), 497–517.

Goffman, E. (1959). *The presentation of self in everyday life.* New York: Doubleday Anchor.

Greimas, A. (1987). *On meaning: Selected writings in semiotic theory.* (Trans. P. and J Perron. F. H Collins). Minneapolis: University of Minnesota Press.

Habermas, J. (1998). *On the pragmatics of communication.* Cambridge, MA: MIT Press.

Halliday, M. A. K., & Hasan, R. (1985). *Language, context, and text: Aspects of language in a social-semiotic perspective.* Oxford: Oxford University Press.

Heaton, L., & Taylor, J. R. (2002). Knowledge management and professional work: A communication perspective on the knowledge-based organization. *Management Communication Quarterly, 16*(2), 210–236.

Katambwe, J. M & Taylor, J. R. (2006). Modes of organizational integration. In F. Cooren, J. Taylor and E Van Every, eds., *Communication as organizing: Approaches to research into the dynamic of text and conversation.* Mahwah, NJ: Lawrence Erlbaum.

Krippendorff, K. (1998). Ecological narratives: Reclaiming the voice of theorized others (Unpublished Working Paper): Annenberg School of Communication, University of Pennsylvania.

Labov, W., & Fanshel, D. (1977). *Therapeutic discourse: Psychotherapy as conversation.* New York: Academic Press.

Latour, B. (1987). *Science in action.* Cambridge, MA: Harvard University Press.

Latour, B. (1994). On technical mediation—Philosophy, sociology, genealogy. *Common Knowledge, 3*(2), 29–64.

Lave, J. (1988). *Cognition in practice.* Cambridge, UK: Cambridge University Press.

Lave, J., & Wenger, E. (1991). *Situated learning: Legitimate peripheral participation.* Cambridge, UK: Cambridge University Press.

Maturana, H. (1997). *La objetividad: Un argumento para obligar (Objectivity: A compelling argument).* Santiago: Dolmen Ediciones.

Maturana, H. R. (1991). Science in daily life: The ontology of scientific explanations. In F. Steier (Ed.), *Research and reflexity: Self-reflexivity as social process* (pp. 30–52). Newbury Park, CA: Sage.

McPhee, R. D. & Zaug, P. (2000). The communicative constitution of organization: A framework for explanation. *Electronic Journal of Communication, 10* (1/2), www.cios.org/www.ejc/v10n200.htm.

McPhee, R. D. & Iverson, J. (Chapter 3, this book). Some perspectives on the communicative constitution of organizations. In A. Nicotera, & L. Putnam (Eds.), *The communicative constitution of organization: Centering organizational communication*. Mahwah, NJ: Lawrence Erlbaum.

Newcomb, T. (1953). An approach to the study of communicative acts. *Psychological Review, 60*, 393–404.

Orr, J. (1996). *Talking about machines: An ethnography of a modern job*. Ithaca, NY: IRL Press.

Orton, J. D. & Weick, K. E. (1990). Loosely coupled systems: A reconceptualization. *Academy of Management Review, 15*(2), 203–233.

Ricoeur, P. (1981). *Hermeneutics and the human sciences* (Trans. J. B. Thompson). Cambridge: Cambridge University Press.

Ricoeur, P. (1991). *From text to action* (Trans. K. Blamey, J. B. Thompson). Evanston IL: Northwestern University Press.

Robichaud, D., Giroux, H., & Taylor, J.R. (2004). The meta-conversation: The recursive property of language as the key to organizing. *Academy of Management Review, 29*(4), 617–634.

Schegloff, E. A. (1991). Conversation analysis and socially shared cognition. In L. B. Resnick, J. L. Levine, & S.D.Teasley (Eds.), *Perspectives on socially shared cognition* (pp. 150–170). Washington, DC: American Psychological Association.

Shannon, C. E. (1948). A mathematical theory of communication. *Bell System Technical Journal, 27*, 379–428; 623–656.

Sigman, S. J. (Ed.) (1995). *The consequentiality of communication*. Hillsdale, NJ: Lawrence Erlbaum.

Stohl, C. (1995). *Organizational communication: Connectedness in action*. Thousand Oaks, CA: Sage.

Suchman, L. (1995). Making work visible. *Communications of the ACM, 39*(9), 56–68.

Suchman, L. (1996). Constituting shared workspaces. In Y. Engeström & D. Middleton (Eds.), *Cognition and communication at work* (pp. 35–60). Cambridge, U.K.: Cambridge University Press.

Taylor, J. R. (1999). What is "organizational communication"?: Communication as a dialogic of text and conversation. *The Communication Review, 3*(1–2), 21–63.

Taylor, J. R. (2000). What is an organization? *Electronic Journal of Communication, 10*(1/2). www.cios.org/www.ejc/v10n200.htm.

Taylor, J. R. (2001a). The "rational" organization reconsidered: An exploration of some of the organizational implications of self-organizing. *Communication Theory, 11*(2), 137–177.

Taylor, J. R. (2001b). Toward a theory of imbrication and organizational communication. *American Journal of Semiotics, 17*(2), 1–29.

Taylor, J. R. (2005). Engaging organization through worldview. In S. May, & D. K. Mumby (Eds.), *Engaging organizational communication: Theory and Research.* Thousand Oaks, CA: Sage.

Taylor, J. R., & Cooren, F. (1997). What makes communication "organizational"? How the many voices of the organization become the *one* voice of *an* organization. *Journal of Pragmatics, 27*, 409–438.

Taylor, J. R., & Robichaud, D. (2004). Finding the organization in the communication: Discourse as action and sensemaking. *Organization, 11(3),* 395–413.

Taylor, J. R., & Van Every, E. J. (2000). *The emergent organization: Communication as its site and surface.* Mahwah, NJ: Lawrence Erlbaum.

Taylor, J. R., Cooren, F., Giroux, N., & Robichaud, D. (1996). The communicational basis of organization: Between the conversation and the text. *Communication Theory, 6*(1), 1–39.

Watzlawick, P., Beavin, J. H., & Jackson, D. (1967). *Pragmatics of human communication: A study of interactional patterns, pathologies, and paradoxes.* New York: W.W. Norton.

Webster's New World Dictionary. (1964). Cleveland and New York: World Publishing.

Weick, K. E. (1979). *The social psychology of organizing (revised ed.).* Reading, MA: Random House.

Weick, K. E. (1985). Sources of order in underorganized systems: Themes in recent organizational research. In Y. S. Lincoln (Ed.), *Organization theory and inquiry* (pp.106–136). Beverly Hills, CA: Sage.

Weick, K. E. (1995). *Sensemaking in organizations.* Thousand Oaks: Sage.

Weick, K. E., & Browning, L. D. (1986). Argumentation and narration in organizational communication. *Yearly Review of Management of the Journal of Management, 12*(2), 243–259.

Wenger, E. (1998). *Communities of practice: Learning, meaning and identity.* New York: Cambridge University Press.

Zilber, T. B. (2002). Institutionalism as an interplay between actions, meanings and actors: The case of a rape crisis center in Israel. *Academy of Management Journal, 45*(1), 234–254.

7

THEORY BUILDING

Comparisons of CCO Orientations

Linda L. Putnam and Robert D. McPhee

The chapters in this volume juxtapose different approaches to CCO through incorporating a common framework. Each chapter articulates a particular version of CCO while it appropriates the four flows from Chapter 2.

Even though the four-flow framework is not entirely isomorphic with each orientation, it serves as a springboard to compare and contrast different approaches to CCO. This chapter synthesizes these orientations through examining how they employ the four flows, describing how they identify and explicate important features of CCO, and noting distinctions in how they conceptualize communication in CCO. Finally, the chapter concludes with some underlying themes that all the approaches share, ones that provide directions for future theory development. Our goal in this chapter is to acknowledge the affinities between orientations while striving to preserve their differences.

Adapting and Responding to the Four Flows

Addressing McPhee and Zaug's (Chapter 2) four flows provides a springboard to explicate important features and distinctions in CCO. A brief summary of how each chapter incorporates the four flows sets up these topics. McPhee and Zaug contend that four distinct flows of interaction processes constitute organizations. Membership negotiation focuses on linking members to each other and to the organization and establishing organizational boundaries. Self-structuring refers to interactions aimed at the design, implementation, and control of organizational processes. The third flow, activity coordination, centers on interdependent work and adapting interactions to work situations and problems. Finally, institutional positioning entails interactions aimed at situating the organization in its larger environment. Each flow has its own dynamic structure that is analytically separate from the other flows.

McPhee and Iverson (Chapter 3) embrace and extend the four flows by noting how CCO occurs differently for each flow. The four flows are generic communicative processes that bridge the local and the global and that intersect as well as operate separately. While all four flows are necessary for CCO, self-structuring seems most directly related to constituting the organization as a whole.

In Chapter 4, Browning, Greene, Sitkin, Sutcliffe, and Obstfeld emphasize the intersections of the flows and how different combinations constitute organizing in diverse ways, even though they start at the same place. They uncover an important finding; that is, the flows become more complex as they unite in a loose, synergistic way. Contradictions such as fixed flexibility arise at the intersections of the flows and signal the development of new organizational forms, particularly as they reconstitute different institutional positions among the Air Force, the technicians, and the Civilian Depot.

Cooren and Fairhurst (Chapter 5) challenge the role of agency in the four flows and focus on explaining how communication integrates the human and the organization, rather than vacillating between the two types of agency. Their chapter takes a bottom-up perspective on the four flows to demonstrate how the organization surfaces in the micro-associations between human and nonhuman interactions.

In Chapter 6, Taylor introduces tight and loose coupling as ways to explain connections among the flows, but Taylor seems to privilege activity coordination as a fundamental CCO process. For Taylor, coorientation through language use leads to the emergence of structures that are tightly coupled. Through self-structuring, these coorientations coalesce and extend into communities of activities (or an organization) that are loosely coupled and distinct from the members of any other community. As these communities become interwoven in continuously renewed sets of relationships, they develop into intercommunity coorientations and interorganizational systems. Thus, Taylor differs from McPhee and Zaug in seemingly privileging a particular flow and in making connections between the flows to trace the development of CCO. Browning, et al. differ from Taylor in locating the organization at the overlap or point of synergy among the flows.

Developing CCO Theories

The seven chapters in this volume identify and explicate important concerns in developing CCO theories. In particular, each one wrestles with the notion of what an organization is and how organizing processes produce patterns that endure over time. Each chapter also focuses on the nature and origin of structure as an important component of CCO. Finally, the chapters in this volume reframe the micro–macro divide as concerns for bottom-up and top-down approaches to theory building. Figure 7.1 compares and contrasts the different approaches on these issues.

Nature of Organizations

CCO approaches describe the "whole" and depict how the whole comes to be in different ways. For McPhee and Zaug (Chapter 2) and McPhee and Iverson (Chapter 3), the organization is a system or complex set of social relationships in which the four flows and the rules and resources linked to them become enacted across time and space. Thus, the organization surfaces as a sign or a resource that mediates actions and functions rather than an agent or an entity. A sign becomes the referent point that makes the social system meaningful. Each of the four flows constitutes this resource in different ways. Browning, et al., in Chapter 4 concur with this position, but they see the organization emerging from the intersection of two or more of the four flows. The organization, thus, grows out of the overlap among the flows rather than from each flow constituting sites in different ways. In effect, Browning, et al., differ from McPhee and Iverson in treating the organization as a single loosely-coupled system that unites and syncretizes different flows.

Features of CCO Theories	McPhee & Zaug	McPhee & Iverson	Browning, et al.	Cooren & Fairhurst	Taylor
Organization as a whole	Social interaction system	System of complex social relations	Uniting of flows; synthetic and syncretic flows	Strings of associations from hybrid actions	Communities of activities and sensemaking
Nature of structure	Mutual influence and relevance among four communication flows	Contextual; duality of structure; draws on past rules and resources	Overlap among four flows	Stabilization of interactions between humans and nonhumans	Coorientations drawn from properties of communication
Approach to theory development	Deductive	Deductive	Inductive	Inductive	Deductive
Types of communication	*General* All types of communication flows of interaction episodes	*General* Multiple forms of social interactions and practices	*General* Improvisational routines, meanings, tacit rules, information flow	*General* Role of nonverbal; interactions between humans and nonhumans	*General* Texts, interaction episodes, grammars, retrospective sensemaking
Role of communication in CCO process	Necessary conditions	Characteristic process	Characteristic process	Necessary conditions	Necessary conditions
Locus of communication	Local and distantiated through four flows	Hermeneutic circle of local interactions and distant sites	Local situated interactions; overlap of four flows	Dis-local; collapses local and distant	Local coorientations and distant meta-story
Time and space distantiation	Draws on rules and resources of the past	Sites, the four flows are spatially distant	Memory traces of past practices	The present is contained in the past and in the future	Texts abstracted from interactions that extend across time and space
Representation and referencing	Identity negotiation	Representing or referencing a sign or image	Representing the Air Force while referencing entrepreneurial activities	Speaking on behalf of hybrid actions	Speaking for one community while participating in another

Figure 7.1 Mapping CCO theories

Taylor (Chapter 6) views the organization as a community of activities and sensemaking that emerges through coorientations. The whole, then, develops in the same way as the parts through a coorientation process that transfers agency from individuals to a collective. Distinguishing between a community of activity and a complex system of social relations (McPhee and Iverson) seems almost like splitting hairs. At the level of the collective per se, these CCO approaches seem very close. Yet, McPhee and Iverson differ from Taylor in placing emphasis on the communicative constituted rules and resource that serve as building blocks for the four flows in this system.

Moreover, the two approaches appear similar in how the organization is recognized. For Taylor, the collective emerges through reflexive monitoring or retrospective sensemaking as participants become aware of the "we." Thus, a transcendent rationality becomes linked to the organization as a whole, one that resembles a meta-story or narrative. This sense of the whole has a referential quality that seems very similar to McPhee and Iverson's notion of a sign.

In contrast, Cooren and Fairhurst (Chapter 5) treat organizations as strings of associations that result from humans interacting with each other and with nonhumans to produce texts that transcend time and space. Organizations, then, are comprised of memory traces of past associations, coordinated activities, and interactions between humans and things. The conception of a whole in this definition seems less well-formed than treating organizations as systems or communities of activity. However, these approaches agree that some type of whole emerges from CCO processes.

Origin and Nature of Structure

Another feature that the four chapters address is the origin and nature of structure. For Taylor (Chapter 6), structures are implicated in interactions, such as speech acts, narrative schema, and grammatical structures. Thus, the properties of communication, including the sequences, patterns, and history of interactions, serve as the origin and nature of structure. For example, Taylor notes that particular grammatical patterns, interaction episodes, and texts capture "the a priori system of forms of organization" as they coorient individuals to getting things done (Taylor, 1993, p. 78).

Cooren and Fairhurst (Chapter 5) extend this work by adding nonhuman entities to the origin and nature of structure. Nonhuman entities contribute to developing structures through dislocating and stabilizing interactions. Human actors orient to such nonhuman texts as contracts, objects, and documents to stabilize schemes of action. It is this stabilization of actions and interactions among humans and nonhumans that produce structures.

In contrast to these approaches, McPhee and Zaug (Chapter 2) cast the nature of structure as the four communication flows and the mutual relevance among them. Browning, et al. (Chapter 4) expand on the mutual relevance among the four flows and locate structures in the overlap among them. McPhee and Iverson (Chapter 3) situate these flows in a structurational view in which language mediates experiences through a duality of structure (Giddens, 1984). Actors rely on local experiences to produce and reproduce the structural rules and resources that they draw on in their interactions. In their view, even though language is clearly patterned and sequenced, the effect of any illocutionary act, such as declaring or performing, depends on unknown conditions and unintended consequences in the social context, not on innate structural forms. Thus, structural relations emerge from contextual-based interpretive practices. For these approaches, then, the origin and nature of structure is rooted in the four flows (McPhee and Zaug), overlap among the flows (Browning, et al.), duality of structure that draws on past rules and resources (McPhee & Iverson), interactions between human and nonhuman objects (Cooren & Fairhurst), or the structuring properties of communication (Taylor).

In effect, identifying what a collective is and what becomes stabilized or structured are common features in each of the chapters. Organizations emerge as complex social systems, strings of association from hybrid actions, overlaps of different flows, and communities of activity and sensemaking. In like manner, these chapters view communication as simultaneously stabilizing and dislocating structural patterns. Through focusing simultaneously on the processes of organizing and developing collectives, these chapters take issue with common notions about micro and macro levels.

Reframing the Micro–Macro Debate

Overall, these approaches challenge the age-old debate about the divide between micro–macro levels. This debate also surfaces in the division between the local and the global; organizing and organization; and local accomplishments and enduring systems (Fairhurst & Putnam, 2004). Micro analyses typically begin with interactions among individuals in bounded episodes that move to relationships among processes as ways to accomplish complex organizations (McPhee & Poole, 2001). Theorists who favor macro orientations often treat the organization writ large as distinct from and dominant over local interactions while scholars who privilege micro local interactions often marginalize or collapse the macro into the micro.

CCO theorists also differ in how the micro and macro come together, as evident in approaches that cast micro-processes as individual laminations or layering of conversations (Boden, 1994) or as interaction episodes that are integrated into systems through producing and reproducing rules and resources (McPhee, 1988; McPhee & Poole, 2001), or as imbrication of emerging structures that become unquestioned routines (Taylor & Van Every, 2000). Thus, CCO scholars struggle with whether to collapse the levels, treat them as separate layers, scale up, or cast them as multiple processes that occur in different arenas.

Some scholars even avoid using the terms "micro" and "macro" because the words connote reified levels (Taylor & Van Every, 2000). In fact, grounded-in-action scholars remain indifferent to the micro–macro debate because they believe that society does not happen at different levels or that individual actions are not building toward higher or lower levels (Fairhurst & Putnam, 2004).

CCO theorists in this volume reframe this debate as differences in bottom-up and top-down approaches to theory building. This reframing moves away from the notion of levels by centering on how to construct CCO theories. The issue, then, becomes the point of entry for analyzing organizational processes rather than whether the theory is grounded on the micro level or focused on macro institutions.

Deductive versus Inductive Theory Building

Bottom-up and top-down approaches link directly to different ways of engaging in theory building. Deductive approaches set forth logical requirements from the top-down and then show how processes of social interaction meet these requirements while inductive scholars develop theory by searching for organizing relationships and then reasoning up from them. In this volume, McPhee and Zaug (Chapter 2) and McPhee and Iverson (Chapter 3) ground their theory development in concepts such as fields of messages or "flows" (Lash & Urry, 1994) and in a recasting of Parson's functional scheme (Parsons & Smelser, 1965). Hence, they follow a deductive process of developing underlying logics and exploring ways in which chains of interaction surface in broader organizational domains.

In Chapter 6, Taylor also embraces a deductive approach through drawing on coorientation theory to examine how collective identity or a community of activities emerges and becomes separated from situated interactions. Coorientation, however, is a construct that Taylor and his colleagues developed in inductive ways from examining the organizing properties of individuals who orient to each other to get things done (Robichaud, Giroux, and Taylor, 2004; Taylor & Robichaud, 2004, 2007). Thus, Taylor's approach relies on the inductive properties and practices of language users while deductively examining organizations as meta-texts that represent communities of activity.

In contrast, Cooren and Fairhurst (Chapter 5) and Browning, et. al. (Chapter 4) adopt inductive approaches to theory development. Cooren and Fairhurst use a bottom-up approach to supplement and critique deductive analyses and to show how humans engage with nonhumans in organizing that spans space and time. Cooren and Fairhurst (Chapter 5) aim to bridge the gap between the inductive and the deductive through scaling up from micro-associations and reasoning downward through hybrid actions that string these associations together. Similarly, Browning, et al. use inductive argument to uncover how combinations of different flows produce system complexities. Both chapters proceed in an inductive manner through revealing interaction patterns that capture the adaptive nature of organizing as well as discover features that emerge in the process.

The issue, though, is not whether to move deductively from an assumed organizational whole to its component parts or inductively from interaction processes that constitute the organization as a complex social form. Both directions are clearly necessary to explain CCO processes. The deductive path is always tempting to scholars who start with a conceptual problem which they aim to address; the inductive path, though, adds complexity and grounded experiences to theory development. The field needs both modes to advance CCO and to add variety to theoretical explanations, yet both should be open to critique for what they conceal as well as reveal.

Conceptualizing Communication in the CCO Process

As noted above, the chapters in this volume identify issues that are central to building CCO theories—describing the organization as a whole, accounting for the origin and nature of structure, and explaining interaction processes through inductive and/or deductive approaches. Communication is central to CCO and the chapters in this volume index the types of communication that have CCO potential, the role that communication plays in these processes, and the locus of communication in CCO. These descriptions fall into the following polar choices: specific versus general forms, necessary conditions versus characteristic processes, and situated local versus contextually distant communication.

Specific versus General Forms

Some CCO scholars believe that particular communicative acts or narrow properties of language constitute social structures (Taylor, 1993; Taylor & Van Every, 2000). Thus, to examine CCO, scholars need to focus on the syntax, speech acts, or particular symbols. For instance, the speech act, "I now pronounce you husband and wife," is famous for constituting the marital relation. Similarly, the signing of an organizational charter might constitute an organization legally. Linguistic structures and symbolic acts, however, depend on contextual practices. Thus, the meaning of language use and the interpretation of a ritualistic event depend on situating practices in context.

Unlike the early work on CCO, contributors to this volume suggest that most or all organizationally relevant communication has constitutive force; thus, the authors favor a generalist as opposed to a specialist communication position. Specifically, in Chapter 5, Cooren and Fairhurst emphasize nonhuman contributions, thus underscoring the role of nonverbal communication in constituting organizations. Taylor in Chapter 6 incorporates a variety of communicative forms that contribute to CCO, including language properties, the practices of language users, texts as abstracted from interactions, episodes, and retrospective sensemaking. Browning, et. al. in Chapter 4 add the flow of communication, improvisational routines, and meanings aligned with rituals and tacit rules. Thus, as McPhee and Zaug contend in Chapter 2, grounding constitution in a narrow range of linguistic structures or selecting only certain communicative acts as having CCO potential is likely to fail.

Necessary Conditions versus Characteristic Processes

Approaches to CCO also differ as to whether they center on the conditions necessary for communication to constitute organizing or whether they focus on how communication shapes particular characteristic processes of organizations. McPhee and Zaug in Chapter 2, Cooren and Fairhurst in Chapter 5, and Taylor in Chapter 6 situate their work on the conditions that are necessary for communication to constitute organizations. The authors develop their orientations through addressing the question, "What communicative processes or contributions must be present for an organization (or organizing) to exist, endure, or have essential organizational features?" For McPhee and Zaug, the communicative constitution of organizations requires all four types of message flows or interaction processes. Complex organizations exist in the relatedness of these flows.

For Cooren and Fairhurst, a necessary condition for CCO is interactions between humans and nonhumans that produce a string of associations through hybrid actions. These associations have staying power and the capacity to transcend time and space. For Taylor, the communicative processes that must be present for organizing to endure are coorientations that extend across time and space and develop into communities of action.

McPhee and Iverson in Chapter 3 embrace the opposite pole and focus on the way communication defines the characteristic processes of organizations. This position emphasizes the properties that typify powerful modern organizations and how they become truncated or altered in small-scale forms. Thus, McPhee and Iverson focus on how each flow, as a typical but varied process, actually accomplishes constitution via organizational communication. Browning, et al. take the same path but with a very different style, one that stresses how theory must respond to the complexity of organizations. Through the use of examples, they demonstrate that particular overlaps of flows are inevitable in complex organizations.

Overall, emphasis on the conditions necessary for CCO or on the characteristic processes of CCO are both valuable in answering two questions, specifically, what is organizing and what is so peculiar about modern complex organizations? Even though the chapters in this volume typically focus on one or the other of these questions, the mutual relevance of these chapters indicates that each has important implications for the other.

Situated Local versus Contextually Distant Communication

Constitutive theories that place a primary emphasis on local interactions contend that many separate social interactions manifest an organization through episodic processes. At one end of this continuum, if communication is organizing, purely and totally, then researchers can study an organization by studying specific episodes. Early CCO work adopted this stance in arguing that situated and local practices such as double interacts, layered conversations, narrative grammars, and particular speech acts could capture what is essential about organizations (Boden, 1994; Cooren, 2000; Taylor, 1993, Weick, 1979). Similarly, imbrication, which refers to emerging structures that become unquestioned routines, might position CCO in locally situated, individual communication episodes (Taylor, 2001).

The chapters in this book, however, contend that focusing on local, situated interactions is not enough to account for CCO. These chapters contribute to the opposite pole; that is, CCO necessarily involves multiple, interconnected communicative episodes that become distant from each other in context. For instance, in one conversation a supervisor might assign a subordinate a task while in the second interaction, he/she reports back to the supervisor on completion of this task. These episodes are internally related—for instance, the first one becomes an instance of "supervision" (as opposed to "attempted supervision") because of the more distant, contextually-rooted second one.

In a similar way, Taylor in Chapter 6 emphasizes that local or situated coorientations become nested in communities of activity that are distant and contextually-based. Through sensemaking, each community develops a transcendent rationality or meta-story that becomes removed from but loosely linked to local interactions. Cooren (2006) and Cooren and Fairhurst in Chapter 5 underscore the importance of contextuality in describing strings of association that transcend time and space across local episodes. In a similar way, McPhee (1985, 1988) points out how organizational structure as a communication phenomenon exists in multiple sites that are distant from the local interactions that constituted them. Thus, each CCO orientation in this volume highlights the critical role of distant and contextually-rooted social interactions.

The subtle differences between these approaches, however, merit discussion. Specifically, Cooren and Fairhurst in Chapter 5 collapse the local and the distant, by arguing that every local interaction episode is "dis-local." Dis-local means that each set of interactions carries both the present and the distant in the discourse. In this approach, then, memory traces and material and textual effects "transcend" within the local. In contrast, McPhee and Iverson in Chapter 3 treat locally-situated interactions as functioning differently in each flow and developing different CCO processes. These processes cannot simply be integrated and are distinct from the organization that emerges from them as a social system.

The critical issue that surfaces from this discussion is, what sort of contextual structures are involved in interactions that contribute to CCO? Does local constitution dominate CCO as an explanatory force at the macro-level? If constitution occurs in multiple distanciated sites, a key challenge for communication scholars is how do these sites become integrated? Among the chapters in this volume, Cooren and Fairhurst

(Chapter 5) may have the clearest response to this question. They contend that nonhuman agencies put the local out of place and carry the stability of an organizational whole, but perhaps only if accompanied by stable sensemaking practices. But what happens across diverse sites? If integration occurs in multiple ways, as McPhee and Iverson suggest, then how are these sites integrated? These questions raise additional issues that future CCO theorizing should address.

In summary, the chapters in this volume take important steps in advancing the role of communication in CCO. First, all concur that a myriad of linguistic, nonverbal, and symbolic interactions contribute to CCO. Moreover, different forms of communication, such as linguistic properties, nonverbal symbols, and interaction episodes, work together in complex ways to constitute organizations. Some theories emphasize the conditions that are necessary for CCO to emerge while others focus on the ways that communication defines characteristic processes of complex organizational systems. Finally, these chapters advance CCO theories through emphasizing the way that local situated interactions become distant and how this distantiation contributes to CCO.

Underlying Themes and Future Directions

In addition to issues central to CCO theory development, three features emerge in these chapters as concerns for future thinking about CCO— transporting interactions across time and space, representing and referencing organizations, and the materiality and embodied practice.

Transporting Communication across Time and Space

Each of the chapters in this book underscores the importance of transporting organizational communication across time and space. Transporting across time and space is similar to local and distantiated communication, but it focuses on what time and space mean in this process. McPhee and Iverson in Chapter 3 use the appealing term "sites" to indicate that flows of communication are temporally and physically situated. The relationship among these sites is critical and flows from one locus and time period have the potential to instantiate practices and structures in another point and time, thus creating distance from the initial communication that produced the flows. For example, storytelling in membership negotiation instantiates boundary-defining practices that span time and space. Browning, et al. (Chapter 4) illustrate this time spanning by showing how the pilots and technicians negotiate entrepreneur boundaries while "never putting the pilots at risk." Memory traces of past practices that protected the pilots instantiate these interactions while they simultaneously negotiated and legitimated new roles.

In like manner, Cooren and Fairhurst in Chapter 5 emphasize the importance of transporting interactions across time and space. In their view, organizations emerge in strings of associations in which "the here and now interactions are contaminated in the there and then and will become a new here and now." Similarly, for Taylor (Chapter 6), texts are the forms of communication that extend time and space and are abstracted from situated interactions.

Thus, these approaches set forth related, but slightly different models of space and time. For Cooren and Fairhurst, actors are immersed in interactions that span space and time while for McPhee and Iverson, rules and resources produced are separated from interactions across space and time. However, both approaches demonstrate that spanning time and space is central to understanding CCO.

The issue of space, however, seems underdeveloped in these theories. With the exception of McPhee and Iverson, who treat the four flows as temporarily and physically distinct sites, the other approaches mention space without developing it. Thus, one key feature that seems necessary for a CCO model is a form of transporting interactions across time and space: An important agenda for future research is conceptualizing the role of space in CCO theories.

Representing and Referencing the Organization

Representing or referencing the organization also emerges as a fundamental feature in CCO perspectives. This process is central to McPhee and Zaug's (Chapter 2) fourth flow, identity negotiation, as a part of institutional positioning. As a CCO process, representation refers to speaking for others or referencing the whole, for example, as a sign (McPhee & Iverson, Chapter 3). A sign is necessary to develop an image so that actors can represent the organization to a variety of audiences and can distinguish it from other collectives. Referencing also occurs in the first flow, membership negotiation, as members speak on behalf of the "we," reference a group that is immediately present, or negotiate difference or distinctiveness for the "we."

Speaking on behalf of others is also critical to Cooren and Fairhurst's (Chapter 5) approach. They treat organizations as hybrid actions constituted by associations among many different actors in which someone or something speaks on behalf of others. They illustrate how physical signs and furniture arrangements in buildings convey messages about entering and exiting, security checks, and surveillance measures. Thus, the nonhumans speak to visitors and represent tenants and managers who are not physically present when visitors enter.

For Taylor in Chapter 6, organizations exist in ecological communities of practice that coorient their activities through inter-community communication. Organizations become bilingual and speak for one community while participating in another; hence, representative voices pass judgment on a community while presenting the organization to others in its environment. Browning, et al. in Chapter 4 offer an example of these representations and how they shift the balance of power among communities. In their entrepreneurial activities, technicians and pilots function as separate but interrelated communities who form a power block separate from the Air Force, yet they simultaneously represent the military to the Civilian Depot. These representations distance technicians from their low-level hierarchical roles in the Air Force and grant them power through aligning them with the pilots in negotiating entrepreneurial activities.

The process of representing and speaking on behalf of multiple communities seems vital to CCO. While it is part of two flows, membership negotiation and institutional positioning, it is tied to multiple audiences and interfaces with diverse communities of activities. It extends beyond individuals as boundary spanners and beyond membership negotiation to constitute inter-communities. It seems pivotal to CCO processes of drawing and dissolving boundaries, forming distinct but interlocking communities, and reshaping institutional relationships. Future theorizing about CCO needs to develop this feature in much greater depth.

Materiality and Embodied Practice

In a similar way, these chapters touch on but minimize attention to materiality in CCO. McPhee and Iverson in Chapter 3 note that self-structuring involves physical manipulations of material objects and Taylor in Chapter 6 advocates that CCO theories need to examine how communication interfaces with practical problems in the material world. This occurs through the ways that conversations and meanings move away from situated interactions into texts. Thus, texts mediate between situated interactions and material facets of organizational life (Taylor & Van Every, 2000). While these approaches clearly avoid collapsing the material into the social or divorcing the material from the nonmaterial, they provide only limited guidance as to how CCO interfaces with material reality.

Cooren and Fairhurst in Chapter 5 give direct attention to the role of nonhumans in the CCO process. Nonhumans as a category refer to material objects such as documents, bodies, physical structures, material resources, and recording devices. Because physical objects remain after conversations end, interacting with these objects and making sense of these interactions stabilizes CCO. Although Browning, et al. do not discuss materiality per se, they illustrate how interacting with a physical object, such as a brief four-page document, led the technicians to interpret the AFI policy as non-binding and open to negotiation. This brevity and lack of detail in a physical document fostered different patterns of CCO.

The issue for CCO, it seems, is to recognize how material objects and communication are mutually intertwined in practice (Laclau & Mouffe, 1990). Cooren and Fairhurst take the lead in this respect. However, more attention needs to be paid to embodied practices and the contingent and semiotic aspects of objects (Heath & Luff, 2000). Consistent with Cooren and Fairhurst's approach, this recommendation requires observing work practices, not just for tracking social interactions, but for understanding how these routines are embodied, the role of the body in these practices, and the way nonhumans play independent roles in CCO.

Other scholars have argued that constitution theories treat the material, and especially the natural environment, as malleable for human use and as passive (Rogers, 1998). Cooren and Fairhurst in Chapter 5 counter this notion that objects are passive through granting them agency in the CCO process. They demonstrate how humans shape material objects and how material objects affect communication in the CCO process. However, they seem to preserve the ideal/material binary in which words and social meanings make objects into signs. As Rogers (1998, p. 248) notes, "When we see an object, we see it through the screen of language, and hence what we see is the meaning. The object itself becomes a sign (i.e., it appears to stand in for meaning)." This segmentation preserves hierarchical relations, especially ones among masculine and feminine relationships that are socially and culturally linked to such concepts as nature, the body, and matter.

Rather than presuming that objects and the natural world are signs mediated through language, CCO theorists might treat materiality as a multiplicity of forces which participate in communicative processes (Rogers, 1998). Adopting this assumption would shift the focus away from how humans and nonhumans interact to how each affects the other, develops fluidity in the production of practices, and penetrates boundaries between them. The focal point on materiality is on a dialogue between them in which each develops CCO in its own right, but in nonlinear and unpredictable ways.

Cooren and Fairhurst in Chapter 5 begin this process by tracking how the decision to install a sign-security system in an apartment complex grew out of multiple meetings, how interactions from two years ago continued to influence organizing through the sign and security devices, and how these objects invited visitors to check in at the front desk and dissuaded them from entering without being identified. What is missing is how each affected the other in constituting organizing, what variations existed in using the security system, and how did the material objects alter the nature of organizing in unpredictable and nonlinear ways. Thus, material reality is not a singular entity; but rather it becomes an independent player in the CCO process.

Mapping CCO Theories

This chapter engages in theory building about CCO through arraying the options, comparing the chapters, and drawing distinctions among the approaches. Our analysis of the different chapters reveals nine features that seem important in developing CCO theories. These nine features appear in Figure 7.1, which compares and contrasts the five CCO approaches.

A close examination of this figure reveals a number of similarities in CCO orientations. Specifically, each of the approaches adopts "a communication in general" stance by treating all forms of communication as important in the process of constituting organizations. Even though some approaches put more emphasis on the properties of language (Taylor, Chapter 6) and others on interactions with nonhumans (Cooren & Fairhurst, Chapter 5), all types of communication contribute to CCO.

In addition, each of the approaches emphasizes the importance of communication episodes that span time and space and are distant from local interactions. They differ in how this occurs—through texts, memory traces, dis-locating, past practices, or constitutive rules and resources—but they see communication as situated in local interactions that become distant in time and context from initial episodes. The CCO approaches in this volume also appear similar in underscoring the importance of representation and referencing of the whole, through constituting organizations as signs, hybrid actions, the "we," and communities of activities. Thus, even though each chapter offers different views as to how communication constitutes organizations, they draw their approaches from similar concerns and have parallel stances regarding these features.

The chapters in this volume, however, differ in their approaches to theory development, the role of communication in the CCO process, and how communication develops structuring patterns linked to the organization as a whole. Cooren and Fairhurst in Chapter 5 build their theoretical explanations in an inductive manner through casting the organization as a product of associations that are dis-local and become hybrid actions. Thus, the whole of an organization is a loose collection of strings of associations that have become stable through interactions between humans and nonhumans. Similarly, Browning et al. (Chapter 4) move inductively from pairs of communication flows to demonstrate how organizing and the collective whole emerge from uniting the flows. The inductive nature of theorizing in these approaches provides strong insights about the constitution of structures but leaves gaps in accounting for sets and interrelationships among organizations. How do different clusters or communities of associations interrelate?

The remaining three chapters engage in theory building in deductive ways. McPhee and Zaug (Chapter 2) and McPhee and Iverson (Chapter 3) begin with the organization as a system of complex social relations and move to explain how the four flows emerge in interaction patterns that lead to different ways of structuring organizational processes. In Chapter 6, Taylor builds theory from organizations as communities of activities and sensemaking, but he aligns coorientations with the development of these communities. The difference in these approaches returns to a critique of the four flows model; that is, what accounts for mutual relevance and influence among the flows?

What seems particularly important about the four flows model is the idea of sites. Sites in this sense captures the notion of physical location in ways that the other theories do not. Thus, future CCO theory development should attend to the notion of distantiation through space, as well as through time. In addition, CCO theory development needs to devote greater attention to materiality, especially the ways that the body, nature, and physical objects interact and influence CCO, independent of language and sign systems.

Overall, the field has changed dramatically since the inception of discussions about CCO. Scholars have moved away from simple explanations that communication enacts interlocking behaviors and structures that constitute organizations. They have developed alternative theories for how constitution occurs, what forms the organization as a whole, and what features seem critical for CCO, theory development. Through building on chapters in this volume and similar publications, the next decade of CCO work has the potential to make major leaps in understanding the beguiling phrase, "communication constitutes organizations."

References

Boden, D. (1994). *The business of talk: Organizations in action*. Cambridge, U.K.: Polity Press.

Cooren, F. (2000). *The organizing property of communication*. Amsterdam/ Philadelphia, PA: John Benjamins.

Cooren. F. (2006). The organizational world as a plenum of agencies. In J. R. Taylor & E. J. Van Every (Eds.), *Communication as organizing: Empirical and theoretical explorations in the dynamic of text and conversation* (pp. 81–100). Mahwah, NJ: Lawrence Erlbaum.

Fairhurst, G. T., & Putnam, L. L. (2004). Organizations as discursive constructions. *Communication Theory, 14,* 5–26.

Giddens, A. (1984). *The constitution of society: Outline of the theory of structuration.* Berkeley, CA: University of California Press.

Heath, C., & Luff, P. (2000). *Technology in action.* Cambridge, U.K.: Cambridge University Press.

Laclau, E., & Mouffe, C. (1990). Post-Marxism without apologies. In E. Laclau (Ed.), *The making of political identities.* London: Verso.

Lash, S., & Urry, J. (1994). *Economies of sign and space.* London: Sage.

McPhee, R. D. (1985). Formal structure and organizational communication. In R. D. McPhee, & P. K. Tompkins (Eds.), *Organizational communication: Traditional themes and new directions* (pp. 149–178). Beverly Hills, CA: Sage.

McPhee, R. D. (1988). Vertical communication chains: Toward an integrated view. *Management Communication Quarterly, 1,* 455–493.

McPhee, R. D., & Poole, M. S. (2001). Organizational structures and configurations. In F. M. Jablin, & L. L. Putnam, (Eds.), *The new handbook of organizational communication: Advances in theory, research, and methods* (pp. 503–543). Thousand Oaks, CA: Sage.

Parsons, T., & Smelser, N. J. (1965). *Economy and society.* New York: Free Press.

Robichaud, D., Giroux, H., & Taylor, J. R. (2004). The metaconversation: The recursive property of language as a key to organizing. *The Academy of Management Review, 29,* 617–634.

Rogers, R. A. (1998). Overcoming the objectification of nature in constitutive theories: Toward a transhuman, materialist theory of communication. *Western Journal of Communication, 62,* 244–272.

Taylor, J. R. (1993). *Rethinking the theory of organizational communication: How to read an organization.* Norwood, NJ: Ablex.

Taylor, J. R. (2000). What is an organization? *Electronic Journal of Communication, 10*(1/2). www.cios.org/www.ejc/v10n200.htm.

Taylor, J. R. (2001). Toward a theory of imbrication and organizational communication. *American Journal of Semiotics, 17,* 1–29.

Taylor, J. R., & Robichaud, D. (2004). Finding the organization in the communication: Discourse as action and sensemaking. *Organization, 11,* 395–413.

Taylor, J. R., & Robichaud, D. (2007). Management as metaconversation: The search for closure. In F. Cooren (Ed.), *Interacting and organizing: Analyses of a management meeting* (pp. 5–30). Mahwah, NJ: Lawrence Erlbaum.

Taylor, J. R., & Van Every, E. (2000). *The emergent organization: Communication as its site and surface*. Mahwah, NJ: Lawrence Erlbaum.

Weick, K. E. (1979). *The social psychology of organizations* (2nd ed.). Reading, MA: Addison-Wesley.

Author Index

Albrow, M. 6, 15
Alessandro, D. 106, 112
Allison, G.T. 54, 84
Alvarez, R.C. 169, 182
Appendini, K. 50, 84
Armor, D. 103, 115
Aronsson, K. 78, 80, 84
Ashcraft, K.L. xii, 1, 7, 17
Austin, J.L. 2, 15, 131, 147, 164, 165, 182

Bakan, J. 54, 84
Bargiela-Chiappini, F. 1, 15
Barley, S. 72, 84
Barnard, C. 6, 15, 38, 45
Barthes, R. 2, 15
Beavin, J.H. 162, 186
Benveniste, E. 60, 84
Berger, P.L. 103, 141, 147
Bernzweig, J. 103, 115
Boden, D. 1, 2, 15, 24, 29, 45, 55, 83, 84, 118, 122, 145, 147, 166, 180, 182, 193, 197, 205
Bodor, T. 136, 148
Boje, D.M. 1, 15, 64, 84, 169, 182
Borisy, A.A. 106, 113
Bougon, M.G. 1, 15
Braverman, H. 74, 85
Bright, A.D. 103, 112
Brown, J.S. 84, 177, 182
Browning, L.D. vii, xiv, 1, 7, 14, 15, 89, 90, 92, 105, 107, 112, 115, 169, 178, 179, 180, 182, 183, 186, 188, 189, 190, 192, 194, 196, 197, 200, 201, 202, 204

Bruner, J. 1, 15, 170, 183
Bryson, J.M. 72, 85
Burke, K. 145, 147
Burleson, B. 102, 112
Bybee, J. 165, 183

Callon, M. 140, 145, 147
Canestraro, D. 136, 148
Casson, M. 100, 112
Chapman, P. 1, 18
Cheney, G. 5, 17, 34, 40, 45, 47, 82, 85
Child, J. 43, 45
Christensen, L.T. 82
Christy, R. 90, 114
Cicourel, A.V. 120, 144, 147, 148
Clegg, S. 18, 121, 148
Cohen, I.J. 59, 85
Conrad, C. 6, 16
Cooren, F. ix, xi, xiv, 1, 2, 5, 7, 14, 15, 16, 18, 30, 47, 51, 60, 85, 120, 124, 132, 136, 139, 140, 143, 148, 152, 157, 159, 160, 163, 171, 174, 183, 184, 186, 188, 190, 191, 192, 194, 196, 197, 198, 200, 201, 202, 203, 204, 205, 206, 207
Corman, S.R. 27, 42, 46
Crosby, B.C. 72, 85
Cushman, D.P. 2, 16
Czarniawska, B. 1, 16, 169, 183

Daft, R.L. 119, 148, 152
Davies, B. 81, 85
Deetz, S. 6, 16, 25, 26, 45, 121, 147, 148

Subject Index